Declining the Stereotype

Contemporary French Culture and Society

edited by Richard J. Golsan, Mary Jean Green, and Lynn A. Higgins

Declining the Stereotype

Ethnicity and Representation in French Cultures

Mireille Rosello

Dartmouth College
Published by University Press of New England
Hanover and London

Dartmouth College
Published by University Press of New England, Hanover, NH 03755

Printed in the United States of America
5 4 3 2 1
CIP data appear at the end of the book

Contents

Figures

Acknowledgments

Reading the final version of this book gave me the impression that I was leafing through a photo album of friends and colleagues to whom I owe so much. Each of the chapters is the result of direct collaboration with one or more scholars and I want to thank them here. I owe the beginning of this project to Ali Behdad, who proposed "new orientalism" as a theme of reflection: he made me discover that I had an unresolved critical ax to grind with stereotypes. I would like to thank Dina Sherzer and Phil Powrie for providing the stimulus to work on films and images, and Russell King for organizing a conference on French cinema. I am grateful to Madeleine Cottenet-Hage for inviting me to explore the links between stereotypes and delinquency, to Larry Kriztman for making me think about history and stereotypes, and to Jonathan Hart for giving me a wonderful reason to think about the relationship between stereotypes and gifts. Thanks to Michel Laronde for encouraging me to work on Emile Ajar and Didier Van Cauwelaert and for his own research on stereotypes.

I much benefited from the brilliant feedback I received from colleagues and students in conferences and seminars. I particularly want to thank the group that attended the 1995 National Endowment for the Humanities summer seminar organized by Françoise Lionnet and codirected by Nelly Furman. I also want to thank the finalists at the University of Southampton and the students who enrolled in the seminar on postcolonial images at the University of Nottingham in 1996.

My gratitude also goes to scholars whose work I have learned to respect and admire while working on this book. Sander Gilman's books have accompanied each step of my research and inspired the whole project in many uncountable ways. I also want to thank Ruth Amossy, Pierre Barbéris, Jean-Louis Dufays, Frank Felsenstein, Alain Goulet, and Christian Plantin. And special thanks to Richard Dyer (a question of wavelength). I am much indebted to the work of Houston Baker, Homi Bhabha, Leo Bersani, Judith Butler, Paul Gilroy, and Gayatri Spivak, constant sources of inspiration and reflection. I much appreciated the trust and intellectual support I received from my editors, Mary Jean Green, Lynn Higgins, and Phyllis Deutsch. And I am grateful to Timothy Mennel for his meticulous copy-editing and elegant initiatives.

Even if they are not necessarily directly quoted here, thank you to those dear friends without whose support and encouragement this work might have still existed but as an empty and meaningless enterprise: for their unflinching support and for making life in academe less of a puzzling mystery, thank you to Françoise Lionnet and Ronnie Sharfman, Elisabeth Mudimbe-Boyi,

Thomas Spear, Christian Garaud, Christiane Baroche, Florence Myles, Jean-Xavier Ridon, Alec Hargreaves, Pat Hargreaves, Liz Constable, Marie-Paule Ha, Michael Worton, and Ross Chambers. Special thanks to Colin Davis, who translated Marie Féraud's story with characteristic sensitivity and elegance.

And finally, thank you to Jean Mainil for being such a wonderfully irritating, perfectionist (obstreperous, he says) work companion. I owe him, among other rather crucial things, the title of this book.

Declining the Stereotype

Introduction

The Reluctant Guest

Declining the Stereotype is about what we can do when we find ourselves invited to participate in a type of cultural ritual we would much rather not condone. What tactics do you adopt when someone, among your guests or among your family or close friends, expects you to agree with typically violent stereotypes about another individual or group, presenting them as incomprehensible or dangerous or deviant others? I suspect that we have all been forced, at times, into the shoes of the reluctant witness whose embarrassed or astonished silence is misinterpreted as a form of acquiescence.[1]

It is always possible for a speaker to recruit the stereotyped other as an understanding listener and accomplice of the stereotyping discourse; you may have even found yourself in the infuriating and frustrating position where you are forced to listen to stereotypes about a group to which you think *you* very obviously belong. An overtly gay person may be invited to agree with the supposedly legitimate disapproval of a straight interlocutor. A Jewish guest may be asked to swallow his or her host's anti-Semitic stereotypes with dinner, the French relative of Arab origin may be entrusted with more or less carefully worded revelations about anti-Arab feelings in his or her own immediate surroundings, he or she, of course, constructed as the exception to the rule.

I propose to treat the reluctant witness as an emblematic figure who can teach us fascinating lessons about how to address the issue of ethnic stereotyping. I focus specifically on contemporary documents of French expression where the stereotype of the ethnic other is confronted and reappropriated from different angles and positionings. I concentrate on recent fiction, films, and written narratives where stereotyped subjects endeavor to resist representations of their own identities or of others' while refusing to position themselves on the outside or on the margins. The reluctant witness knows that there is no outside, especially if two speakers share the same language, the same linguistic crucible where stereotypes have slowly formed over centuries of intertextual references.

France is therefore implicitly asked to give a schizoid self-portrait of its current fears and anxieties, as well as its hopes and optimism. It is no secret that the social fabric of late twentieth-century France is a patchwork of races and ethnic groups that does not unanimously celebrate diversity. If French suburbs are, on paper, a wonderfully multiracial melting pot, a theoretical celebration of hybridity, the reality of the encounter between different races, religions, and cultures is far from peaceful and harmonious. Even if the sensationalist apocalyptic predictions favored by certain factions of the mass media are greatly exaggerated, it is just as silly to pretend that the *banlieues* are prosperous cradles of diversity, bilingualism, biculturalism, mutual respect, and tolerance among different waves of more or less well settled immigrants. Racist stereotypes cannot wish multiracial cohabitation away, but conversely multiracial cohabitation has little effect on the practice of stereotyping. In the France of the 1990s, figures of the reluctant witness include people whose participation in the cultural, social, and political life of the nation is both undeniable and rendered problematic by their own history and the history of the country in which they live.

The "black/blanc/beur" trio and its implications

I have privileged several evolving stereotypical matrices that are responsible for the construction of such embodied abstractions as the Arabs, the blacks, and the Jews, even if the categories in question do not make sense, even if the paradigms thus created are incommensurable. From the perspective of the reluctant witness, what is crucial is the historical moment at which he or she intervenes.

For example, in the fifties and the sixties, the stereotypes attached to the large population of North African immigrants reflected a certain set of problems of a certain historical moment: the typical Arab was male, single, separated from his family, and usually a construction worker or an employee of the Régie Renault, the car manufacturer that came to symbolize the links between French industries and immigration at the time when Jean-Paul Sartre dominated the cultural scene. Racist representations and counternarratives addressed very specific issues, such as the severe shortage of decent accommodations that made the Arab workers extremely vulnerable to the so-called *marchants de sommeil* (sleep merchants) who shamelessly exploited the housing crisis by renting squalid rooms to multiple inhabitants for exorbitant rents. Another issue of the moment concerned the thousands of North Africans who were parked in sprawling shantytowns around cities while also involved in the erection of those *cités* or housing projects that would become sociological, urban, and political time bombs in the 1980s and 1990s. As long as the Arab was depicted as an illiterate construction worker who lived and worked in the mud, counternarratives attacked the prevalent myth according to which "these people" enjoyed living in filth. In the late fifties and early sixties, for example, l'Abbé Pierre was trying to solve the problems not of the homeless but of the *mal-logés* who had no hope of finding decent housing. In 1970, Guy Bedos, a *pied-noir* (European North African) comic wrote skits about the supposedly well-meaning attempts to correct the urgent problems of unsightly shantytowns. Pretending to celebrate the management's determination to address the issue and to share with the public his admiration for the creative solutions adopted around Paris, Bedos exclaimed that the shantytown has finally disappeared now that "Ils ont fait construire un mur" ("They have built a wall around it").[2] Such stereotypes and counterstereotypes would have little relevance today, not because housing problems have disappeared, but because changing conditions have produced different racist and antiracist images.

Today, French citizens of North African origin live in the same subsidized projects as everyone else (the shantytowns and *cités de transit* [transit zones] were finally bulldozed at the end of the sixties), but new narratives have emerged about their supposedly idiosyncratic dwelling practices.[3] Throughout the seventies and eighties, popular films and sensational media articles gradually imposed phantasmagoric visions of bloody lambs sacrificed in bathtubs, covers of magazines have focused complacently on apparently huge crowds of men caught at that very moment of prayer when their position makes them faceless and invisible, accentuating the impression of anonymous numbers, and since the 1989 *affaire du foulard* (the Islamic scarf controversy that created strange new alliances and new frictions between antiracists, staunch defenders of secularism, and feminists), photographers have produced endlessly repetitive portraits of female adolescents whose political veil seems to have been put in the same cultural bag as the Odalisques of nineteenth-century orientalist painters.

Since the beginning of the 1990s, the Arab living in the suburbs has been systematically suspected of being in cahoots with international terrorist organizations that are said to send emissaries, recruit youths, pack them off to military training camps in Afghanistan, and then enroll them in their holy war against Western cultures. The image has obviously changed quite radically since the seventies, but this evolution can hardly be said to be an improvement. It is, however, quite clear, that in the 1990s the reappropriation of stereotypes cannot tap the same cultural resources as in the sixties or seventies. Of course, the *travailleur immigré* (migrant worker) of the seventies was already suspected of belonging to the FLN (the Algerian *Front de Libération Nationale*).

At the time when Gillo Pontecorvo's *La bataille d'Alger* (The battle of Algiers) was produced in 1966, two stereotypical constructions coexisted:[4] the myth according to which only an extreme minority of Arabs wanted to be independent while the vast majority remained faithful and grateful to the colonial motherland; and the incompatible and terrifying rumor according to which every Arab was a *Fellagha* or Algerian rebel and therefore a potential terrorist. Such images are clearly obsolete, even if stereotypes have at least as many lives as cats.

Today, the young French citizens of North African origin are both more clearly insiders and perhaps about to be more violently ostracized than their parents' generation by poverty, unemployment, and new racist fears. The so-called Beurs and children of Beurs are not immigrants; their parents and sometimes grandparents left Algeria or Morocco or Tunisia.[5] They have received the same education as every child born in France, even if socioeconomic discrepancies cast severe doubts about the reality of this. As amply demonstrated in the eighties', there is such a thing as a Beur literary generation. At the same time, Beurs remain outsiders as well, torn between the realization that their parents' dream of future returns is a myth and the desire to determine whether their persistent malaise may be solved by voluntary cultural or religious identification processes. Meanwhile, anti-Arab racist stereotyping is one of the favorite rhetorical games of the French National Front, whose leaders shamelessly exploit any incident involving people of North African descent to fuel the smoldering fires of xenophobia and racism. The scapegoating of the Arab is a reflex that is not deterred by the fact that the definition of the "Arab" in this case makes no sense whatsoever.

As reluctant witnesses to persistent anti-Arab stereotypes, French citizens of North African origin or Francophone Maghrebi clearly have a privileged understanding of the range of possible reappropriative techniques. For example, it may be a sadly familiar reality for Beur writers that bouncers routinely single out people that they interpret as Arabs and refuse to let them into bars and discos. But for the public who appreciates the autobiographical novels or the films made by those who have been described as "second-generation immigrants," this behavior may create the opportunity to discover the existence of such practices and the possible responses to such exclusionary measures (Begag 1989, 170 ff.; Chibane 1993).

Similarly, stereotypical representations of black people have both evolved and remained anachronistically similar since Aimé Césaire, Sedar Senghor, and Léon Gontran Damas decided to rally behind the word *Négritude* between the two world wars. Let us think, for example, about the endearing, childish, harmless, yet potentially rabble-rousing Africans portrayed in Hergé's *Les aventures de Tintin au Congo* (The adventures of Tintin in the Congo) (Hergé, 1946, 1974). Even after the elimination of violently racist comments from the 1974 edition of this book, the images remain profoundly coherent.[6] His portraits of black and white people are caricatures of a certain type of imagined relationships between races, a story told not only by comic strips but also by many contemporary discourses: advertising campaigns also used stereotypical images to sell rum, or chocolate, or the famous chocolate-flavored breakfast powder, Banania. In France, anyone would be familiar with the yellow Banania box and its unavoidable "L'ami Y'a bon," which infuriated Senghor (fig. 1). The smiling Senegalese Rifleman enjoying a spoonful of Banania is an unforgettable cultural icon branded with the same intensity into the minds of white and black French and Francophone people. In 1940, in a "Poème Liminaire" dedicated to Damas, Senghor wrote:

> Vous Tirailleurs Sénégalais, mes frères noirs à la main chaude sous la glace et la mort [. . .]
> Vous n'êtes pas des pauvres aux poches vides sans honneur
> Mais je déchirerai les rires Banania sur tous les murs de France. (Senghor, 55)
>
> [You, Senegalese Riflemen, my black brothers with your warm hands buried under ice and death . . .
> You are not paupers with pockets empty of honor
> But I will rip all the Banania laughters off the walls of France]

And whether or not that particular poem has influenced the history of the brand's advertising campaigns, it is obvious that Banania's packaging has rapidly evolved and moved away from the picture of a naive black face. They now privilege a typical shade of yellow (supposedly the color of bananas, one of the ingredients of Banania powder) and a stylized smile of happiness whose ideological implications remain completely transparent. Images have changed radically, but the memory of previous representations lingers in the collective unconscious. For example, the child narrator of Azouz Begag's autobiographical narratives reads a book called "Tintin et Milou chez les sous-développés du Congo" (Tintin and Milou among the underdeveloped people of the Congo) (Begag 1989, 26). The explicit rewriting of the title suggests that the text and its message are far from obsolete, even if their stereotypical content is by now identified and criticized.

People whose skin color makes them likely to be constructed as blacks will usually find that stereotypes don't go any further than that. The advent of Negritude was a historical moment when the reappropriation of stereotypes by black intellectuals took a certain turn: the colonized elite refused to use their education to sing the praises of assimilationist policies and deployed their creative energies in the creation of other images and representations that could themselves easily be accused of being stereotypical. When Senghor reclaimed the beauty of a hypothetical black soul and the cultural marvels of a mythic Africa, critics were quick to point out that he was stereotyping and simplifying. And of course, they were right. But they sometimes failed to acknowledge the necessary mimetic energy of all counterstereotyping narratives.

Figure 1. The evolution of the packaging of the Banania box. *Source:* Jean Garrigues, *Banania une passion francaise.* Paris: Du May, 1991. Reproduced by permission of CPC France.

1re DEJEUNER SUCRE
BANANIA
BANANIA
POIDS NET 500 GRAMMES

BANANIA
TOUT UN REGIME
DANS UNE TASSE
BANANIA
PETIT DÉJEUNER RECONSTITUANT
médicalement

y a bon..
BANANIA
LE PETIT DÉJEUNER FAMILIAL

y'abon
BANANIA
LE PETIT DÉJEUNER DYNAMIQUE

1kilo
BANANIA
UN REPAS LE MATIN

BANANIA
LE BON PETIT DÉJEUNER ÉQUILIBRÉ 1kg

Negritude was not as primarily concerned, for example, with exploring differences between Creole and African cultures. Since the sixties and seventies, among writers, playwrights, sociologists, and historians, Francophone black literatures and cultures have been more systematically divided into at least two separate territories of research. Francophone African and Caribbean literatures are clearly thriving, but it could be argued that shortly after 1946, when Martinique, Guadeloupe, and Guyana were turned into French departments, they followed two completely distinct paths, reflecting diverging historical realities. While African writers satirize dictatorships and postcolonial states, a whole series of novels by Caribbean authors has explored the potential of creolization and *métissage* (cultural and ethnic hybridity),[7] and their increased visibility within French literatures has been recognized symbolically by literary prizes and canonization. The general public probably knows about at least one or two Martinican writers by now: for example, Aimé Césaire and Patrick Chamoiseau have recently received a certain amount of media attention. But how is a reluctant witness supposed to interpret the facts that Chamoiseau's *Texaco* received a Goncourt Prize in 1992 (albeit a disputed one)[8] or that Césaire's *Cahier d'un retour au pays natal* suddenly appeared as one of the texts of the French *baccalauréat*? Are we to suspect that the sudden desirability and popularity of creoleness is a new wave of intellectual negrophilia? And how are we to reconcile this phase of intense interest in Caribbean literatures with the equally intense rejection of black people from Mali or Senegal or Zaire, whom stereotypes have very successfully constructed as suspicious illegal immigrants?

Jewishness, on the other hand, continues to remain an elusive signifier in French cultures. Paradoxically, the challenge here may be to question an absence of representation that is easily confused with an absence of stereotyping. The lack of stereotypes can also be the expression of a stereotype of invisibility. The proverbial French distaste for what are perceived as Anglo-Saxon models of community-based identification may have something to do with how Jewishness is consistently constructed as an invisible ethnicity. The relative arbitrariness of such narratives of invisibility should have been seriously qualified by the type of anti-Semitic representation that proliferated just before and during the Second World War; the authors of caricatures published in right-wing magazines were obviously convinced that Jewish identities were easily recognizable, even if the supposedly tell-tale signs constantly oscillated between biological features and socioeconomic or symbolic attributes (Delporte 1993). Today, in films such as Mathieu Kassovitz's *Métisse* (1993) for example, the elusiveness of Jewishness is exposed as yet another potentially harmful construction when the ethnicity of the supposedly generic "white" member of a multicultural trio is packaged as a surprise for the viewer: often the "black, beur, and blanc" trio turns out to be a black, Beur, and Jew trio

(Ajar 1975; Beyala 1992, 1995; Kassovitz's *La Haine* [1995], and *Métisse*). By incorporating issues of Jewishness into an overall plot of invisibility, what that identity consists of often remains unformulated, metonymically suggested by a few allusions to rituals, a name, or an accent. As in all Western cultures, the construction of Jewish identities today cannot be dissociated from the memories of the Holocaust, which has obvious and less obvious consequences on the way in which current stereotypes can be opposed or perpetuated in novels, films, museums, and so forth. Unlike blacks and Arabs, Jews are not represented as immigrants, even if the myth of the Wandering Jew is still as recognizable (if as irrelevant) as ever. Culturally speaking, an immigrant and a wanderer do not occupy the same place on the chessboard of social and symbolic roles. Although comparisons between the Shoah and two centuries of slavery are attempted regularly, such risky parallels are often thwarted by insuperable obstacles and taboos. Several forces pull in different directions: some voices are finally accepting responsibility for France's deportation of French and foreign Jews during the war. It is remarkable that during his second term, French President François Mitterrand abolished the tradition of officially bringing flowers to the grave of Marshal Pétain (head of the collaborationist Vichy government), but it is perhaps just as remarkable that every president of the French Republic had done so until then. Scholars who have published revisionist theses have indeed generated heated debates and much indignation. Some have sometimes incurred administrative sanctions; others have been instrumental in the passing of the 1990 law against anti-Semitism and hate speech and also in the writing of recent new testimonies. Still, it is perfectly mind-boggling that such discourses find any base to emerge a mere fifty years after the end of World War II. Meanwhile, two generations of Jewish children whose parents or grandparents were deported are struggling with the difficulties of collective and individual survival, forced to take on board the realities of international politics but also torn between the syndrome of what Alain Finkielkraut calls the "Imaginary Jew" and the necessity to preserve some fragile and fragmented versions of what it was, is, and will be to be Jewish and French at the same time (Finkielkraut 1994).

Looking at the way in which French and Francophone Arabs and blacks living and working in France are represented or represent themselves in novels, films, sociological studies, and the media is not an essentialist decision to privilege ethnicity. The logic is reversed: I have had to accept the fact that most reluctant witnesses of stereotypes tend to learn how to reuse stereotypes in striking and imaginative ways, and it is thus no coincidence that most of the examples of sophisticated moments of reappropriation are provided by subjects who have an intimate knowledge of what it means to have inherited the ambiguous status of insider-outsider and all the contradictions of still-evolving postcolonial and post–World War II conditions. As Françoise Lionnet puts it, because the postcolonial subject is "multiply organized across cultural boundaries . . . [it] becomes quite adept at braiding all the traditions at its disposal, using the fragments that constitute it in order to participate fully in a dynamic process of transformation" (Lionnet 1995, 5). Some forces in France as well as in Europe seem tempted by the possibility of re-creating a transnational commercial empire based on redrawn boundaries, while others try to draw the painful lessons of the colonial past and to welcome the creation of internally diverse cultural areas. Part and parcel of that debate—and no longer the external object of our solicitude or hostility—those whose parents or grandparents were immigrants but who are still anachronistically represented as "others" by the same old batch of ridiculously inappropriate stereotypes have perfected sound methods of declining scandalous invitations to tolerate the intolerable.[9]

Consciously creolized and hybrid subjects may be very skeptical about the virtues of creolization and hybridity, but they may also have been forced to develop strategies that people who think of themselves as naturally belonging to the dominant group (we could call them less consciously creolized subjects) would be well advised to learn.[10] As Gayatri Spivak puts it, "they too want to inhabit the national subject by displacing it" (1993, 145).

How to decline invitations and stereotypes?

The double movement of inhabiting while displacing can be achieved through a combination of the two meanings of the word "declining," for if "declining" evokes delicate decisions and potentially strident political statements when referring to what we do to invitations, the same word also refers to an apparently innocent and quite socially meaningless activity. I am thinking about what we do to German, Latin, or Greek nouns when we learn the grammatical rudiments of such languages. To list all the possible variations of a given word might seem completely unrelated to the problematic issue of ethnic stereotyping. What could be more harmless and more apolitical than to recite "rosa, rosae, rosam" in an attempt to memorize all the possible forms of a given word? Here, the attention seems to be exclusively on grammar, on formal mechanisms, on what in language appears to be most alien to the messy realm of ideology and human conflicts. Remembering that stereotypes are also or perhaps above all a manifestation of what is mechanical in our language, I will treat declensions as an interesting combination of fixed roots and variable endings, as a crossroads where form and function meet and where the principles of sameness and difference are united as two aspects of the same reality. "Declining" a word means acknowledging the various formal identities that one element of language must adopt depending on its position and role within a larger linguistic unit. "Declining" here means paying attention to the relationship between one word and the rest of the sentence.

I plan to treat formal declensions as a metaphor: one sense of "declining" involves paying attention to the formal characteristics of the stereotype so as to control its devastating ideological power. In practice, this type of declining encompasses ironic repetitions, carefully framed quotations, distortions and puns, linguistic alterations, double entendres, and self-deprecating humor.[11] Declining a stereotype is a way of depriving it of its harmful potential by highlighting its very nature.

The other meaning of "declining" allows us to take on board one of the difficulties encountered by the reluctant guest. The paradoxical violence of stereotypes uttered in public is that they are often presented as a chance to make us prove our loyalty to the speaker but also as an opportunity to be accepted as part of a group. Here is an open invitation to belong, to be welcomed by a supposedly unanimous community. Here is a chance to declare your allegiance, as if that moment of decision itself constituted some powerful moment of ecstatic communion. In the presence of a stereotype, you are asked implicitly or explicitly to approve, to agree, to nod, and to feel understood and properly positioned as a legitimate member of a group whose identity is well defined and legitimately celebrated. At the beginning of the century, Walter Lippmann ironically imagined stereotypes as medieval walls behind which we feel protected and safe, and the image has not lost any of its relevance.[12]

Part of the difficulty is that stereotypes are constructed as effecting a pleasurable form of togetherness.[13] Their violence is difficult to address when the stereotyper thinks that he or she is extending a helping hand, a benevolent signal to join in. Oblivious to its authoritarian implications (my own identity is predicted and imposed), the stereotype lets me in, or rather implies that it is unthinkable that I may wish to decline. The trouble is, of course, that we usually have no reason to fear inclusion and that we spend much time and energy trying to design inclusionary strategies. Cultural theorists who seek to read transnationally are rightly concerned with the increasing number of marginalized individuals whose powerlessness can be described accurately as a lack of access to the benefits provided by the wealthier nation-states. When we deal with national or ethnic or gender communities, exclusion almost systematically entails the loss of rights, the loss of privileges, or in the most extreme cases, the loss of all dignity and hope. As a result, the moment when we wish *not* to be included may find us disarmed and confused as to what strategy to use. Whoever wishes not to participate may not have practical and theoretical resources available because willing nonparticipation is the exception to the rule.

Even in the most mundane circumstances, it is never pleasant to decline an invitation. Accepting is not only the path of least resistance, it is the polite thing to do.[14] Declining is, at best, a difficult art, and invitations become formidable Gordian knots when the desire to decline is mitigated by the feeling that our objective will not be best served by a pure and simple refusal to appear, to speak, or to express an opinion.[15] I am sure that we can all remember a situation where an invitation was made nightmarish by our strong opposition to everything that the event represented. At the same time, accepting the challenge of unwanted marks of inclusion may be perceived as a treacherous yet necessary gamble: If I willingly exclude myself, I may be protected from the very real dangers of collaboration and complicity, but the opinions that I would like to promote are then not defended, and even my absence can be retranslated as implicit approval.

When the managers of Régie Renault invited Tahar Ben Jelloun, a well-established Moroccan writer acclaimed in Parisian literary circles, to deliver a series of conferences to its high-ranking executives on the topic of racism, should he have refused for fear that his presence would sanction a hypocritical and devious enterprise? Was it not obvious that the goal was to capitalize on a much-publicized event whose political and intellectual objective was ostensibly to do something against racism and more subterraneanly to generate more profit for the firm by reducing friction between white executives and the traditionally large percentage of workers of Arab origin? Would Ben Jelloun's presence unwillingly contribute to the perpetuation of racist stereotypes by exonerating Renault from any future criticism? Was his silent approval paradoxically bought by an invitation to speak? On the other hand, if Ben Jelloun had simply refused to cooperate, another type of familiar silence and invisibility would have prevailed. His response was more complex than a simple yes or no: the author accepted the invitation and then published a critical account of the experience, putting both his role and that of Renault in perspective. The result is *Hospitalité Française* (1984), in which Ben Jelloun confronts not only anti-Arab stereotypes but the construction of what constitutes a stereotype in different contexts. Consequently, the dialogue between the invited author and the self-contained audience is made public. Ben Jelloun's voice and his hosts' opinions are now discussed in a forum that relativizes the speaker and his audience's position.

> Le contremaître qui disait des Tunisiens, "ils ne sont pas des hommes mais des reptiles" se mettait en colère lorsque je lui faisais remarquer que c'était cela le racisme, mépriser l'Autre au point de lui refuser la qualité d'Homme. (Ben Jelloun 1984, 54)

> [The foreman who said, about Tunisians, "They are not men, they are reptiles," would get angry if I pointed out that racism was precisely that: despising Others to the point of denying their humanity.][16]

I propose that Ben Jelloun's account of his encounter with the foreman's stereotypes embodies a typical, important, necessary, and yet highly problematic tactic of reappropriation: here, what I call "declining" is an ambiguous gesture of refusal and participation at the same time. The trace left by the declining posture is a complex piece of writing where both the stereotype and its critique cohabit so intimately that no safe barrier can be erected between the two. For not only was Ben Jelloun invited, during the session, to listen to a statement that its author would certainly not identify as a stereotype, but he is also forced to repeat a version of that stereotype in order to denounce it. What version of the stereotype reappears in print and how that reemergence constitutes a more or less effective tactic of reappropriation is what I will analyze here.

When responding to the generalization about Tunisians, Ben Jelloun declined to address the specific meaning of the comparison between men and snakes and focused on the function of stereotypes. That is the tactic of appropriation that I want to emphasize; the desire to oppose stereotypes as meaningful statements is a self-defeating attempt. To declare them wrong, false, to attack them as untruths that, presumably, we could hope to replace by a better or more accurate description of the stereotyped community, will never work. As tempting as the correcting reaction may be, it is often a misguided effort that fails to analyze the structure of stereotypical statements (their grammar so to speak) and the specific form of social harm they can do; my underlying hypothesis is that we need a politics of grammar. This book asks not only "What can I do against stereotypes" but also "What can I do *with* a stereotype? What kind of mental, intellectual, social and literary activities can I deploy in the face of a stereotype?"

Answers to such questions or the questions themselves can only be formulated if a theory of stereotyping informs our constant search for appropriate tactics. And because stereotypes are inscribed in language, one issue immediately looms large: Do we have to choose between studying stereotypes in literature and stereotypes in real life? Do we have to resist either ethnic stereotypes or literary stereotypes? And if books distinguish between the two phenomena, do they reflect or invent two distinct realities?

The framing of the issue constitutes the theoretical genealogy of this book, which I situate at the crossroads between two theoretical traditions: I suggest that research on stereotypes falls into two different categories: some studies approach stereotypes from an angle that I would loosely call semiotic, others look primarily at the political and social repercussions of stereotypical representations. The former category is inscribed in a tradition started with Roland Barthes's *Mythologies* (1957) and *The Pleasure of the Text* (1973) and concentrates almost exclusively on the literary and formal characteristics of stereotypes or the role of stereotypes in literature.[17] Although quite different from each other, all the recent studies seem to share a fascination with the various types of stereotypes and an interest in classifications (that is, the differences between a cliché, a *lieu commun,* a commonplace, a topos, and a theme and the stereotype's role in these forms).[18] Historically, the most often studied forefather is Gustave Flaubert, especially his *Dictionnaire des idées reçues* and *Bouvard et Pécuchet* (1881) and generally speaking there is much interest in the end of the nineteenth century with its predilection for the genre of the *sottisier* or collection of laughable statements.[19] The metaphors used to describe stereotypes often treat the object of study as a sort of organism: a disease of language, with a form of congealed speech and expression, a transplanted organ. In other cases, the world of trade and commerce is tapped, the stereotype being likened to a type of borrowing or debt. The overall impression is that the main danger is slow petrifaction, gradual immobility, eventual necrosis, and the death of just about everything pleasurable: thought, originality, beauty, independence, literature. The stakes are high: stereotypes lead straight to terminal boredom, to a sort of Baudelairian ennui that you would not even wish on your nastiest colleagues.

Should this latest statement be taken as a flippant dismissal of the theories in question, let me hasten to reformulate: I am convinced that every value we hold dear is at stake. The studies recently written in French are indispensable because they teach us awareness of the formal structures of stereotypes, of their grammatical qualities, of their formalist side if you will. They help us, for example, identify stereotypes as a form of repetition. And this is in no way an innocent or apolitical discovery: once stereotypes are identified as forms of victorious repetitions, despair may well set in because I suspect that there is no known antidote to death by repetition.

But I also think that literature is not the only victim of stereotypes, and that social practices, governmental policies, relationships between communities, and every other level of communication are threatened by the same phenomenon. Stereotypes are especially tragic when they resurface in the social text. Which is why I would like this book to operate at the intersection between the Barthesian lineage and a second theoretical approach that pays a bit less attention to "what is it, and how does it work" and concentrates more specifically on "who does what to whom, how and when."[20] I thus propose to work in the area of overlap between books that study the politics of grammar and those that study the grammar of politics.[21] What I found precious in authors such as Sander Gilman, Frank Felsenstein, and Richard Dyer, for example, is that their books offered models of analysis of the relationship between stereotypes and race, stereotypes and sexuality, stereotypes and the violence of exclusionary social policies. Cultural inheritors of Walter Lippmann's "fortresses" rather than of Barthes's setting "mayonnaise," they are interested in the social construction of reality.[22]

Working at the intersection means giving up on the distinction between a literary stereotype and an ethnic stereotype; research on the formal similarities or dissimilarities among clichés, commonplaces, and stereotypes within different historical or literary contexts have just as much to teach us as those texts that examine the social and ideological uses and abuses of ethnic stereotyping. Whether they appear in literary texts or in other cultural productions, whether they are written or spoken, stereotypes always imply a theory of identity. A stereotypical character in a novel may be a literary failure if the passage is banal and predictable or a successful satire if it is negotiated as a comically exaggerated portrait. But whether the blame or praise falls back on the author, on the character, or on the text itself, the principle of the stereotype supposes that there is a norm and that the stereotyped figure falls either within or without it. Otherwise, the stereotype is meaningless: to drive like the French only makes sense if we understand not only what it is to drive but also to drive safely or dangerously, what it is to drive in different countries as a national or as a foreigner, what it is to comment on the experience—the list is virtually endless (see fig. 2).

A stereotype calls upon a knowledge of certain recognizable social structures and identities. That much is more or less obvious. But what is rather puzzling is that a stereotype can implicate us as participants not in a community (as insiders or as outsiders) but simply in the knowledge that the community is familiar with certain gender roles, ethnic roles, professional roles, class consciousnesses, and so on. In other words, we are not recruited as members: It is not even important whether we agree or not with the values alluded to by the stereotype. As Dyer puts it, "the effectiveness of stereotypes resides in the way they invoke a consensus" (1993, 14), but the consensus is a hypocritically welcoming ragbag. We do not have to believe that the French, or even a few French people, drive like dangerous maniacs. Knowing about the role is enough to appreciate the virulence of the image and for our own memory to become a host to systems of stereotypical inclusion and exclusion. For a theory of identity can always be used to exclude, to police borders, to grant or deny rights to individuals. Dyer even claims that "this is the most important function of stereotypes; to maintain sharp boundary definitions, to define clearly where the pale ends and thus who is clearly within and who is clearly beyond it" (1993, 16).

In that sense, it is not a sophism or an exaggeration to claim that critical attention to stereotypes sooner or later becomes a study of ethnic stereotypes and a concern about the ways in which stereotypes reappear in and as social practices. It would be a serious misunderstanding to assume that literary stereotypes are less dangerous that others: a so-called literary stereotype could be more accurately described as a stereotype that happens to appear in a literary text. As literary critics, we may decide that literary stereotypes must be studied as one of the possible types of literary discourses, but as cultural critics we may consider that it is more relevant or urgent to treat stereotypes as the primary object of study, and we may then decide to scrutinize a given ethnic

Figure 2. "The perfect European should be . . ." Reproduced by permission of Whiteway Publications, Ltd., and J. N. Hugues Wilson.

stereotype through its different manifestations, in literature, in films, in history, or in the texts of laws and local or national social policies.

Thinking of racist stereotypes as cross-disciplinary entities that affect the language of many different discursive formations has direct implications on the tactics of reappropriation we choose to counteract their racism. When I suggest that stereotypes always imply a theory of identity, I do not mean that stereotypes *are* a theory. The rejection of stereotypes is not coterminous with the fight against racist or sexist images. It is worth keeping in mind that some (most?) theoretical systems are precisely full of stereotypes and that attacking those systems as a whole is not reducible to denouncing their stereotypical nature. Nor is a stereotype likely to disappear if we discredit the theory it supports. Debunking the scientific basis of the idea of "human races" may not necessarily affect the production of racist imagery. I do not think it is very useful to argue with stereotypes, to try and confound them, to attack their lack of logic or common sense. Ethnic stereotypes are always at the service of some ideological system, but they cannot be reduced to the system. Consequently, I suggest that stereotypes are more usefully confronted as a contestable way of speaking, of using language, as an objectionable style, rather than as an opinion whose content we disagree with. Precisely because, in the end, I do not believe for a minute we can really separate style and opinion, but that in practice we often fall prey to the tendency or the temptation to concentrate on the obviously offensive ideological implications.

We could then imagine stereotypes as having a purely formal, purely linguistic molecular structure, so to speak. If we looked at enough stereotypes, we could most probably create some without attaching them to any specific group or ethnic community. Not that this contentless core identity is any cause to rejoice, since it allows stereotypes to pop up everywhere, like runaway gremlins, in those very discourses that are supposed to fix the limits of what it is legal to do or say and think, if we accept that saying and thinking are speech acts.

As Jan Nederveen Pieterse puts it in *White on Black* (1992), stereotypes "tend to function as self-fulfilling prophecies. The targets of stereotyping are maneuvered into certain roles, so that a vicious circle develops, in which reality seems to endorse the stereotype" (11). Stereotypes and representation are mutually interconnected, a point of view which, as Ruth Amossy puts it "flagrantly contradicts public opinion which opposes the stereotype to the accurate reproduction of reality" (Amossy 1984, 689). And if stereotypes are a branch of the art of representation, they have to be treated not as the opposite of truth but as one of the narratives that a given power wants to impose as the truth at a given moment.

Reading stereotypes as art, however, is almost impossible when the stereotypical narrative is proposed by a completely delirious and paranoid source: the more violent the stereotype, the more inclined we will be to invoke reality, common sense, the truth of "real" people, even if we put reality between the quotes of poststructuralism.[23] We know that, as many theoreticians have demonstrated, stereotypes "tell us far more about the endemic beliefs and prejudices of those who are the *stereotypers* than they can reveal about the *stereotyped*" (Felsenstein 1995, xiv). And yet the more violent and potentially dangerous the stereotyping force, the more difficult it is to accuse the stereotyper of madness.

A tragic paradox of stereotyping is that the most violent stereotypes are produced by some seriously mad and powerful people or institutions. If the stereotype is indeed the stereotyper's self-portrait, we should then remember that when a whole ethnic group is diabolized, there is a distinct possibility that the source doing the diabolizing has gone seriously mad, become dangerously paranoid. At that moment, it is probably far too late to invoke reality, to oppose the stereotype with pacifying discourses, with appeals to things as they really are. The trouble is that the stereotype itself functions like a screen, and it is very tempting to react to what it pretends to state as the obvious. In other words, when the stereotype seems at its most vulnerable to our common sense, it may be far too late to start opposing the stereotyping individual or institution who has had time to become both mad and extremely powerful.

The mission of our reluctant witnesses, therefore, is to ask under what circumstances it is possible and desirable to decline even the invitation to denounce the stereotype. Sometimes, the most disturbing ruse of the stereotype is its invitation to launch a virulent critique against its obvious weaknesses. In that case, the trick is to learn when to save time and energy: some stereotypes are not worth denouncing, or rather, they act like political baits. Sometimes, all our ideological reflexes will respond to a stereotypical statement in the name of a truth we can name. And sometimes, the result of the intervention will prove to be a disastrous betrayal of the type of solidarity we would like to encourage. It is counterintuitive, relatively pessimistic, and yet probably urgent to suggest that a crucial part of the fight against ethnic stereotypes lies in ascertaining carefully when and where we have a responsibility not to fall into the trap of immediate reaction. It may not always be appropriate to think that explicit intervention is the opposite of nonintervention, and I here propose to find examples of when a principle of nonreaction cannot be equated with either indifference or even compliance with stereotypical assumptions about a given group.

Declining as (non-)intervention

Going even one step further, I suggest that once we have determined which stereotypes are better left alone, we concentrate on even more disturbing stereotypes that thrive on being denounced; every time someone opposes them, they gain in strength and consolidate their cultural positions as pseudo-truths. Ignoring them and refusing to give them audience does constitute an effective form of rebuttal. Declining them actively involves complicated gestures of rewriting, strategies of recontextualizing that I will illustrate in the following chapters.

Chapter 1 concentrates on developing a theoretical construct of what I see as the most dangerous aspect of stereotypical discourse: its infectious nature. I argue that stereotypes contain a sort of built-in antidote against all attempts at discrediting them. As a result, resistance to stereotypes is often self-defeating; at the very moment I try to contradict, dismiss, or eradicate scandalous ethnic stereotypes, I sometimes end up monumentalizing them, erecting the pedestal from which they will continue to dominate the cultural landscape. Since resignation to the tyranny of stereotypical thinking is clearly not an option, I conceive of this volume as a cautious exploration of the narrow roads that cultural critics can travel when they want to continue to oppose ethnic stereotypes while being quite conscious of the immense power of self-perpetuating images.

The chapters following this theoretical declaration of independence from stereotypes belong into two main families of tactics. Chapters 2 and 3 give examples of direct intervention deployed in a series of contemporary films, stand-up comedy routines, novels, and short stories. I focus on instances of conscious cultural reappropriation of ethnic stereotypes. Typically, the mood there is exuberantly triumphant or good-humored and tongue-in-cheek, the tone is resolutely upbeat and the characters rarely take themselves seriously. Chapter 2 looks at three similar examples: Mehdi Charef's *Le thé au harem d'Archi Ahmed*; a short story ("Les Ray-Ban") about delinquency by French sociologist Marie Féraud; and the work of Smaïn, a popular humorist of Maghrebi origin whose routines address the issue of nationality and origin. Smaïn reappears in chapter 3 as one of the main heroes of the self-parodic "blanc, black, beur" trio in a 1987 comedy by Serge Meynard, *L'oeil au beurre noir*. All these primary sources make fun of the stereotypical view that all Arabs are thieves, play with the figure of the delinquent, and reappropriate the image of the Other as thief. Here, declining ethnic stereotypes amounts to casting oil on the fire, as the heroes take the risk of repeating stereotypes even though they are fully aware of the danger of contamination. Those texts add to our cultural models the idea that the use of ideological lubricant is an effective tactic against stereotypes. At the same time, the characters propose a critique of their own activity: they know that they have no control over the very slipperiness they appropriate. The theft of stereotypes, like stereotypes themselves, respects no community limits, no essence. It is a form of smuggling rather than a legitimate example of border crossing.

In the next two chapters, I turn to the apparently paradoxical consequence of the definition of stereotypes as self-perpetuating units of language and ideology. In certain contexts, the best way of opposing ethnic stereotypes is to refuse to intervene. Needless to say, when the only possible tactic is a form of self-imposed paralysis, the tone is likely to change, but comedy does not necessarily disappear, even if it is now set against a background of subdued pessimism and occasional sadness. Chapters 4 and 5 provide examples of when and how it is possible to propose nonintervention as a form of reappropriation. In chapter 4, I bring together another of Marie Féraud's short stories, "Oh, le pauvre malheureux!" and one of Baudelaire's prose poems, "La fausse monnaie." The comparison suggests that sometimes silence and abstention are not caused by cynical indifference but are the only way to avoid the bitter irony of self-defeating repetitions. Both texts explore the delicate relationship between charity and stereotypes and they come to sobering conclusions about what not to do when confronted with a specific type of stereotyping. Coline Serreau's film *La crise* goes even further, making a puzzling and thought-provoking point about the possible harmlessness of apparently devastatingly dangerous ethnic stereotypes. Chapter 5 thus concentrates on a rather tricky example of cultural homeopathy, Serreau's favorite metaphor for reappropriation of social dysfunctions. In *La crise,* the comic confrontation between allopathic and homeopathic ideals takes on symbolic significance. Here, ethnic stereotypes are both a symptom and Serreau's limited, tentative and disillusioned remedy. She cynically though tenderly proposes that we accept the existence of those stereotypes and clichés that have achieved a sort of formal perfection: the utterance, in a comedy, of a formally perfect stereotype turns the stereotype into a caricature of itself and forces the viewer to read it as a form of defamiliarized statement—that is, a form of art, or perhaps a form of cinematographic sport.

The last chapter examines three particularly imaginative textual performances where declining stereotypes involves almost exclusively a focus on language. Emile Ajar's *La vie devant soi*, Calixthe Beyala's *Le petit prince de Belleville,* and Didier Van Cauwelaert's *Un aller simple* are three comedies about the tragic consequences of stereotypes on the life of three children who are (or are thought to be) of foreign origin. At first, listening to their narration, the reader may get the impression that the characters are curiously indifferent to the fact that stereotypes cripple their practical, social, and emotional lives. But it soon becomes apparent that Ajar, Beyala, and Van Cauwelaert share the same principle of reappropriation of stereotypes: following Barthes's recommendation, they "cheat" on language. As a result, they attack the very core of stereotypical statements: they undermine their memorability, or, rather, they capitalize on that very memorability, inserting an element of critique within the congealed stereotype that will continue to circulate like a mutant organism. Although ostentatiously limited to the realm of language, of syntax, this kind of intervention may well be the most powerful of all, even if it is limited by the difficulty of translating the authors' sophisticated and highly personal literary games into other languages.

The comic lesson in complicity offered in all these texts suggests that the heroes have learned a valuable lesson of independence: on the one hand, as dominant or marginalized subjects, we are constantly invited to use and abuse the immense reservoir of stereotypes that human memory has slowly accumulated over centuries. On the other hand, it is possible to find effective ways of declining the invitation without excluding oneself from the pleasure of cultural feasts.

Chapter 1

Stereotypes and Iterativity

> Le fascisme, ce n'est pas d'empêcher de dire, c'est d'obliger à dire.
> (Barthes 1978, 14)
>
> [Fascism is not forbidding someone to speak but forcing someone to speak.]

Literally speaking, then, what is, or rather what was, a stereotype? And how do technical details matter if I am searching for ways of reappropriating ethnic stereotypes? I am not too keen on finding the one and only true authentic origin of the word itself; rivers have many sources. Often, looking for the origin of a key word does not prove very meaningful and does not generate much more than the feeling that a necessary mission has been accomplished. The desire to find out when, where, and why the word "stereotype" was used for the very first time may well be guided by the illusion that a phenomenon can be controlled once its source is identified. In the case of stereotypes, however, going back in time along one of the branches of the river yields interesting surprises, since the literal and the figurative meanings of the word are linked by a revealing degree of irony and self-contradiction.

When I envisage stereotypes as a technical development, the literal meaning, as is often the case, seems innocent enough. A stereotype is, at first, one of the professional printer's tools: quoting from a nineteenth-century technical manual, Isabelle Rieusset-Lemarié writes,

> Avant toute chose, la stéréotypie est un procédé typographique "qui consiste à convertir en un seul bloc de fonte des pages composées en caractères mobiles." (Rieusset-Lemarié 1994, 15)
>
> [First of all, stereotyping is a typographic technique "consisting in transforming the pages constituted of mobile type into a unique slate of cast iron."][1]

Instead of printing a series of carefully composed lines, the typographer took a negative image of that page by pressing it into a soft cardboard mold, called the *flan* in French and then cast a whole block whose semantic content was obviously fixed once and for all, ready to be faithfully reproduced on thousands and thousands of copies. The first experiments date from the beginning of the eighteenth century, but the technique became immensely popular only during the second half of the nineteenth century. According to the French *Encyclopaedia universalis*, between 1850 and 1900 almost all books, periodicals, newspapers, and other printed matter were produced this way. The stereotype itself consists in the passage from discrete characters lined up to constitute sentences and paragraphs to one single matrix of reproduction (Martin 1996).

Naturally, like the result of any other technical advance, stereotypes are not just inanimate objects; they are steeped in ideology, they are endowed with a multifaceted ideological, political, commercial, and social soul. And if we change the question slightly from what a stereotype is to why it was necessary to invent them or why they were so successful during the second half of the nineteenth century, the cultural repercussions of the technique become more apparent. At first it may seem counterintuitive to add one extra stage to the chain of production of any item, yet in the case of stereotyping the making of the mold constitutes an intermediary level, since a new layer of material is inserted between the paper and the original type. Why, then, was it deemed effective, why was a simplification involved? As Gérard Martin puts it:

> les lignes de caractère en plomb . . . s'usaient relativement vite à cause de la pression appliquée sur elles par les presses et de l'action abrasive exercée par le papier. Cet inconvénient a été accepté comme un mal nécessaire aussi longtemps que les tirages n'ont pas dépassé quelques centaines d'exemplaires. Il a commencé à paraître insupportable au XVIIIe siècle. (*Encylopaedia universalis,* 1996 CD-ROM)
>
> [the lines of lead type . . . wore out relatively fast because of the pressure exerted by the press and the abrasive contact with the paper. This drawback was accepted as a necessary evil as long as only a few hundred copies of a text were printed. It gradually became intolerable in the eighteenth century.]

Here was the seed of the ironic reversals between the literal and the figurative meaning of "stereotype": the details of the original technique of stereotyping are relevant to a study of contemporary ethnic stereotypes because the inventors of stereotypes have succeeded beyond their wildest dreams. Before stereotypes came into play, the support they used to disseminate ideas was fragile, making the ideas themselves vulnerable. And now, when we think about a stereotype, we search in vain for a way to get rid of ideas that seem to have become completely autonomous from their support, resistant to time, space, and any material limitation. Stereotypes were precisely created to protect ideas from the wear and tear of materiality. Today, we use the same word to refer to an idea that has managed to bypass the original problem of materialization and mass circulation.

Having infiltrated everyday culture, stereotypes now refer to something that refuses to die even if it has outlived its own relevance or significance. And the concept itself has proved particularly catching: the word "stereotype" shows no sign of being semantically threatened by the fact that the printing industry is gradually replacing even automated typography with computerized technology.

The curious way in which the metaphorical use of "stereotype" comments on the original technical discovery seems like a warning: from the very beginning, stereotyping is marked by a principle of ambivalence. The stereotype facilitates the transmission of ideas, images, and concepts, but it does so by freezing a certain stage of the production of the text. Similarly, stereotypes are very successful particles of language and ideology that cannot be reduced to or dismissed as the mechanical repetition of trite clichés or delirious narratives about certain races or communities. Like a block of cast iron, they form a whole that cannot be dissolved and whose main purpose is to be repeated endlessly. There again, the ambivalence of the stereotyping process resurfaces: a term referring to a splendidly successful process almost immediately acquired a derogatory figurative meaning partly because, both literally and metaphorically, the stereotype is systematically implicated in the issue of repetition that has long confounded thinkers who have tried to adjudicate the relative values of originals and copies.

I suggest that the relative values of literal and metaphorical repetition are themselves accurately represented by the distinction some critics make between images or texts (or between visual and written narratives). At one level, we can say that the stereotyping process turns the text into an image because it transforms the symbolic freedom of endless assembling and dissassembling into a symbolic lack of flexibility. Not surprisingly, then, many studies of stereotypes rely heavily on images as if the visualization of certain ideas was the ultimate actualization of the metamorphosis of separable signs into one fixed entity.

Scholars interested in postcolonial studies and especially in the intersection between imperialism, (de)colonization, and the representation of race and gender have a large selection of relevant collection of images at their disposal: Malek Alloula (1986) proposes to return to the sender all the orientalist postcards manufactured in the Maghreb during the colonial period.[2] Sander Gilman (1985, 1988) uses medical drawings and reproductions of paintings, Felsenstein (1995) analyzes eighteenth- and nineteenth-century engravings, and Jan Neverdeen Pieterse (1992) draws from a vast array of disciplines to analyze the portrayal of blacks from the Middle Ages to the present.[3] Anne McClintock (1995) takes a critical look at puzzling representations of domesticity and empire via the evolving images of soap. Since the 1990s, cultural studies in French have been enriched by a series of illustrated volumes, books on the stereotypical implications of advertising campaigns (Garrigues 1991 or Bachollet et al. 1992) or on the role of political cartoons (Delporte 1993).[4]

While looking at published images, however, it is crucial to remember that neither texts nor images are completely enslaved by technical processes of reproduction. Clearly, we valorize the possibility of preserving the mobility of signs, and moving little pieces of lead on a line becomes a metaphor for living thought. But it is a metaphor and not a truth.[5] Yes, a stereotype fixes things, but it is important to distinguish between metaphorical fixity and literal thoughtlessness. The distinction between something that can, at any time, be recomposed and changed and the fixed result of the transformation of a message into one solid block—that is, into an image—has influenced our theories and may at times prevent us from adopting the most effective tactics in the face of those stereotypes we do respond to.

For example, in *Les crayons de la propagande* (1993), a most useful study of how politics, censorship, ideology, and caricatures interacted during World War II in France, Christian Delporte argues that images are indelible while texts fade from people's memories. During World War II, he says,

> Pendant quatre ans, les Français furent abreuvés de mots et d'images. Les premiers s'estompaient avec le temps ou s'imprimaient dans la mémoire comme autant de slogans appelant à la haine et au meurtre. Les secondes laissaient des traces plus indélébiles. Si l'on pouvait parcourir distraitement un éditorial pétri d'outrance, ignorer un article en page intérieure rédigé par un obscur journaliste, passer rapidement devant un kiosque sans être attiré par des titres d'une violence devenue banale, il était quasi inconcevable de faire l'impasse sur le dessin qui, tout autant que la manchette du journal, provoquait l'oeil et suscitait le réflexe. (178–79)

> [For four years, the French were gorged with words and images. The former faded with time or were branded in memories like so many hatemonging slogans and incitations to murder. The latter left more indelible stains. It was possible to skim absentmindedly through a violently extremist article, to dismiss a story written by an obscure journalist and buried in the middle of the paper, to walk past a news agent booth without being drawn to the by now routinely violent titles, but it was inconceivable to ignore the cartoon that, like the headline, was meant to be eye-catching and triggered reflexes.]

Delporte's book concerns the specific influence of political cartoons. It is therefore quite understandable that he should oppose words and images as two qualitatively different media. According to him, images stay alive, while words are eventually forgotten. I am not sure that I agree with a distinction that even he seems to deconstruct: according to the passage I just quoted, both words and images apparently left traces in people's memories as if they had been printed on blank slates (some words were "branded" into people's memories as slogans). It was also possible to read images as texts (he claims that cartoons functioned like headlines; they were obviously interpretable), and it was also an option to glance at texts in the same manner as we take a quick overall look at an image. Historically, I think it is easy to demonstrate that some images have faded from collective memories in the sense that they would be either meaningless or completely uninteresting today while some texts have remained alive.

The cultural production of images and that of texts cannot be studied independently; they belong to the same discipline. During World War II, images and words fed on each other, their authors sharing some of the same ideological units whether they agreed with each other or not. Yet Delporte's idea that a qualitative difference separates what is remembered from what fades from memory is a flexible theoretical tool that I reformulate as follows: If some images are branded into people's minds, it is because they share with stereotypes the high degree of memorability and iterativity that comes from the transformation of assembled individual units into one apparently solid unique block of meaning. Some texts will function exactly in the same manner if they use the same mechanism, and some images can certainly not operate like stereotypes.

One particularly didactic combination of words and pictures presents itself as a lesson in reading images, or rather as a warning of the relationship between stereotypes and representation: a poster reproduced in Pieterse's *White on Black* (1992) where the top part is explained by a text written underneath as in those ads for cigarettes that also warn you that you are (deliciously?) playing with fire. The picture represents two men running in the same direction. We are meant to "see" a white man in a police uniform running after a black man dressed in civilian clothes. But after reading the caption, we are also asked to change our minds and realize that the white man is running behind the black man, in pursuit of someone else who is not represented in the picture. Under the image, the text reads: "Another example of police prejudice? Or another example of yours?" Then, in smaller print, "Do you see a policeman chasing a criminal? Or a policeman harassing an innocent person? Wrong both times. It's two police officers, one in plain clothes, chasing a third party" (Pieterse 1992, 208). This is a good example of how text and image can not only supplement each other but also function as increasingly complex layers of interpretation. The whole point of the story is that it is crucial to pick one's words carefully when describing what looks obvious: the designer wants us to fall into a trap. Naturally, the idea that the reader is "wrong" to have come to conclusions about the respective identity of the characters is slightly unfair. We may want to ask instead whether it is a coincidence that the black man is represented as running ahead of the white man and without a uniform. We may also ask why we are supposed to interpret an image from which a third party has been erased. Would it have been meaningful to make decisions about that "real" criminal's race?) At the same time, as a poster that advocates the recruiting of ethnic minorities, it certainly demonstrates that no matter how race is used and interpreted in the image, it cannot be said to be irrelevant.[6]

There is another more or less useless and even dangerous paradigm at work here: namely, the assumption that the opposition between positive images and negative images can function equivalently to the opposition between stereotypes and more truthful representations. This does not mean that all stereotypes are equally harmful or harmless, but rather than opposing good texts to bad) images or even bad stereotypes to good images, it is worth introducing notions of power, domination, and legislation into the equation.

Stereotypes are like weapons: left in a drawer, they cannot kill. The trick is to realize that in that little parable the important element is the drawer, not the weapon.[7] When ethnic stereotypes are taken or left out of the drawer, then we need real help. As Gilman says, "Certainly, no stereotypes have had more horrifying translations into social policy as those of 'race.' Tied to the prestige of nineteenth century science, the idea of racial difference in the twentieth century became the means of manipulating and eventually destroying entire groups" (Gilman 1985, 129).

Representating slavery and abolition, representing the Jews, representing immigrants, representing the ethnic Other is the same as fiddling with the key to more or less dangerous drawers. At the beginning of *The Myth of Aunt Jemina* (1994), Diane Roberts insists that stereotypes are directly linked to social policies and legislation. Regretting that the United States has consistently both mistreated and negatively stereotyped its African-American minority, she writes:

> Controlling the representation means controlling the culture: if blacks are the ignorant, over-sexed savages of pro-slavery literature, then laws must be made to keep them from the whites they might harm—or seduce. If they are Christ-like loving innocent souls, they must be educated and brought along, slowly to citizenship, and if they are intelligent resourceful mature beings they must be granted the full rights of citizenship. Representation is ultimately involved in power. (7)

Roberts is absolutely right to suggest that representation and power simply cannot be separated. After all, laws are texts, sometimes narratives, and they are interpreted by readers. The law writes itself as a series of little narratives, and judges may be considered professional interpreters. It would also be insanely idealistic to assume that laws are written by abstract agencies that have not been exposed to the same stereotypes as all the members of the group that recognizes the law as an emanation of its own collective principle. Just as some laws survive the historical context that made them necessary and linger on, sometimes obsolete, sometimes completely archaic and irrelevant but still usable because interpretation allows us to both be faithful to and alter a text, some stereotypes seem to defy all attempt at denouncing their meaninglessness in a contemporary context. Some stereotypes and some laws tell the story not only of what a certain imagined national "we" believes but also of what we used to believe. The history of how fast ethnic stereotypes and legislation change in relation to each other may well be worth studying as the single corpus of one unified research project or even one discipline. The results would certainly provide us with a new way of measuring the relative respect shown to certain communities by a dominant culture.

On the other hand, I doubt that there is an arrow going from stereotypes to legislation. Richard Dyer's image of a vicious circle seems more accurate, if more pessimistic: "the stereotype is taken to express a general agreement about a social group as if that argument arose before and independently of the stereotype. Yet, for the most part, it is from stereotypes that we get our ideas about social groups" (1993, 14). At first sight, Dyer's lucid vision may lead us dangerously close to the desperate quicksands of double binds and aporias. But Roberts's powerful insistence that there is perfect coordination between stereotypes as cause and laws as mandatory effects may work as a precious invitation to act. Yet her position also raises a number of difficulties: for example, we have seen that it is quite possible for a culture to contain contradictory stereotypes about ethnic groups. It is therefore difficult to assume that the law would necessarily privilege the right one, so to speak. Besides, there is a danger involved in such a process: we would have to assume that a good image is a good image and that a bad image is a stereotype. Finally, it is difficult to know if one text clearly precedes the other; can we really tell whether the law or the stereotype comes first? Should the law follow the changing of mentalities or should it force people to recognize that some of their opinions have become illegal?[8]

The optimistic take on this dilemma holds that nobody needs to choose between changing the law and changing stereotypes. It can easily be the same activity infiltrating the different facets of our daily routine. Richard Dyer says, for example, that he constantly moves back and forth between a study of how stereotypes function in social thought and how they function in fiction (1993, 11). We could assume that there is indeed no contradiction at all between the two practices. One of the points of this study is that each judge or senator or voting citizen or member of an association or community is also a consumer and producer of images and texts. A person who is actively involved in the drafting of a new bill of law also goes grocery shopping, talks to neighbors, reads books, watches television, or goes to the movies. Effort and vigilance will produce the same kind of results as joyful participation in the life of symbols. The relationship between stereotypes and legislation will never take the form of a magic moment of epiphany, which does not mean that we cannot continue to act as though such moments were possible.

The pessimistic flip side is that no law can eradicate stereotypes and that the relationship between representation and power is a very messy and relatively uncontrollable business. The other piece of bad news is that this messy business seems to beg for a theory of timing: How long before a stereotype disappears? How long before a law intervenes? How long before a perfect moment of balance? But this desire to count, to measure, to calculate time is probably another dangerous trap: monitoring the lifetime of a given stereotype as a way of predicting the trajectory of others may well be a theoretical distraction, another desperate attempt at controlling, at erecting the same barriers around stereotypes as the stereotype creates around people to begin with. And yet, how comforting it would be to imagine stereotypes as a human body or even as a sort of bacteria whose active life span could be measured and predicted on a relatively accurate basis. Figures, however, when applied to stereotyping patterns, are incredibly discouraging and puzzling. As Diane Roberts sadly notices: "We in the U.S. have had at least three decades of powerful passionate images of black women (and men) to complicate and challenge three hundred years of stereotypes and yet the best-known black woman's face in the land looks out from a box of pancake mix" (Roberts 1994, 1).

Why, for example, don't we celebrate the image of Rosa Parks, the woman who started the 1955 Montgomery bus boycott when she refused to give her seat to a white man?[9] Roberts has very good reasons to be distressed by the triumph of archaic (or at least old-fashioned) stereotypes, and I am not sure that there is an answer to her specific question about the difference between three decades and three hundred years. Could it be, after all, that three decades is too short in stereotype years? Does it take three centuries of counterimages to erase three centuries of stereotypes? Gilman and Felsenstein debunk stereotypes that have persisted, against all odds, since the Middle Ages (Gilman 1985; Felsenstein 1995). Must we assume that stereotypes are eternal, that they never completely die but that they lie dormant in the collective unconscious, waiting to emerge in the right context?[10] When science-fiction films scare us with alien forms of life that can survive for billions of years in hostile conditions only to resurface and threaten a little group of nice, civilized, and vulnerable human beings, could they be presenting us with an accurate vision of the devastating longevity and power of stereotypes?

The oblique way of answering the question is to ask why certain stereotypes seem to be more easily inherited than others. The fight to control representation cannot be equated with either a fight against negative images or the formulation of a more comprehensive theory of stereotyping. A close analysis of stereotypes may provide us with tactics and solutions that can be used when we are working on the delicate relationship between prescription and representation, but it would be illusory to hope that a magic formula can be discovered.

In fact, it is strategically and theoretically more useful to imagine stereotypes as a type of images endowed with power and to determine where this power comes from. Stereotypes come with a high power of persuasion, circulation, and memorization. That may be why they last so long. Rosa Parks could presumably be turned into a stereotype, but even as a stereotype she would not necessarily or definitively dethrone Aunt Jemima, nor would her political power necessarily be increased. When the historical character lives on in people's memories as a stereotype, it is not necessarily a tribute to the individual's original message. The fact that Rosa Parks is a "real" historical character certainly does not pose an insuperable obstacle to her stereotypification. As the French political movements of the far right have recently demonstrated, Joan of Arc can easily be stereotyped (hijacked, as some have put it) as the incarnation of nationalist values. It could be said that it is the fate of all historical characters to survive only as stereotypes once they have been swallowed and spat out as national symbols by the machine of historicization.

Does this then mean that stereotypes are simply the most pervasive and unavoidable cultural phenomena? Barthes, in his unmistakenly elegant and poetic style, attacks "the stereotype" as if some abstract entity called "the sign" was to blame, whatever the context, whatever the situation, whether or not someone suffers from the ideological, cultural, or political consequences of stereotypes. In 1973, in *Le plaisir du texte*, he writes:

> Le stéréotype, c'est le mot répété, hors de toute magie, de tout enthousiasme, comme s'il était naturel, comme si par miracle ce mot qui revient était à chaque fois adéquat pour des raisons différentes, comme si imiter pouvait ne plus être ressenti comme une imitation: mot sans-gêne, qui prétend à la consistance et ignore sa propre insistance. (69)
>
> [A stereotype is a word repeated without any magic, without any enthusiasm, as if it were natural, as if this recurrent word were miraculouly always adequate for different reasons, as if imitating were no longer perceived as imitation: an inconsiderate word, that claims substance and ignores its own insistence.]

When Barthes writes about stereotypes, I recognize and find quite seductive his familiar critique of every sign that tries to draw its authority from a supposedly "natural" origin, and this attack is quite legitimately leveled at stereotypes. But Barthes's richly metaphorical definition of the stereotype is slightly problematic: first of all, it is tautologically negative. The stereotype is undesirable because it is defined as such, because it rhymes with a total "absence of magic" and a "lack of enthusiasm." The question then becomes, Why would anyone want to use such pathetically defective signs? If stereotypes are obviously useless, why are they so widespread, so resistant to all kinds of counternarratives, including the invocation of the usually quite powerful "reality" or "truth"? Could it be that Barthes's definition underestimates or even ignores that we (that is, not only others) may find much pleasure and comfort by using stereotypes. Accepting this, couldn't we then try to salvage this element of pleasure and comfort by using stereotypes strategically, like other potentially dangerous signs?

For Barthes, the stereotype is a sort of intruder, an "inconsiderate sign" *(mot sans-gêne)* whose overwhelming presence "insists" on being noticed. While such anthropomorphizing takes into account the seemingly uncontrollable strength of images, clichés, and preconceptions that cannot be dismissed as individual idiosyncracies, at the same time, severing all links between stereotypes and speaking subjects may not be the best system of resistance against what Barthes imagines as their intrusive "rudeness." What I propose instead is to distinguish between stereotypes and the ways in which they are used. After all, being *sans-gêne* is quite a welcome feature in comedians and satirists. Being sans-gêne is not systematically a political statement, but it could also be the name that irritated powers give to subversiveness. As for being devoid of magic, just think about rabbits: before being pulled out of magicians' hats, rabbits are dull and stupid animals, devoid of magic, obsessed with self-repetition.

Five years later, in *Leçon* (1978), Barthes's metaphors are even more negative. His contempt for stereotypical thought spawns strangely ambiguous yet quite evocative images of scavenging, delinquency, perhaps even of prostitution. Repetition is no longer a dull and ordinary activity lacking brilliance and magic; repetition is now a monster, an abnormal and deviant thing or creature.

> Les signes dont la langue est faite, les signes n'existent que pour autant qu'ils se répètent; le signe est suiviste, grégaire; en chaque signe dort ce monstre: un stéréotype. Je ne puis jamais parler qu'en ramassant ce qui traîne dans la langue. (15)
>
> [The signs that constitute language can only exist when they repeat themselves; signs are gregarious followers; in each sign, a monster is asleep: a stereotype. I can only speak by picking up what's lying there, in language.]

The rich polysemy of the verb "*traîner*" (to lie around or to loiter, to hang out) is a remarkable moment of rejection: while insisting that no one can avoid stereotypes, Barthes still creates images of filth, exclusion, and disorder. Language is visualized either as an untidy room where things have been left lying around, or perhaps as a group of slightly suspicious people who are hanging out, apparently up to no good. The verb may well evoke echoes of the word "*traînée*," a particularly violent and sexist term of abuse that implicitly equates the stereotype with everything that the norm hates and fears about the woman who either sells her body or is accused of being free.

Barthes relegates the stereotype to the trash can of thought and language, and this attitude makes it impossible to invent a theory of recycling. In Barthes's metaphorical universe, stereotypes look like perverse organisms that are quite happy to assume their status as monsters. I suggest that this may be one of their ruses: by appearing to be the systematically unredeemable and disgustingly trite leftovers of intelligent language, stereotypes deprive us of the power or desire to use them, to put them to work for purposes different from what was originally intended. Instead of considering stereotypes as a fatality, I would like to claim the right to use them. Rather than feeling superior to the stereotype or stereotyper whose hidden agenda is exposed, rather than seeking to replace (bad) stereotypes with more luminous and magic truths, I am looking for a theory that will allow me to recycle them.

Confronted with the dullness of stereotypes, Barthes advocated a mimetically dull science that would carefully record the slow process of diseased linguistic solidification and finally witness a sort of death by immobility.

> Il serait bon d'imaginer une nouvelle science linguistique; elle étudierait non plus l'origine des mots, ou étymologie, ni même leur diffusion, ou lexicologie, mais les progrès de leur solidification, leur épaississement le long du discours historique; cette science serait sans doute subversive, manifestant plus que l'origine historique de la vérité: sa nature rhétorique, langagière. (Barthes 1973, 69)

> [It would be useful to imagine a new linguistic science; it would study, not the origin of words (etymology), nor even their circulation (lexicology), but the progress of their solidification, their thickening throughout historical discourse; that science would probably be subversive, exposing more than the historical origin of the truth: its linguistic and rhetorical nature.]

But is it really the case that all stereotypes can be compared to a flow of ideas progressively losing its desirable fluidity? Even the value of fluidity may be a stereotype, and it would be easy to invent a context where Barthes's suggestion loses its immediate commonsensical appeal. Instead, we should recognize that some stereotypes are all the more dangerous and harmful because they *are* full of enthusiasm and creativity and appear to radiate with transcendental truth, precisely a sort of magic that turns us into children begging for more of the same story and not grown-ups asking for explanations and historicization and rationalizations.

Here, I will treat stereotypes as respectable narratives that it is not demeaning to read and analyze. I take them seriously as valuable objects or study rather than as laughable exaggerations and obvious falsehoods. Consequently,

I plan on claiming or reclaiming whatever magic potential they continue to hide behind their hypocritical I-am-stupid-and-I-know-it signed confession, and I will propose a ludic, subversive, and reappropriative use of stereotypes.

One direct consequence of that resolution is to recognize that there is a stereotype of the stereotype: the stereotype is always bad, simplistic, idiotic. Most recent scholarly studies agree: the word "stereotype" functions performatively as a gesture of refutation. Rhetorically, the argument is lost if one of the protagonists can be accused of stereotyping. Ruth Amossy recognizes that the stereotype "has attracted bad publicity" (1984, 700). Richard Dyer remarks that "the word 'stereotype' is today almost always a term of abuse" (1993, 11). I find Dyer's use of the word "abuse" sobering. Normally, when I think of an author denouncing a stereotype, especially an ethnic or racial stereotype, I immediately assume that it is the stereotyper who is wielding "abuse." It is quite useful to realize, if we plan to make a careful and educated use of the term, that the word "stereotype" itself can be brandished as a discrediting weapon. Jean-Louis Dufays goes one step further at the beginning of his monumental collection, *Stéréotype et lecture* (1994). Agreeing with other critics that stereotypes have acquired a bad reputation, he also points out that the reception of stereotypes is neither universal nor completely independent from preexisting socio-economic categories:

> [Les stéréotypes] on le sait, n'ont pas bonne presse. Qu'il s'agisse de clichés de langage, de poncifs thématiques ou d'idées reçues, la banalité, sous toutes ses formes, est de nos jours unanimement honie par la classe intellectuelle. (7–8)

> [As we all know, (stereotypes) have a bad reputation. Linguistic clichés, thematic commonplaces, or preconceived ideas, the banal under all its guises is unanimously spurned by intellectuals.]

It is quite a meaningful gesture to acknowledge that a certain class of readers tends to find stereotypes particularly distasteful. That approach has the advantage of focusing on one often unformulated aspect of definition of stereotypes: statements, remarks, attitudes, or images can only be identified as stereotypes if a reading and judging agency is present.

No self-respecting scholar would imply that stereotyping activities are the exclusive province of one social class or one racial group. The issue of who has the right or power to define a statement as a stereotype has received proper attention and, as a result, recent criticism is neither self-righteous nor dogmatically prescriptive. As Pierre Barbéris argues, for example,

> L'illusion ce serait: le stéréotype, c'est quelque chose que je vois que je désécris et à quoi j'échappe. Ou: le stérétoype, c'est les autres. Parce qu'on est toujours embarqué. (1994, 9)

[The illusion would be: stereotypes are something that I see through, that I unwrite, and that I avoid. Or else: steretoypes equal others. For we are always already on board.]

This does not mean that everything is relative and that I should simply live and let live, but it may be crucial to verify which values are involved in my criticism of stereotypes. Stereotypes are very easy to identify, quote, and denounce, and yet they are impossible to eliminate. More disturbingly, those who loudly oppose stereotypes may be their best allies, their best chance of survival. As cultural critics, we can posit that our point of departure, our horizon of exploration, is the limits of defamiliarization as a countertactic: proving that the stereotype itself is a stereotype does not make it go up in a puff of smoke. I am not saying that defamiliarization is useless—in fact, quite the opposite. It is crucial to write books that anchor different stereotypes in their own changing historical contexts. Because stereotypes parade as eternal bits of human wisdom, studies that analyze their evolution implicitly or explicitly juxtapose their pseudo-immortality with their social irrelevance. But what I want to avoid is the comfortable illusion that simply reading texts that denounce stereotypes is itself a successful enterprise of reappropriation.

Although it is true that by understanding and remembering what scholars and historians have said about stereotypes they have studied in texts and films and images, we can gain knowledge about how stereotypes function, reading books is not enough. Teaching them is not enough. Teaching them and assuming that I have been contributing actively to a global fight against ethnic and sexual stereotypes is like imagining that I have trained for a marathon after watching the Olympics on television. And feeling good about it is definitely irresponsible. Teaching books that study (and therefore include) stereotypes is neither good enough nor a straighforward and easy solution. For, paradoxically, such teachings convey "new" stereotypes about gays, Jews, blacks, and mad people.

I don't think it is an effect of my own naïveté that I was not familiar with some of the images attached to Jewishness in eighteenth-century England (Felsenstein 1995). And I will certainly not make a list of those stereotypes I discovered about madness and blackness and sexuality in Gilman's volumes. As for what it may or may not mean to wear a red hankerchief in the left pocket of your jeans if you are a gay man in the 1970s, I will leave it up to you to look up Hal Fisher's 1978 *Gay Semiotics: A Photographic Study of Visual Coding among Homosexual Men.*

More seriously, I think it would be a disaster to frame some of the "new" stereotypes I have discovered and to indulge in a renewed moment of more or less morbid fascination with cruel images. In this specific instance, I would be perpetuating in vain what I perceive as the endemic problem of any detailed analysis of stereotypes, including this one. Neither do I think that it is a catastrophic by-product of those books to have put stereotypical ideas in my mind: stereotypes need not be taboo as long we recognize that they are highly dangerous rhetorical tools and that we should treat them like bottles of poison in a kitchen cabinet. In other words, as long as each stereotype is accompanied by a metadiscourse about stereotypical language, as long as each stereotype is placed under constant surveillance, there is no reason to suppose that radical acts of censorship are always preferable. Stereotypical poison does not die, and even if we are perfectly aware of its presence, existence, and even obsolescence, we may want to treat stereotypes as evolving systems and make a point of constantly monitoring them, checking for signs of alarming changes in the relationship between representation and power, images and domination.

Clearly, once we have explained exactly which ethnic stereotypes have saturated literatures and cultures at certain times, which populations have been targeted and by whom, and which voices have embraced or denounced them, it is still not possible to stop and hope that the war against stereotypes has been won. First of all, to use Gramscian images, because it is hardly a war but rather an eternal series of skirmishes and latent conflicts between ambivalent factions (Gramsci 1971).

Ethnic stereotypes function like many other cultural constructions that predicate a collective identity shared by all the members of a given group. The definition of the group can be based on race, ethnicity, religious belief, on gender or sexual preference, but the result is almost always comparable: when opposing bias or confronting stereotypes, it is difficult not to preach to the partially converted. Unlike Barthes, I do not recommend the creation of a new discipline of stereotype studies that could at times overlap with or be included in other areas of studies such as gay and lesbian studies or queer studies or ethnic studies or African studies. As the critics of early twentieth-century Africanists warned, displaying the riches of African art will not silence the colonizer's guns. Similarly, Leo Bersani worries about the "discrediting of a specific gay identity" by studies that genuinely seek to celebrate gayness and sometimes lead to what he calls "degaying."

> We have erased ourselves in the process of denaturalizing the epistemic and political regimes that have constructed us. The power of those systems is only minimally contested by demonstrations of their "merely" historical character. They don't need to be natural in order to rule; to demystify them doesn't render them inoperative. If many gays now reject a homosexual identity as it has been elaborated for gays by others, the dominant heterosexual society doesn't need our belief in its own naturalness in order to continue exercising and enjoying the privileges of dominance. (1995 4–5)

So what is it about the formal structure of stereotypes that can recruit the enemy and turn him or her into an unwilling ally? First of all, rejecting stereotypes is too vague a project as long as we don't focus on their illusory timelessness. And here, the two key words are time and memory. Whether it is in order to understand or at least to control the phenomenon, we may want to ask: What is it that makes stereotypes almost immortal? They have obviously not always been called "stereotypes," but some ready-made assumptions have survived centuries of major cultural, political, and ideological changes. If you are Jewish, does it help to know that medieval texts circulated the same pernicious rubbish as the little schoolchildren who enlightened you about your community (Felsenstein 1995, xiii–xiv)? If your skin is black, is it any consolation that *Le Pen* rehashes the same old theories as Arthur, Comte de Gobineau's 1853 essay on *The Inequality of Human Races* (Gobineau 1967)? Let us propose instead that the stereotype seems endowed with an almost self-generating nature. Once uttered, a stereotype can be branded in an individual's mind and start an almost autonomous life as a repeatable unit of ideology.[11]

Even a person plagued with an appallingly bad memory remembers stereotypes without any problem. Stereotypes are wonderfully successful bits and pieces of language; they are memorable. They may be compared, studied in parallel with rhyming poetry, advertisements, nursery rhymes, and so on. Their memorability is directly linked to their timelessness; a vicious circle develops whereby memorability leads to timelessness, which in turn, because human cultures hoard the past, increases memorability. The alliance between memory and time in this case can be pinpointed as both the cause and the effect of stereotyping practices, what I will call their "iterativity." Because of their strong iterative force, they travel from mouth to mouth, from text to text, from discipline to discipline without losing much of their original shape and strength, as if, parasites themselves, they need not worry about the deterioration other statements suffer from circulation and transmission processes.

Characterized by iterativity, stereotypes have often been identified as cases of repetition gone crazy, as a disease of the same, of the always already said. As such, they have inspired countless literary masterpieces but always in a relatively pessimistic and cynical way. Flaubert's pathetic and annoying pair of friends, Bouvard and Pécuchet, immediately comes to mind, but other authors have capitalized on the realization that stereotypical forms of language are not destroyed by satirical treatment. In her study of Flaubert's *Le Dictionnaire des idées reçues*, Anne Herschberg-Pierrot cites one of Jean Paulhan's brilliant little emblematic narratives, the tale of cousin Henriette and of her influence on her family, the Langelons. "Incident de langage dans la famille Langelon" tells the story of how a family was contaminated by stereotypical language in spite of their desire to reject it as trite and automatic. When cousin Henriette comes back from Canada, she is mocked and ridiculed by her relatives because her sentences are saturated with proverbs. But gradually, Henriette's habits infect the family like a contagious linguistic disease, for whenever they try to make fun of Henriette's idiosyncratic way of speaking, the Langelons end up sounding exactly like her. As Herschberg-Pierrot logically concludes: "Dire des stéréotypes et les dénoncer ne sont que deux aspects d'une même énonciation" (Using and exposing stereotypes are the two sides of the same act of enunciation) (Herschberg-Pierrot 1988, 24). To go one step further, it could be said that the decision to denounce a stereotype leads inexorably to a moment when the stereotype has to be uttered and that even this type of meta-utterance, this distanced repetition of a framed stereotype involves a minimum, unconscious yet unavoidable element of allegiance. If we included stereotypes in our conversation even as examples, even as the target of our jokes, others could be primarily sensitive to the presence of those questionable statements; their interpretation of our position may then complicate what we take as unambiguous criticism. In Paulhan's story, the Langelons are completely contaminated by Henriette's stereotypical way of talking, and only their neighbors and friends—those who listen to stereotypes now uttered by the mocking family—remain lucid, puzzled, and uncomfortable.

According to Paulhan, the Langelons' failure was unavoidable because of what he perceives as a crisis in language, an "incident" as the title of the story puts it:

> Elle répétait tout le temps les mêmes phrases. Or, les répétant à leur tour, et fût-ce avec ironie, à propos des événements les plus dissemblables, ils ne prenaient pas garde qu'elles devenaient insensiblement le nom de ces événements. D'où l'écart de sens et l'ironie s'effaçaient peu à peu.
>
> [She used to repeat the same sentences over and over again. And as they repeated them too, even ironically, about completely dissimilar events, they did not realize that gradually those sentences were becoming the name of such events. From which distance and irony slowly disappeared.][12]

The dangerous level of ambiguity in the Langelons' tactic is exacerbated by the unstable quality of any critical distance. The stereotype is a form of enunciation that thrives on the possibility of confusion between the descriptive and the prescriptive—that is, on the death of irony. The erosion of irony is a tremendous risk to assume when the stereotype in question is malevolently racist, and Paulhan quite cleverly insists on the invisible, involuntary, and gradual qualities of the transformation of the mocked stereotype into the adopted stereotype. It is not quite clear what he means here by the "name" of an event, but the suggestion that steretoypes can become the names of events is both disturbing and fascinating. Most of the time, events are defined as and through stories and narratives, not names. Or is Paulhan implying that when events are indeed identified by a proper name it is because they have been branded with a steretoype, or rather impregnated or infiltrated or infected with the incessant repetition of a steretoype? Is it the case, then, that we should beware those historical moments that we tend to identify with one or two very specific nouns and adjectives? Is "the French Revolution," for example, an event whose "name" was originally an ironic stereotype? And what implications does this suspicion have for ethnic steretoypes?

When trying to oppose ethnic stereotypes, one of the most delicate problems will therefore be to find an adequate and strategic response to what Homi Bhabha, in his study of colonial stereotypes, calls the "fetishistic nature" of stereotypes. He writes:

> The stereotype . . . is a form of knowledge and identification that vacillates between what is always "in place" already known, and something that must be anxiously repeated . . . as if the essential duplicity of the Asiatic or the bestial sexual licence of the African that needs no proof, can never really, in discourse, be proved. (Bhabha 1994, 66)

But even though the stereotype can never be proved, this lack of final and definitive anchorage in the truth does not represent a weakness. The stereotype does not function like a suspect: What the jury says is irrelevant; there is no innocence, no guilt involved. There is no reason to be comforted by the impossibility of verifying the truth of a stereotype since, as Bhabha hastens to point out, the absence of proof is not enough to eliminate the "anxious" repetition of those sentences that successfully pass as declarative statements. In other words, the "truth" of a stereotype—its identity—cannot be found in what is said about the ethnic group but in the specific features of the statement itself.

I suggest that the identity of an ethnic stereotype is a very abstract quality, a formal characteristic that we could conceptualize as a level or as an intensity rather than as content. That is, an ethnic stereotype is above all defined by a high degree of iterativity. An ethnic stereotype is like a form of contamination; it is a strong element of iterativity that insinuates itself like some sort of bacteria to a general statement about a group or a community. The stereotypical infection then turns this nondemonstrable statement into an instantly memorable formula that parades as common sense, truth, and wisdom. In the next stage, the ideological content, the supposedly descriptive element of the stereotype—that is, what the stereotype says about a certain racial or ethnic group—then appears to be the stereotype itself. However, the fact that I focus on and react to *what* is said is another of the ruses of the stereotyping machine. Behind the smoke screen of what the stereotype says about a certain ethnic group, the identity and immense resilience of the stereotype resides in its apparently indestructible degree of iterativity.

Even if I become aware of this particular problem, what can be done? Repeating is the most powerful form of enactment. Repeating is a speech act endowed with the maximum authorized level of power. I cannot quote stereotypes without acting in their favor. But if I don't quote, how can I address the issue of ethnic stereotypes without hovering ten thousand theoretical feet over the debate that precisely requires immediate intervention? Am I not effectively threatened with aphasia once I admit that stereotypes are just as likely to borrow my voice as a channel of transmission? (Moreover, I can scarcely imagine that readers would be interested in a book that never gave an example or illustration). A few years ago, I thought it was particularly funny and ironic that the members of the Meese Commission, working on possible ways of censoring pornography, were forced by virtue of their mission to expose their souls to reams after reams of horribly thought-provoking material (Steward 1991, 253–72). I now find myself stuck on the other side of the mirror: I know that I cannot study stereotypes without being affected by their high level of quotability. But burying one's head in the sand does not seem to make them go away either.

When I decide to oppose a stereotype, I usually become the victim of this confusion between what is said and what is repeatable. Assuming that I want to discredit a given stereotype about a specific ethnic group, if I do not recognize that the survival of a stereotype depends more on its repeatability than its demonstrability, I may confront the ideological element and try to demonstrate that a particular; statement is not true. As a result, I find myself treading on the narrow line between a speech act and a quoted speech act that has not lost its power; saying "All Arabs are *x*" and "It is not true that all Arabs are *x* is scarcely different from the point of the view of the stereotype. Attacked as a unit of truth, it takes its revenge by forcing speaking into an act of mimesis. I am forced to actually repeat the statement that activates the stereotyped idea. If we look at what Bhabha does in the passage above, the ruse of the stereotype appears plainly: in order to denounce stereotypes about "the Africans, the Asians," Bhabha must repeat, at least once, what he must assume "we" all know—not what we all know about Africans, but what we all know about what our culture says about Africans. The trick, of course, is that, although the truth of a stereotype lies in its successive repetitions, there is always a first time for someone. And this is all the more important as that first time is all it takes.

Naturally, every reader knows that Bhabha does not subscribe to what he says, but the iterativity of stereotypes traps him in a double bind: there is no possible innocent reference to a stereotype, and there is no stereotype to denounce until it is quoted. As soon as it is mentioned, the stereotype starts functioning within the critic's discourse, a little like a ticking time bomb. It is not possible to cite it without unleashing its stereotypical power. In a sense, that is one of the possible definitions of a stereotype: something that cannot be properly quoted, if by "quoting" we mean containing between diacritical marks, within codified boundaries, the words of some criticized Other that I want to oppose. Because of its performative and malleable qualities, however, the stereotype easily crosses such barriers.

It is even possible that quoted ethnic stereotypes gain more from being quoted than the critic from illustrating his or her point since their strength resides in the duplicity of their presence and in their ability to contaminate their environment. We can never tell for sure in what capacity they are invited, since the reference to a stereotype *is* a stereotype. When we try to contain them within a theoretical apparatus, we often end up framing stereotypes, thus attracting attention to them by placing them in positions of centrality that increase their capability for self-transmission. Bhabha himself cannot completely eliminate the risk of seeing his own text provide a support for delusional and malevolent generalizations that resurface through his own writing, as if the letters of an old palimpsest gradually reappeared.

Stereotypes do not allow scholars to pin them to the wall like some dead insect. Their venom is intact and can infiltrate any text that wants to contain it. As products attacked by a negative advertising campaign sometimes manage to benefit even from the discursive space that tries to destroy them, stereotypes will probably survive all attempts to erase them from the face of the earth. But it may even be worse. According to some critics, when stereotypes do not disappear, they extend their hold over yet larger cultural territories. According to Sieglinde Lemke, the ethical balance of such a transaction is clearly a deficit. At the end of a review of Jan Nederveen Pieterse's *White on Black*, Lemke concludes that the author has not sufficiently guarded his text from the danger of contamination between stereotypes and a critique of stereotypes. And Lemke sadly concludes that *White on Black* is an example of "the unfortunate irony" generated by "an account of the stereotype that is itself a stereotype" (1993, 154).

But if the structure of stereotypical discourse poses formidable obstacles, stereotypes are not completely invincible either. It is quite useful to be aware of their infectious power, but it is also out of the question to remain silent forever. What is quite clear is that there is no pure victory, no pure fight, no hope of clearing the air forever. Nevertheless, all stereotypes are not equal and they do not require the same response from socially responsible subjects. What we need to ascertain is when to intervene and when to avoid the trap of feeding the mimetic machine of stereotypical constructions. Sometimes, nonintervention may be the best tactic. Sometimes, it is necessary to take the risk of being "stereotyped," as it were, of being traversed, contaminated, spoken by stereotypes.[13]

As Sander Gilman recognizes, "the need for stereotypes runs so deep that I do not think it will ever be thwarted; nor do I think that it will ever be converted to purely harmless expression" (1985, 12). I agree that it is useful to treat stereotypes as the expression of a need rather than as the manifestation of a social evil. It is true that their ineradicable presence can never be converted into "purely harmless expression." So perhaps it is crucial to distinguish between different levels of harmlessness; if we cannot hope to transform stereotypes into "purely" harmless statements, surely we can decide whether or not to intervene depending on the degree of violence or innocuosness of certain ethnic stereotypes.

For example, it is prudent not to rely on a tacit confusion between stereotypes and negative images: certain positive images are ethnic stereotypes. Bhabha suggests that it is much more important to scrutinize the relationship between stereotypes and domination rather than operate a classification of positive or negative images. Speaking more specifically about colonial discourse, he writes: "the point of intervention should shift from the ready recognition of images as positive or negative, to an understanding of the processes of subjectification made possible (and plausible) through stereotypical discourse" (1994, 67). We thus may want to ascertain very carefully whether or not an apparently complimentary series of adjectives is not just as dangerous as certain racial slurs.[14] On the other hand, certain antiracist interventions are clearly stereotypical, and once again it is not always obvious whether we should happily launch a crusade against the clumsiness of such a campaign.[15]

To insist that stereotypes are not necessarily harmful is very tempting. But whose interest would it serve? That human thought is consistently saturated with stereotypes may be true, but that is beside the point. Through a study of what stereotyped people do in the face of steretoypes, through a study of the activities they deploy, we will see how a stereotype can been turned into a *relatively* harmless event, or at least deprived of most of its effectiveness. In the following chapters, I have privileged situations where a given stereotype has lost *some* of its power, at least temporarily, due to the intervention of a careful dosed mixture of positive and negative declining.

The belief that we can, even provisionally, in certain contexts, change the valence of certain stereotypes implies a leap of faith. Each of the following chapters tells the story of a more or less successful attempt to map the space of what Ross Chambers calls "room for maneuver" (1991). As Pierre Barbéris writes:

> Le stéréo n'existe pas en dehors d'un système de relations qui le constitue. . . . Il y a toujours de la liberté possible, à l'intérieur d'un système de nécessité. Mais cette liberté, cette possibilité est toujours précaire et relative. (Barbéris 1994, 9)

> [The stereos do not exist outside a system of relationships that constitutes them. . . . There is always a margin of liberty within a system of necessity. But this freedom, this possibility is always precarious and relative.]

Chapter 2

Stealing Stereotypes

Mehdi Charef, Marie Féraud, and Smaïn

All the texts analyzed in this chapter have one feature in common: They play with the stereotypical figure of the petty thief, of the juvenile delinquent.[1] Each text adopts a slightly different tactic of reappropriation, but in each case the ultimate goal is to rebut a particularly vicious stereotypical commonplace: the image of the Other as thief. One of the ways in which to fight back is to operate a reversal that is also a form of overbidding: rather than rejecting the image, some texts either fight the way in which the image is constructed (how does one define a thief?) or steal the negative image and put it to a different use. Instead of denouncing the user of stereotypes that accuse them of being thieves, some characters prefer to give up on the idea that there is a neutral place from which to oppose the ideological premises of stereotypical discourses, and they operate a sort of counter "double mimesis."

"Double mimesis" is the phrase used by Kaja Silverman to describe complex processes of identification proposed by imperial Englishmen to natives during the colonial period. In her analysis (1989) of Lawrence of Arabia's *Seven Pillars of Wisdom*, she suggests that the native is expected to construct his own identity by mimicking the version of himself provided by the white man's impersonation of the Arab.[2] Our postcolonial era adds an ironic twist to double mimesis: The distinction between natives and colonizers has all but disappeared in contemporary France. Now French citizens of North African origin see their identity imagined and projected onto imaginary and real screens as a list of stereotypical features (a look, an accent, a predictable behavior, certain sets of beliefs). For example, in order to successfully portray an Arab character, stand-up comics will adopt accents that are meant to be recognized as foreign. When we see Smaïn, one of the most popular Beur figures, acting out something that we are expected to identify as an authentic first-generation immigrant's accent, the effect is immensely troubling: it is as if

Aimé Césaire suddenly started speaking "petit nègre," as if Sédar Senghor had opened a speech with "y a bon" or had started speaking like one of the black characters, in Hergé's *Tintin au Congo*. Today, Francophone people of North African origin, regardless of their nationality, have the option of playing with stereotypical images. Instead of resisting the schizophrenic splitting of audience created by the denouncing of stereotypical voices (I, as a listener, denounce you, the speaker, as a creator of stereotypes), they not only pretend to go along with the stereotype as truth, they also offer a perfect performance of who they are supposed to be.

Perfecting the art of producing counterstereotypical stereotypes is no mean feat, because the images proposed to the Arabs and their children are both predictably negative and extraordinarily complex, multifaceted, and sometimes self-contradictory. Often they take the form of lists. When I hear the media announcing yet another special program on social issues (another *Marche du siècle* on *banlieues, état d'urgence*, for example), I often find myself reverting to the age when small children play with litanies of words. All French children, at one time or another, have presumably been exposed to this strange game that consists of reciting endless and meaningless lists of words triggered, as if by magic, by someone uttering the word "*Marabout.*" As a culturally competent subject, you know that "Marabout" does not refer to anything in particular; you are probably even too young to wonder if there is any connection with Africa and other cultures. What you do know, at that point, is that you are supposed to remember how the game works: you are expected to add, as fast as you can, without getting any of the words wrong, "Marabout, bout de ficelle, selle de cheval, cheval de course, course à pied, pied à terre, terre de feu, feu follet, lait de vache . . ." Translating here would be pointless: What counts is that the first syllable of each word sounds the same as the last syllable as the previous word but also that it is not enough to remember the formula as if it were one of Oulipo's literary games. The list is set once and for all; knowing how it works will not save you from the dishonor of not knowing how to continue correctly. There are, I am sure, variants to the game and I suspect that each player would adamantly defend their own version as the only legitimate one, for the litany is not just a way of testing one's memory.

It is not by chance that this senseless list tends to superimpose itself over current-affairs television shows, there is a political way of describing the pleasure involved in such apparently futile recitations. The Marabout-bout-de-ficelle list is part of a canon, and the pleasure experienced in the faultless reproduction of words deprived of their semantic content is not so much a test of one's memory as a ritual demonstration of one's identity as a legitimate member of the group. Not knowing how to recite this meaningless list signifies a lack of cultural knowledge that may then sanction more or less severe, more or less permanent forms of rejection. It may look as if I am dignifying a silly childish habit with a lot of theoretical meaningfulness, but I am indeed suggesting that the juxtaposition of idiocy and cultural competence in the reproduction of a nonimprovisable list has everything to do with the production of stereotypes.

Try using the word "Maghreb" or "Arab" in France today. Try inserting them in a sentence, innocently, as if by chance. Even if your interlocutors are sophisticated users of language who indulge in the pleasure of nuances, even if they are cautious and able with words, you may find that you have inadvertently started what we could now recognize as a "Marabout" syndrome. Say the word "Arab" and you will have pressed a discursive and cultural button, unleashing a Pavlovian herd of images: "Arabs" or "Beurs" or "Maghrebins" equal Islam and fundamentalism and mosques and crowds and suburbs and fanaticism and fundamentalism and racism and antiracism and fear and insecurity and immigrants and illegal aliens and Pasqua's laws and S.O.S. Racisme and the Algerian war. The reflex is all the more fascinating as it lies well beyond any ideological opposition between right-wing and left-wing politics. Even more remarkable perhaps is that when this list is perceived as a stereotype, when scholars decide to oppose the principle of amalgamation, their own discourse seems infected with the same agent: lists reappear under their critical pens, triumphant, practically unchanged. Rémy Leveau and Catherine Withol de Wenden admit that the ideological landscape is marred by "l'existence d'enjeux-clés comme l'insécurité et l'immigration" ("the existence of keywords such as insecurity and immigration") (1988, Leveau 103). Olivier Roy warns us against the dangers of confusing "l'immigration, le racisme, les beurs, les ghettos, l'ethnicité et l'islam" (immigration, racism, Beurs, ghettos, ethnicity and Islam) (Roy 1991, 37). Both sociologists' intention is clearly oppositional, but the list survives criticism unscathed. Roy's, Leveau's, and Withol de Wenden's sentences are swallowed by the universe of repetition. Like stereotypes, of which I suspect that they are often a category, lists contain an antidote against contradiction.

Because it can only be repeated, recited, because it suffers from amnesia (its own logic of fabrication and ideological structure crave oblivion and transparency), a list is not unlike a stereotype. And lists are a particularly irritating version of stereotypes because they hide beneath sheer quantity to mask their lack of nuances and complexity. Like stereotypes, they are a discourse of truth that sells its arbitrariness and political bias in a seductive gift wrapping of commonsensical immediacy. We are not to question the legitimacy of each repetition, it is always already too late to object. As Jean-Marie Touratier puts it:

> Il y a du stéréotype quand il y a interdit sur le questionnement de la répétition. Mieux, lorsqu'il y a oubli, scotomisation de toute répétition, leurre pour faire miroiter qu'il n'y a pas, qu'il n'y a jamais eu répétition. (Touratier 1979, 10)

[There is stereotyping when questioning repetition is forbidden. Better still, when forgetfulness and unconscious exclusion affect all repetition, when a lure makes us believe that there is no repetition, that there never was any repetition.]

A list, like a stereotype, counts on the hypnotic power of repetition. It hopes that each repetition will confirm its incantatory charm (Bhabha 1994). And even as we become aware of the principle, we continue to allow repetitive and formulaic statements to build up around politically sensitive issues ("immigration," "race," and, of course, "racism") because silence is clearly not an option.

In other words, it is worth asking why so many texts and films by Beur writers or directors portray their heroes as thieves as long as we do not immediately jump to the conclusions that postcolonial Beur authors suffer from an obvious case of self-deprecating alienation. In fact, that may be the least likely answer. Consider the following statement made by Hedi Dhoukar, a respected critic of Beur cinema: speaking about delinquency, Dhoukar suggests:

Moins qu'un thème, c'est une réalité toujours présente dans la plupart des films. Tous les personnages principaux des films de Mehdi Charef sont des délinquants ou se livrent à des actes qui en font objectivement des délinquants. Il s'agit de vol ou de proxénétisme dans la plupart des cas. (Dhoukar 1990, 154)

[It is less a theme than an all pervasive reality in most films. All the main characters in Mehdi Charef's films are delinquents or commit acts that objectively make delinquents out of them. Most of the time, they are thieves or pimps.]

It would be easy to be shocked into a defensive interpretation of the sad "reality" that even Beur directors present us with images of Beurs as delinquents (in the process implying that their perception should somehow be "different"). But falling into the trap that consists of explaining, excusing, condemning, or even celebrating that "reality" is but one of the possible readings of the passage. Instead, we could ask what kind of mechanism transforms a theme into a reality or vice-versa. We may also note that the critic introduces a distinction worth pursuing between being a delinquent and practicing delinquency, a split reminiscent of Michel Foucault's opposition between sexual identities and sexual practices, as in the case of gayness, for example. One may also wonder what is the exact connotation of the word "objectively" in Dhoukar's statement. Many texts that present us with the image of an ethnic delinquent provide precisely the innovative answers to the questions in Dhoukar's formulations. It is crucial to ask whose reality has the power to become a theme (that is, a recognizable, recurrent, immediately apprehensible image). In the case of delinquency, it is urgent to consciously analyze why identity and practices are sometimes collapsed and sometimes carefully distinguished; this self-conscious mental process is inseparable from a better awareness of who has the right to decide "objectively" what exactly constitutes a delinquent practice.

One of the possibilities of rewriting the "objective" stereotype of the ethnic thief involves a type of reasoning that could accurately be called deconstructive. Farida Belghoul's *Georgette* redefines stealing by showing that our commonplace understanding of theft implies important and unformulated preconceptions about the insider-outsider opposition and about the limits of private property. When the narrator, a young female child, steals money from her mother's purse, she explains: "Je suis pas une voleuse. Le vol existe pas dans une même famille. Mon père le dit à chaque fois que mon frère m'accuse" ("I am not a thief. Theft does not exist within a family. My father says so whenever my brother accuses me") (Belghoul 1986, 19). This, I would claim, is not a case of bad faith, but a moment when we realize that the little girl oscillates between two contradictory sets of rules. The text does not make it clear whether she knows or not that the father's convictions are at odds with a more generally accepted definition of stealing. What he wants his children to learn is that within the limits of some social groups (here, the "family"), the circulation of goods and money is not ruled by the laws of commerce, exchange, and profit that are increasingly applied as universal global moral code. What the son seems to know, however, is that it is possible to refuse the father's boundaries, his notion of who is inside and who is outside. He thus adopts a definition of stealing that is based on a completely different model of property. The passage makes it clear that our analysis cannot rely on the figure of the delinquent, since assuming that we can define delinquency is already a dangerous shortcut. The father's intuitions are crucial and not often theorized on a daily basis: one cannot determine theft without a theory of private and collective property, a definition of who is family and who is not.[3] Unless we interrogate our definitions of "property" and "family," we may fail to realize that explaining the thief's behavior is not so different from (and potentially as racist as) condemning it. *Georgette* points out that we often fail to ask who has the right and the power to propose a definition of theft, of what requirements must be met for a character to be identified as a thief.

Originally, I was tempted to ask the following questions: Why does Mehdi Charef, in *Le thé au harem d'Archi Ahmed*, portray his heroes, Pat and Madjid, as cynical pickpockets? Why does he place them in the middle of a typical "stealing from the bourgeois" scenario that seems as predictable, given the circumstances, as the arrival of the American cavalry at the end of a western? A similar set of problems arises with Marie Féraud and her *Histoires Maghrébines* (Maghrebi stories). She presents her book as a collection of stories or folktales told by the "Maghrébins de Roubaix" (The Maghrebi from Roubaix) (Féraud 1985, 10) among whom she lived for a while. What, then, is the purpose of "Les Ray-Ban," a glaringly atypical and at the same banal story that tells the story of three teenagers who are caught stealing a few pairs of glasses? Also, why does *Hexagone* (1993), Malik Chibane's film that attempts to represent the Beur community in its diversity, insist so much on Sami's habit of "*se faire un caddie*"[4] and on his rather complicated schemes, such as his plan to steal matching pairs of shoes from shops that only display the right or the left foot? Why does Bertrand Blier, in his surrealistic *Un, deux, trois soleil* (1993), present us with a scene where a lonely white home owner leaves money lying around on his table to make sure that some "merveilleux enfant" ("marvelous child") will come and steal from his place?

I am now convinced, however, that such questions fall into a gaping ideological and logical trap. First of all, they assume that juvenile crime is already defined, even as the texts multiply invitations to verify our assumptions. Sami, who decides to "go and get a shopping cart," functions according to his own reinvented norms, and those norms entail the redrawing of the boundaries between public and private space and the definition of property. The film strongly condemns him, but the story presents him as a challenge to our definition of delinquency. Similarly, inside and outside, family and strangers are implicitly rearticulated in Blier's film: when the "merveilleux enfant" finally shows up, steals the money left on the table, and realizes that the owner is watching him, he asks him why he is so generous while all the others threaten him and try to catch him. The white character's answer is "Tu n'as qu'à pas aller voler chez les autres" ("That'll teach you to go and steal from other people's houses"). Again, the apparently paradoxical argument revolves around notions of territory, the difference between "chez moi" and "chez les autres," where otherness is radically reconceptualized in a move that deprives us of known definitions of what is reprehensible about stealing in general.

Taking seriously the implications of Chibane's, Blier's, and Belghoul's fictionalizations, it becomes obvious that the questions must be reformulated. And looking back at the list of examples I have just accumulated, its seemingly unquestionable authority appears suspect. And, transgressing the elementary rule that demands that one keeps the conclusion for the end, I propose that the question of "why so many thieves among ethnic characters?" was blind to the fact that the question itself is the problem, whereas the texts I refer to have already found the solution to the proliferation of stereotypes.

Only after a second close reading of Smaïn's, Marie Féraud's, and Mehdi Charef's descriptions of pickpockets did I finally understand that it was not postcolonial Beur literature and culture as a whole that were fascinated by the picture of the delinquent. Rather, those texts had tempted me, and the temptation was a certain type of interpretation. As a reader, I chose to make sense of the difficult passages by invoking the stereotyped figure of the Arab-as-thief. My reading was the equivalent of translating "se faire un caddie" with "stealing." And such translation is obviously reductive even if it cannot be said to be inaccurate. What the texts suggest instead is that it is pointless to ask them *why* they repeat stereotypes, but that it is possible to answer *how* they repeat stereotypes and what tactic they choose to repeat them while undermining their ideological implications about who is in and who is out, who is rich and who is poor, who owns and who steals.

Glasses and thieves

Histoires Maghrébines (1985) is a collection of folktales, short stories, legends, and news recorded and transcribed by Marie Féraud, a sociologist who worked with the Maghrebi inhabitants in the "Alma-Gare" neighborhood outside of Roubaix in the north of France. In her preface, Féraud proposes the word "*conte*" (folk or fairytale) to describe her texts in order to emphasize the link between her stories and a well-established oral tradition where the community is united around the storyteller and by the activity of storytelling. Marie Féraud systematically refers to her companions as storytellers and to their activity as storytelling, even though more conventional anthologies would have put her texts into very different literary categories. Some of the legends belong to what Western literature would call the fantastic, but other stories revolve around contemporary real characters whose adventures are neither particularly glamorous nor original. Féraud insists on viewing storytelling as a modern practice that says something valid about current social issues. In her preface, she anticipates potential objections of archaism and refuses to distinguish too sharply between modernism and tradition. She refuses the "préjugé tenace [qui] nous présente le conteur comme le dépositaire d'une tradition immuable" [persistent preconception that presents the storyteller as the guardian of an unchanging tradition] (7).

Féraud's story "Les Ray-Ban" says something new about juvenile crime because the economy of the story does not correspond to our expectations: It does not end with a moral, nor does it function as a thriller where we would be invited to identify the good guys and the bad guys hidden behind tragically mixed-up appearances. The text is not looking for unjustly accused innocents, nor for culprits to judge or exonerate. Instead, "Les Ray-Ban" presents us with a new definition of delinquency in a very specific context. The story suggests that each historical context should carefully reconsider the relationship between power, the authorities, and delinquency and make sure that both the law and the delinquent do not find themselves caught in a perverse mirror-situation of mutual imitation.

At first, "Les Ray-Ban" looks as if it conveys a stereotype. The story belongs in a rather unimaginative local news column. We may have the impression that we have heard this before, and unlike all those literary texts about which the critic says, with a certain degree of self-justification, that no plot summary can do justice to their complexity and depth, "Les Ray-Ban" fits in a nutshell. In the late 1970s, in a suburb of Roubaix, three young teenagers—Bongo, Rabah, and Kamel—of different ethnic origins decide to steal a few pairs of then-fashionable Ray-Ban glasses. They are caught red-handed by a supermarket security guard who not only forces them to give the glasses back but also demands that they spend a afternoon cleaning filthy shopping carts, giving a whole new intertextual sense to "se faire un caddie."

I suggest that like the three heroes, Marie Féraud's text can be called delinquent because it manipulates those very images and clichés on which the definition of delinquency rests at a given historical moment; the narrative embezzles a number of cultural stereotypes and proceeds to use the cultural currency of such images for its own purpose. From an ideological point of view, the clever point of entrance of this story into the cultural arena is its apparently naive acquiescence to the notion that the figure of the young ethnic delinquent is unavoidable. The reader will thus spend a lot of time wondering if the author is guilty of good intentions gone sour and has fallen back into the pattern of lists: youth equals delinquency equals immigration equals children of immigrants equals Maghrebi. At first, we may be annoyed by the blatant repetition of a stereotype framed by seemingly respectful conditions of enunciation.

From the beginning of the book, the reader is aware that Kamel, Bongo, and Rabah will not be judged according to criteria that would normally be used to distinguish (or precisely fail to distinguish) between delinquent and honest social actors, between supposedly nonethnic, nonimmigrant "Français de souche" (French people of French origin) and second-generation immigrants. The author does not hide behind some illusory desire for impartiality. Early in the book, it is clear that she has a lot of affection for the "*maghrébins de Roubaix*" who agree to plant a metaphorical "*arbre à palabres*" (palaver tree) in the middle of the city after she produces her tape recorder (10). It is just as clear, however, that her position is not that of the activist or grass-roots militant. She cannot be confused with the voice of members of associations; she has nothing to do with charismatic political figures such as Harlem Désir; she is not a spokesperson. Féraud refuses the title of "author" and insists that she is only presenting us with the collection of narratives. The gesture is different from a conventional manuscript-found-in-a-bottle plot, yet the stories are coded as somebody else's. Féraud is only the ethnographer, the witness, the translator, the facilitator. The self-effacing distance, however, is immediately offset by the author's intimate involvement in the telling of the stories. The narrative voice is never neutral; her listening is a form of witnessing and the fictionalization reflects the fact that the stories are the result of decisive choices, of radical redefinitions of inside and outside, of "themes" and "reality."

In the film *Hexagone*, the resemblance and difference between se faire un caddie and shoplifting is maintained and dramatized by the introduction of the paratext, a glossary, sometimes distributed to the audience at the beginning the film. The textual appendix recognizes that the audience may speak a different language. If we watch the film without looking at the glossary, or if we happen to read the glossary without watching the film, the negotiations and tensions involved in the decision to choose one phrase rather than another disappears. In "Les Ray-Ban," the narrative voice manages to keep the tension alive by forcing both types of descriptions—different types of language—to cohabit more or less harmoniously. Féraud's role as a sympathetic storyteller emphasizes the work involved in moving from "reality" to "theme" by highlighting her position as *both* speaker and listener, both witness and actor, both author and translator.

This uncomfortable vantage point writes itself as a specific narrative technique, an original voice that I would like to call "unreliable free indirect speech." Like unreliable narration, unreliable indirect speech gives us reasons to doubt the veracity of what is presented to us as facts. Free indirect style, on the other hand, seeks to bypass the author or the omniscient narrator; it allows us to hear, without quotes, though in the third person, what one of the characters says or thinks. This technique demands that the narrator make room, at least temporarily, for the point of view of his characters, even if this apparent modesty is often used to criticize or ironize. In other words, a hybrid space occurs where the dominant, powerful voice pretends to let the subaltern speak. But in Féraud's manipulation of this technique, an element of unreliability is introduced. For example, when she introduces her character for the first time, the portrait she offers is clearly schizophrenic and tension ridden.

Bongo is said to be "un grand noir Marocain . . . qui avait une soeur intéressante" (a tall black Moroccan . . . with an interesting sister) (60). This tongue-in-cheek presentation is an example of what I call unreliable free indirect speech: it catapults two completely different levels of language into the same sentence: the first part of the sentence describes the hero's physical appearance and inserts a piece of information about his ethnic origin. The reference to Bongo's color is an apparently matter-of-fact observation whose relevance is not immediately clear. But just as we may be wondering if the author seriously believes that it is possible to introduce identity and race in such an apparently casual way and not have the reader find something clichéd about the hero's depiction (why is Bongo reduced to his physical appearance; why is his skin color privileged?), the first impression is irrevocably modified by the amusing allusion to his sister. When the sister is deemed "interesting," the tone has obviously changed considerably, and it is very unlikely that the statement should have been uttered by the sociologist. The vague yet unmistakable sexual connotation makes it much more likely for the remark to have been overheard. In all probability, that type of comment comes from one of Bongo's male heterosexual adolescent peers, and it is not clear at all that Marie Féraud approves of what is implicit in the teenager's attitude, even if a certain degree of amused and affectionate grown-up indulgence is detectable here. But the most obvious result of the conflation of the two levels of language is its comic effect.

The complete sentence now sounds strangely discordant, as if it had been authored by two different and not necessarily compatible voices. It is as if a space has been created where both Chibane's glossary and Sami's slang can cohabit, as if it had become impossible to say where each voice begins and stops. Two completely different levels of description have fused to produce an incongruous unit, and the resulting tension within Féraud's text underlines the fact that, in spite of the narrator's tenderness for the Roubaisian community, she is quite capable of ironic distance. The space of seamless cohabitation between two voices, the absence of markers of alterity (quotation marks in this case) forces us to rethink who is in and who is out, who is *chez soi* and who is not at home, a crucial redrawing that, as *Georgette* demonstrated, is the key to finding out who the thief really is. When Féraud dispenses with diacritic markers of otherness, she creates an experimental place where it will be more difficult to distinguish between the witness and the delinquent, as well as between quotations and commentary. Although the author's voice does not replace her heroes' version altogether, she does not renounce her place as storyteller either. Her voice is different, yet not separable. Her story speaks of otherness within the boundaries of a unique family.

Having created one space of original textual combination, the text simultaneously chooses to dissolve the stereotypical fusion between ethnic youth and delinquency through another layer of redefinition of theft. In "Les Ray-Ban," delinquency is an oppositional practice, not because it seeks to subvert a contested norm but because it claims that the norm itself is a form of delinquency. Delinquents imitate or borrow models from the very dominant structures that exclude them as outlaws.

Another crucial step toward a redeployment of the stereotype is to insist on an extreme contextual specificity of the concept of delinquency. Féraud is interested in separating the three youths' practices from a supposedly commonsensical and ahistorical definition of delinquency. Their cultural identity, for example, is always problematized. It is out of the question for the story to simply ignore their ethnic and racial specificity, but the text also makes it clear that identity does not explain the episode. Unlike some of the other timeless legends in the book, this short story is very accurately located in time and place. The cultural context is also meticulously recalled, even though the events in question are only a few years old. At the beginning of "Les Ray-Ban," the reader is told that the story occurs at one specific moment in time, a short-lived era humorously referred to as a natural catastrophe: one day, "la fureur des Ray-Ban s'abattit sur la ville" (Ray-Ban glasses fell on the town like a plague) (59). Féraud remembers that the addiction to the fashionable glasses had displaced, at least among teenagers, a "passion des pantalons à pattes d'éléphants" (a passion for bell-bottoms) that "ravageait la ville" (wreaked havoc on the town) (59). The narrator explains that in this period Ray-Ban glasses were every adolescent's fetishistic object of desire, and, perhaps more important, that the gods of ephemeral fashions who influence the youths' behavior are worshiped by all, regardless of their national or ethnic origin."Tout ce que la ville comptait de garçons à mobylette se changea soudain en cow-boy sur Harley Davidson, comme Fonda dans le film avec ses fabuleuses Ray-Ban qui reflétaient le désert Américain" (In town, every kid on his moped suddenly metamorphosed into a cowboy riding a Harley-Davidson, as in the film where Peter Fonda's pair of fabulous Ray-Ban glasses reflect the American desert) (59). With a touch of patronizing yet understanding irony, the narrator's voice explains that no young man can hope to become a certified "*dragueur roubaisien*" (Roubaisian Casanova) without the required props and accessories. Success or failure on the heterosexual scene has everything to do with a carefully constructed image of masculinity, but that construction is not ethnically predetermined.

It is therefore impossible to generalize from the story. The reader cannot extrapolate and use "Les Ray-Ban" to make up a theory on the relationship between delinquency and children of immigrants. Instead, the text recognizes that it is dangerous and inept to work from too broad a concept of delinquency instead of analyzing the mental activity we deploy when we erase the differences between the different types of historical delinquents. Without necessarily going back to the nineteenth-century realist novels and their stereotypical hungry poor sent to the gallows for having stolen some food, it is urgent to verify that our analyses of stereotypes and our sociological studies keep abreast of the swift evolution of urban delinquency over the past two decades. Recently, the young inhabitants of suburbs have dubbed their condition "*la galère*" (literally, "the galley"), as if what was once a punishment (being sent to work in the galley) was now internalized as a way of life. *Galère* includes delinquency and the misery that comes with it, as if the effects of the norm needed no external agent to impose its values.

After World War II, youth delinquency was traditionally associated with those suburbs branded "*banlieues rouges*" because they often elected communist mayors. To conjure up stereotypical images of young, dangerous delinquents, it was enough to mention those red suburbs. In other countries other geographical areas served the same purpose: in Great Britain, northern mining towns evoked the same caricatural images. In 1968, the stereotype flirted with other charismastic embodiments, such as the figure of the student-movement leaders. Young people were now visualized as dangerous activists, "*casseurs,*" who followed mass demonstrations, burning cars, breaking windows. Rebels had a cause and the word "*politisé[e]*" (politicized) sounded dangerously threatening to the so-called silent majority. The worker's son had moved from the banlieues rouges to the boulevards of big cities.

In Marie Féraud's story, 1968 is already a thing of the past. Alma-Gare is portrayed as a self-contained suburb of a self-contained provincial town. Here, the adolescents' delinquency is devoid of a political message; it is not ritualized; more important, it does not have anything to do with the heroes' ethnic identity. In other words, this book is very specifically inscribed right before the beginning of the 1980s (which could be considered the "Beur decade" in terms of novels and autobiographies) and even more clearly before the following moment when *banlieues-films* began to make it clear that *la galère* had definitely turned to hatred and that ethnicity could no longer be deemed irrelevant.

Féraud's heroes exemplify what François Dubet and Didier Lapeyronnie call "conformisme déviant" ("deviant conformism").[5] Dubet and Lapeyronnie distinguish between modern *galère* and the earlier ritualized forms of group activities associated with the working class and much feared by the bourgeoisie. According to the sociologists, so-called delinquent working-class young adults were in fact reproducing a model their parents had themselves gone through. Féraud's characters cannot rely on this element of tradition and cannot count on their family's support. For while the sons of workers were criticized and disapproved of by their community, their subversive practices were in fact contained and relatively controlled, the adults granting them a measure of tolerance and complicity. This background is completely absent from Féraud's story, where only the narrator represents a benevolent adult presence.

As a result, her young adolescents seem all the more likely to be defined as thieves since, unlike Georgette, they lack a territory from which stealing is excluded by the law of the father. Neither 1968 antibourgeois revolutionary students nor young militant Beurs of the 1980s, the heroes of Féraud's stories do not represent anyone; they cannot be used as the origin of a new stereotypical image. Yet their story is precious in its specificity and its stress on a historicization of the notion of juvenile crime because it reveals a rather disturbing aspect of recent patterns of so-called delinquency, an aspect that gets systematically erased in the construction of the stereotype of the delinquent as ethnic other. That revelation (in the photographic sense of the word) is radical because it suggests that there is a fundamental resemblance, a qualitative sameness, between what is presented as delinquency and the system of power that pretends to exclude and marginalize young offenders. The text suggests that not only are the security guard's practices just as illegal or decidedly dubious as the heroes' but that the authorities and the young men share the same values, the same philosophy of life. Not only does *la galère* retain an ironic and unconscious memory of times when lawlessness and punishment were separable, but this way of being in the world now seems to be governed by exactly the same rules and moral codes as supermarkets, malls, and department stores. The father's law is now replaced by the law of supermarkets, where the way in which money and goods circulate suffers no exception, no inside and no outside.

As if to signal to the reader that we have to beware of mirrors and reflections, of double acts and similarities between apparently different systems, the stolen object places the whole episode under the sign of sameness. What the adolescents try to steal from the local Monoprix is the image of fashionable glasses, not even the glasses themselves: "des imitations presque parfaites de Ray-Ban" (almost perfect imitations of Ray-Ban glasses) (60). The glasses are not used to protect the teenagers' eyes from the sun or to help them see better or differently. Like the *miroir aux alouettes* (literally, "the skylarks' mirror"), a piece of glass whose sparkle lures birds toward huntsmen, the glasses function like a deceptive snare: they "miroitaient sous les néons dans l'attente des beaux ténébreux roubaisiens" (they sparkled under the neon lights, waiting for Roubaix's handsome and mysterious young men) (60). The young men are fascinated by a certain image of America fabricated by international consumerism. What they seek to appropriate corresponds exactly to what supermarkets have chosen to import and to sell: what Bongo, Rabah, and Kamel have learned about America is a transnational white stereotype. In another context (particularly pop music and especially French rap), the adolescents could have discovered and adopted another America; they could have become fascinated by the history of minority communities as rap singer MC Solaar claims he was, for example. Even if transnational corporations are just as involved in the marketing of music as they are in the business of exporting fashion items, the transit of different cultural goods produces different patterns. Instead, Bongo, Rabah, and Kamel are attracted to a mythic and commodified version of America that they can neither afford nor cease to be fascinated by.

The second element of resemblance between the young teenagers and the system that supposedly wants to weed out delinquents lies in how this symbolic universe is saturated with deregulated exchanges outside the regular traffic of currency. An economy of bartering dominates the heroes' world, and this system of exchange exists without any control. There are no price tags and no one knows what is fair and what is not fair. What counts is the crudest level of supply and demand. And while the beginning of the story pretends to indulge in the illusion that such practices represent a marginal and marginalized parallel economy, it soon becomes clear that there is nothing else to imitate. The principle of deregulated exchange is generalized among young people and grown-ups, among delinquents and security guards.

At first, it does look as if the swapping of goods functions as a relatively subversive and egalitarian activity. After all, couldn't bartering offer alternative solutions to those who are excluded by a lack of cash flow and find themselves on the margin of capitalism because of its system of class reproduction? For example, early on, it looks as if Kamel will never be able to buy a coveted pair of bell-bottoms. Yet he is able to take his place among the respectable community of "dragueurs roubaisiens" thanks to his talent for math. He obtains "le pantalon à pattes d'élépant du fils du boucher qu'il reluquait depuis des semaines" (the butcher's son's bell-bottoms that he had been ogling for so many weeks) (59) by swaping the object of his desire against his peer's math assignment. Apparently, some sort of immanent justice has somewhat compensated for the original class inequality between the two teenagers, with Kamel's intellectual superiority symbolizing the possibility of further upward mobility. And yet, the exchange is far from being presented as a good deal for Kamel. According to the story (and it is not clear who intervenes here, whether it is the narrator or the teenager himself), the butcher's son agreed to part with his pair of pants only in exchange for "*un nombre impressionnant*" ("an impressive number") of problems (59). For someone who is supposedly good at math, the end result of the operation is not particularly beneficial (or so the authorial voice seems to imply). Kamel remains unaware of the high price he has had to pay. What the story suggests at this point is that Kamel's talents will enable him to do well in school but certainly do not guarantee him commercial prosperity as an adult. Obviously, the cliché of the good math student as potentially successful businessman does not apply to Kamel, whose abilities do not protect him and do not compensate for his original absence of means. The text does not paint him as naive or foolish; he is not less clever than the butcher's son. In fact, his initiative seems to portray him as a flexible thinker capable of adapting to his environment. His imagination creates ripples in the pond of predictable consumption. He manages to instigate the circulation of merchandise outside traditional routes. In spite of his individual skills, however, the fact that Kamel and the butcher's son start out with different cards in their hands never changes. The story does not equate what Kamel does with idealized forms of potlatch. Bartering is not a supposedly more natural and simple practice that could shield the participants from the laws of capitalism. Rather than being presented as the opposite of consumerism and commodification, the exchange principle between two teenagers is the extreme manifestation of a deregulated system, where some abstract entity known as the market is liberated from external ethical and social constraints. Everything is for sale, and the price is imposed by the powerful, by whoever owns more than the others. What happens between the two young men is a form of rehearsal rather than subversion. Their exchange mimics regular trading practices instead of carving out a space of difference and marginality within the norm.

When the theft of the glasses finally occurs, the episode only carries the same type of logic to an extreme. The three youths manage to hide a few pairs under their garments, but they are caught by the security guard as they try to leave. An emotional scene ensues during which threats of calling the police are made, then withdrawn. What the security guard does after capturing the delinquents suddenly looks very familiar if one remembers the previous exchanges. The possible intervention of some sort of outside law in the world of the supermarket never materializes. The security guard obviously thinks that he has the choice to call the police or not, and he finally opts for a different solution. For all intents and purposes, he turns into jury and judge, deciding that he can punish the delinquents himself. And what is perhaps even more remarkable is that his way of doing justice without referring to an independent system of thought and power is, once again, a form of swapping, of bartering, of deregulated exchange. And naturally, just as the butcher's son had been able to impose an exorbitant price because he owned the desirable pants to begin with, the powerful adult lays down the terms of a contract that is extremely favorable to him: in exchange for his not calling the police, and as a way of teaching them a (free) lesson, he will force the youths to work for him all afternoon without any compensation or salary. This afternoon of unpaid labor is interpreted as a lesson and a punishment: "vous resterez jusqu'à la fermeture du magasin. Comme punition, vous allez nettoyer tous les caddies de l'entrée" (you will stay until the supermarket closes. Your punishment will be to clean all the carts in the entrance) (63).

Far from being an exception that disappears with adulthood, this type of unregulated exchange is shown to be standard practice. It perpetuates and increases inequalities between the two parties of a rigged game. In the end, the security guard trades their labor against nothing, but a nothing he manages to make appealing, against a negative promise. Even if we assume that it is in their best interests not to have a police record, even if we pessimistically suspect that the police would not be more indulgent than the security guard, the fact is that the proposed alternative is closer to usury and blackmail than to a lesson in supposedly honest trade. The supermarket as school of good moral conduct is a rather worrying role model, and we may wonder what conclusions the customers/students (another worrying and familiar amalgam) are supposed to draw from this conflation between business and civic sense. Learning how to trade pants and math papers was apparently a most useful preparation for a world that functions on the margins of its own norms.

What the system calls "delinquency" includes the image that power finds in the mirror and that it refuses to recognize as itself. Within that perverse economy that stereotypes the thief as Other and outsider no matter what happens, it could be said that Marie Féraud, like Georgette's father, intervenes in the naming of what exactly constitutes an act of delinquency. For Georgette's father, being an outsider to the family is a prerequisite but not a sufficient condition. In the logic of the supermarket, insiders and outsiders can both be thieves, but the difference between their activity and what the security guard condones is not clear. In other words, faced with the threat of stereotyping young others, this hybrid text suggests, without a hint of didacticism, that the security guard's gesture is a specific form of delinquency. His policy of exchanging the boys' labor against his silence is shown to be quite similar to Kamel's practice of bartering and swapping. What is stolen in this story is the origin of delinquency. Just as no independent and supposedly just law presides over that type of exchange, the security guard is exposed as the origin and sole guarantor of the difference between authorized and unauthorized trade. What he practices is perhaps the very same type of exchange that teenagers are both implicitly urged to copy and punished for imitating.[6]

Le thé au harem d'Archi Ahmed

Another remarkably effective tactic of reappropriation can be found in the works of Mehdi Charef where the stereotype of the thief is consciously embraced. Rather than deconstructing the opposition between the delinquent and the security guard, Mehdi Charef creates characters who embrace the role of the thief and manage to benefit from being interpreted as such. Perhaps better known as a film director, Charef doubles as a novelist.[7] I will here consider *Le thé au harem d'Archi Ahmed*, the print version of his most famous feature film, *Le thé au harem d'Archimède*. Although the crucial scene does appear in the film, the written dialogue betrays some of the characters and sides with others, much as Marie Féraud's omniscient voice criticizes some and defends others. In the novel, the two heroes are Madjid, a young Beur, and Pat, his Caucasian friend. Here, they are about to steal someone's wallet—that is, to engage in what Dhoukar calls an "objective" act of delinquency. But instead of concentrating on whether it is legitimate to describe what the two young men do as an act of delinquency, the text deploys a completely different strategy.

Pat and Madjid have singled out their two victims: a man and a woman traveling in the subway. Charef's characters wait on the platform with the couple, and they innocently follow the two anonymous silhouettes into the car. As they all take places inside, the first part of Pat and Madjid's perfectly coordinated double act is in fact already over, and the couple has not noticed anything. As the man bent over to pick up his suitcase, Madjid deftly removed the wallet sticking out from the back pocket, gave it to his white and blond accomplice, Pat, who then moved to the other side of the car. Madjid stands by the couple, quietly waiting for the real game to begin. In fact, contrary to what a first stereotypical reading, it is only after the theft that the story becomes really interesting.

Madjid regarde le couple reflété dans la vitre. Le gros enfouit son mouchoir humide dans une poche avant de son pantalon. Brusquement il porte la main sur sa poche arrière, du même côté. Il regarde sa femme, l'air affolé.
—Mon portefeuille!
—Tu ne l'as plus? Tu es sûr?
—Non. Regarde dans ton sac.
La dame ouvre son sac, évidemment pour rien. Elle demande:
—Tu ne l'as pas oublié à la maison?
—Je suis sûr que je l'avais: j'y ai mis mes tickets de métro.
Il regarde par terre au cas où . . . Puis se retourne sur Madjid.
Il le dévisage de haut en bas et sans se gêner: un Arabe!
Il prend l'Arabe par le colbac et l'attire vers lui:
—Mon portefeuille, fumier!
Madjid se fait tout petit, tout tremblant, trouillard. Murmure:
—Ça va pas, non? je vous ai rien fait, moi.
Et finalement crie:
—Il est fou, ce mec, il est dingue!
Il voit Pat qui se marre, là-bas. Il continue de crier:
—De quel droit, hein? Je m'en fous, moi, de ton larfeuille. Mais ça y est: ils voient un Arabe, c'est un voleur! (Charef 1983, 106)

[Madjid is looking at the couple reflected in the window. The fat guy pushes his wet handkerchief into one of the front pockets of his pants. Suddenly, he feels the back pocket, on the same side. He looks at his wife, in a panic.
—My wallet!
—Don't you have it? Are you sure?
—Yes. Look in your bag.
The woman opens her bag, in vain of course. She asks:
—Didn't you leave it at home?
—I am sure I had it: I put the tickets in there.
He looks for it on the floor, just in case. . . . Then he turns toward Madjid. He stares at him unashamedly: an Arab! He grabs the Arab by the collar and pulls him toward him:
—My wallet, you scum bag!
Madjid turns into a trembling little thing, a real coward. He whispers:
—Are you crazy? I have not done anything.
Finally, he yells:
—This guy is mad, he's gone crazy!
He sees Pat over there, grinning. He continues to scream:
—Who do you think you are? I don't give a damn about your wallet. Ah, but there you are: they see an Arab, and he is a thief.]

A theft has indeed been committed, and the thief *is* in the same car as his victim, but the scene never becomes Madjid's trial. In fact, in relation to Féraud's story, we could imagine that the Beur character in this scene occupies the place taken by the security guard in "Les Ray-Ban." For the man whose wallet is stolen does not manage to get it back, nor does he avoid a type of situation where he himself is put on the spot as someone who needs a good lesson. Pat, who now holds the wallet, has moved away from the scene, as if creating an implicit inside-outside zone that will reinforce ethnic stereotypes. Madjid, by remaining physically close to this white man whose money he has already stolen, functions as an ethnic bait, another *miroir aux alouettes.* His body acts as a snare, a trap set for whoever is willing to think and act according to the stereotypical matrix (ethnic = delinquent). The stroke of genius in this case is that Madjid is, at the same time, guilty of an act of theft and the victim of a stereotype that accuses all the people in his community of being thieves. At the very moment when a stereotype confuses an act and an identity, one individual identity and a whole community, at the moment when the typical equation between "Arab" and "thief" is deployed in its crudest way, all Madjid has to do is to reappropriate the principle of amalgamation and loudly protest, in the name of all Arabs, when in this context his identity as an Arab is far less relevant than the theft he has just committed. Dhoukar's analysis is uncannily reversed: here is how an "objective act of delinquency" cannot be denounced, because the reader of signs (the victim of the theft) was not capable of making a distinction between the act and the identity (or rather identities) of a fellow passenger.

Madjid is obviously quite aware of the existence of stereotypes, but he does not suffer from them. He has learned how to use them and to send them back to potential aggressors. For him, stereotypes are baits that he uses to tempt other human beings. The man who lost his wallet has lost more than his money; as a self-appointed detective, policeman, and security guard he is clearly clueless. Given his lack of professional skills and the lack of objective evidence, it was to be expected that he would not get his wallet back. The text seems to say that, no matter what, this man was set to lose his money and that this theft could not have been avoided. What could have been avoided, however, is a useless confrontation and the resulting humiliation: "Le gros se retrouve comme un con. Il s'excuserait presque" (The fat guy looks like an idiot. He almost apologizes) (107). Instead of trying to hide, instead of trying to sneak out of the supermarket like Féraud's characters, Madjid has used his knowledge of prevailing stereotypes to stage a remarkable diversion, using the other's ideology as bait. He deliberately put himself in a position that tested the stereotyping reflexes of a "fat guy" who would probably have sworn that he is not a racist.

Madjid recognizes that he operates in a stereotypical symbolic universe and operates within that undesirable system. By accepting the role of the ethnic presence that will tempt the white Other and test the extent of his or her prejudices, he warns us that no one is ever safe from being criminalized, suspected, or stereotyped by a dominant group to which one partially belongs. The inside-outside structure that protects Pat is clearly differential. Madjid clearly suspects that there is no point in inviting the bourgeois to celebrate another culture. On the other hand—and this may be the crucial difference that separates this book from earlier novels where characters schizophrenically integrated the ideal of assimilation—Madjid never seems to suffer from internalized racial prejudice.[8] He is not interested in what the man thinks. He has no desire to convince him that Arabs are not all one thing or another. He does not want to convert a racist. The syntax and grammar of stereotypes are completely familiar to him—in fact, they are part and parcel of that language that is his mother tongue. The distinction between native languages and the colonizer's idiom, of what colonial and postcolonial Maghrebi writers used to call "*la langue adverse*," has ceased to provide adequate representations. It is here replaced with irony and a high dose of cynicism that allow Madjid to steal both the wallet and the stereotype.

We readers are forced into a position that I would compare to the possession of stolen (discursive) goods and to the concealment of criminals; this text turns us into accomplices. Like Pat, safe at the other end of the car, we are both aware of the existence and power of stereotypes and delighted to witness an act of reappropriation. Pat is the model provided by the text to those readers who may ask themselves how to articulate a sense of solidarity and alliance, how to reinvent a code of ethics in the presence of a situation where everyone is guilty of something. Madjid is guilty of stealing money, his victim is guilty of crude racist stereotyping. The former gets away with a double theft and walks away with his financial and symbolic prizes: one wallet, one stereotype. The latter has lost everything and learned nothing.

If this man was the only white character, we might ask whether the passage suggests that stereotypes are easily mirrored and that depending on the reader's ethnic identity, certain types of identification (with Madjid or with his victim) are to be expected. But it is impossible to forget Pat's presence, even if his role is to capitalize on his invisibility as a white man. His presence introduces the function of the excluded third, of the witness, of the spectator. Pat is able to testify, both to the act committed in his presence but also to the undeniable racist behavior of a fellow passenger.

Pat's presence offers the reader the space of a nonessentialist identification process, and his name crystallizes the possibility of escaping the binary opposition between whiteness and ethnicity. "Madjid" is one of those names that in the 1990s continues to sound Maghrebi. At first sight (and this whole episode is precisely organized around what happens if someone acts according to a first impression), Pat is not a Maghrebi-sounding name, but it does not sound typically French either. The short one-syllable nickname could sound vaguely American or could remind the reader of other characters who shorten their names precisely to disguise their North African origins.[9] The novel does not allow the reader to decide one way or the other: What is important is that Pat remains a figure whose identity is invisible or at least unproblematic. And yet he is not indifferent. He has actively participated in the theft and taken significant risks. After all, he is holding the wallet, the only piece of evidence that the white passenger seeks when he searches Madjid. But Pat will not be accused, and no one chooses to bring him into the inner circle where theft and identity become relevant. He witnesses a particularly successful form of manipulation. Like the reader, Pat knows exactly what happens and benefits from the lesson. Even if Madjid has not internalized the devastating effects of the stereotype, Pat cannot ignore that his friend is constantly in danger of being stereotyped. His reading position is informed by his cultural hybridity; he cannot read exclusively as a white or Beur individual because the categories of power and knowledge that draw boundaries around essential identities have been confounded by Madjid and Pat's double act. Similarly, we are invited to put ourselves in a strange ethnographic position from which, whatever our identity, we consider the white middle-class passenger as an object of study. The narration follows the reaction of an ordinary xenophobic Frenchman curiously, as if he were some sort of exotic animal. Not only is his body described in a rather cold and unsympathetic manner ("un gros type, balaise, la quarantaine . . . avec un énorme valise à la main" (a fat burly guy, forty something, carrying an enormous suitcase) (104), but he never really becomes a full-blown character. We know nothing about this man's feelings except perhaps when the text takes an unglamorous snapshot of his physical and mental state: "Il sue" (He is sweating) (104). He does not have a name, we do not know where the couple was going. He is a type, a caricature, an ironic equivalent of the Algerian women immortalized by silly postcards' captions ("une belle Mauresque" ["beautiful Arab woman"]) or of those natives filmed by anthropologists. The narration reinforces the impression by using a type of syntax that will sound familiar to readers of anthropological studies or documentaries. The man is suddenly turned into a representative sample of a whole species when the text says: "Une femme, certainement la sienne, l'accompagne" (A woman, presumably his own, travels with him) (104). The novel refuses to fall into the trap of deciding whether he is a good or a bad victim. Literally and figuratively, the text does not listen to what he has to say as long as he does not engage in a dialogue with Madjid: "Il regarde sa montre et dit quelque chose à sa femme" (He looks at his watch and says something to his wife) (104); "Le gros et sa femme consultent le trajet de la ligne. Ils parlent à voix basse" (The fat guy and his wife check the train itinerary. They are whispering) (106); and later, "Le gros, vexé, glisse quelques mots à sa femme" (Humiliated, the fat guy whispers a few words to his wife) (107). The text, whether maliciously or unconsciously, resorts to visible stereotyping techniques and does not take the trouble of providing this character with a personality or a language until Madjid sees fit to draw around him a confrontational circle of communication.

Despite Madjid's fake apprehensions and powerlessness, within that circle the two men are equal. The battle remains a battle of words and representations. But Madjid is a much better manipulator of stereotypes; he knows how to use them in a more subtle and effective way than his opponent. The theft of the wallet is not justified as a form of historic retaliation, for example, and when the two accomplices go through the stolen wallet, they will be disappointed by its contents. Their victim was pathetically broke. Madjid's gesture is not celebrated as some sort of political statement either. The theft of the wallet, in itself, is a lot less meaningful than the verbal confrontation between the two men. If Madjid is the undeniable winner of the stereotypical game, it is not because he is right, or because he is innocent, but because he knows how to manipulate the dangerous weapon of stereotypes while his adversary is not even aware that he is using it. It is as if he had forced his opponent to play a dangerous game where he who starts always loses.

In order to adopt Madjid's position, it is not enough to be that ethnic Other who must constantly protect himself against stereotypes: It is more important to have become aware of the perverse dynamic that puts each potential victim of ethnic stereotypes in a complex position. Both can suffer from the internalizing of stereotypes *and* use them as if they were a perfectly mastered foreign language. The principle is to have the last laugh, to remain one step ahead in the game of hide-and-seek where identity can no longer be guaranteed to rhyme with power.

After seeing how Madjid tempts someone into using stereotypical images and then steals their power, the logic of the scene becomes crystal clear and the seduction of this game of temptation more apparent. Tempting someone into using stereotypes holds the promise of a moment of laughter that depends neither on identity nor on innocence.

Smaïn's "Le Président Beur"

In "Le Président Beur" (The Beur president), Smaïn goes even further toward the destabilization of baleful confusions between acts and identities when "act" happens to mean "theft" and identity happens to mean "ethnic." This is one of the Beur comic's most famous routines. In the next chapter, I will look as Smaïn's performance as an actor in Serge Meynard's *L'oeil au beur~~re~~ noir*, but here I will draw from his work as a stand-up comic, a series of highly amusing self-contained episodes whose humor consciously warns us against ethnic stereotypes.

Standing behind a tall podium wrapped in the blue, white, and red French flag, Smaïn, doing his best to affect a supposedly Arabic accent yet lapsing from time to time into distinctly Parisian vowels, opens what is obviously going to be a political speech with a question: “Y a-t-il des Français dans la salle?” (Are there French people in this room?). This is both a simple yes-no question and an immediate intrusion into the highly loaded realm of identity. A significant part of the public takes the bait and answers the question. Without wasting any time, Smaïn immediately asks a second question: “Y a-t-il des Arabes dans la salle?” (Are there Arabs in this room?). The public, used to interactive televisual games, knows that they are expected to go along and to help the humorist as he builds up towards some amusing punch line. And yet the principle of mandatory participation cannot completely erase the fact that the questions asked by Smaïn are not innocent. His distinction between “French” and “Arab” is the turf of heated debates, of confrontations and passionate arguments. At this point, we might suspect that Smaïn is heading for a political satire; we might anticipate a sort of reversal that will make fun of xenophobic French people who no longer feel “at home” in France because there are “too many” Arabs. But as in *Le thé au harem*, the audience is implictly asked to recognize that the questions represent a form of bait. Whoever will have refused to play will be rewarded with the last laugh. But let us not jump forward. Until then, the majority of Smaïn’s audience is responsive; they see nothing wrong with the game. The “Arabs” signal their presence after the second question. Obviously delighted with a perhaps even more enthusiastic cooperation than he had hoped, Smaïn now steps down from the podium and gets as close to the audience as he can. Like Madjid standing close to the couple whose wallet has already been lifted, he comes closer and closer to his victims. The trap is set. “Que les Français lèvent la main droite!” (Let the French raise their right hand) he requests.

This time, the public is understandingly a bit more reluctant, and Smaïn must repeat the order to reach the desired objective. He yells, imperiously, “Que les Français lèvent la main droite!” Like the audience, we are wondering what is really going on, but the ritual itself is neither unfamiliar nor innocent. Behind the gesture of raising one’s hand, old powerful ghosts loom large: children in a classroom, or the figure of education minister Jules Ferry’s schoolmasters, whose Republican fervor is just as vividly remembered as their tendency to use their rulers as pedagogical arguments. And beyond the memory of that benign, if authoritarian, character, even more sinister scenarios may come to mind.

For some, this demand for a public acknowledgment of national and ethnic identity will sound uncomfortably reminiscent of supposedly random identity checks that could pave the way for even more radical measures of exclusion and persecution. And yet, the public has paid to be amused. So, they raise their hands without suspecting for a moment that they have yielded to the temptation of the stereotype. For this simple gesture of raising one's hand in response to the identity question has separated the public into two waterproof communities, once again, an inside and an outside around which the definition of stealing will be rearticulated. This principle of division creates a difference between the good and the bad, the thieves and their victims, the foreigners and the nationals. Answering the question "Are you French or Arab?" is a recipe for disaster because it means accepting the implication that the two categories are mutually exclusive when they are more likely to belong to the type of chaotic Chinese encyclopedia cited by Michel Foucault at the beginning of *Les mots et les choses* (1966, 1970).[10] It is impossible logically to oppose French people and Arabs (there are French Arabs and non-French Arabs, French people who are not Arabs, and some Arabs probably belong to the Emperor). Answering Smaïn's question amounts to falling into the trap of a stereotypical construction that pretends it is impossible to be both French and an Arab, or worse, that pretends to know exactly what it is to be French.

Once again, the trap closes on the unsuspecting victim. Some members of the audience happily raise their hands, expecting that this strange request probably carries some sort of prize. But the game is not over yet. Faced with a forest of raised hands, Smaïn continues, just as sternly: "Que les Français lèvent la main gauche!" (Let the French raise their left hand!). This time, the command is utterly incomprehensible, tautologically meaningless, and the familiar ritual is altered beyond recognition. This is not as banal as we thought and some spectators seem to believe so as they slowly lower their right hands, slightly puzzled and perhaps a bit worried by this new development. Can we really win something? Some are beginning to suspect a misunderstanding, some are beginning to doubt that their French identity needs so much publicity. Others, on the other hand, cannot spit out the hook in time. Trapped in the role of actors, spectators, and puppets whose strings are held firmly by Smaïn, they now react like an anonymous crowd controlled by a sort of professional Big Brother whose job is to make them laugh. They can no longer leave the game, even if they are beginning to suspect that the joke may well turn sour. Those who raised their right hands more or less casually, those who did not guess that there was an inaudible test behind Smaïn's words, failed to understand that their first act of cooperation was an experiment where what was measured was their potential indifference to the dangers of such identity checks. Now they really have no other choice but to go all the way. They raise their left hands without knowing what it means to do so. They can do nothing but acquiesce to this apparently redundant display of national identity.

The rest of the story sounds like the triumphant ending of one of La Fontaine's fables: surveying an obedient group of people who have by now assumed the position of surrendering soldiers, Smaïn, barely suppressing a chuckle, suddenly concludes: "Que les Arabes fouillent dans leurs poches!"

(Let the Arabs go through their pockets!). And those two-time French people, who had raised their hands twice to win God knows what kind of prize at this identity game, are suddenly exposed as losers. The lesson is that it is the very careless and ill-considered urge to claim a supposedly desirable identity that places the subject in the very position that makes him or her vulnerable to the dangers that his or her own stereotypical fears have in fact created.

. . .

These texts show that it is possible to reappropriate ethnic stereotypes instead of trying to rewrite them. Smaïn and Madjid manage to weaken the stereotypical rule that would only have been reinforced if an "I" had tried to constitute himself or herself as an exception. It is no consolation to be a "good Indian" in the best of cases, and it is no protection against persecution when systems become mad. Smaïn and Madjid refuse to replace the stereotype with a discourse of truth and prefer to push stereotypes around on the social chess board as if they were manipulating delicate symbolic weapons. They play a new game that is particularly well adapted to the ironic context of postcolonial reassessments: the theft of stereoypes. Rather than trying to resist the ideological implications of ethnic stereotypes, Madjid and Smaïn prefer to add fuel, or rather oil, to the fire, as the French saying goes, just as Charlie Chaplin does in *Modern Times* (1936) when he steals the foreman's can of oil and sprays the assembly line, the workers, and everyone who tries to catch him. Similarly, the petty thieves of *Le thé au harem* or the Beur president steal the ideological lubricant that allows the old system to function smoothly and reappropriate its slippery qualities for their own purposes of laughter and derision. They add to our cultural models the idea that the use of ideological lubricant is an effective tactic against stereotypes. At the same time, they propose a critique of their own activity. They know that they have no control over the very slipperiness they appropriate. The theft of stereotypes, like stereotypes themselves, respects no community limits, no essence. The comic lesson in complicity offered by these texts suggests that the Beur heroes have learned two things: on the one hand, it is impossible not to be traversed by the flow of stereotypes that the dominant culture teaches us (in school, for example); on the other hand, the knowledge of how such stereotypes work is the precondition of reappropriative activities.

Chapter 3

Investing in Stereotypes

Serge Meynard's *L'oeil au beur~~re~~ noir*

> Un Arabe sauve une jeune fille agressée par deux blancs. C'est le monde à l'envers! (*L'oeil au beur~~re~~ noir*)
>
> An Arab saves a young woman from her two white assailants. What is wrong with this picture?

Smaïn has also played with the image of the "typical" Beur in recent comedies such as Serge Meynard's *L'oeil au beur~~re~~ noir* (1987).[1] A commercial feature, it rehearses the by-now familiar topos of the multicultural trio of the so-called *banlieues-films*.[2] Like Mathieu Kassovitz's *Métisse* (1993) and his more pessimistic *La haine* (Hate, 1995) *L'oeil au beur~~re~~ noir* presents us with three characters whose identities are crucial to the development of the plot.

The films tease the audience, both inviting and disinviting essentializing readings of race and ethnicity or culturalist interpretations of class and origin. In *Métisse*, a young Caribbean woman is in love with a white man and a black man, and the film refuses to assume any simple form of racial or class alliance. The black suitor is the son of extremely wealthy African diplomats, and the heroine refuses to listen to his grandiloquent and generalizing talk about their common heritage. After one particularly enflamed tirade, for example, she calmly points out that there are no slaves in his background. As for the tensions between the two men, they are increased by the fact that the "white" lover's ethnicity remains invisible to his rival (he is Jewish) and that he comes from a poor working-class family. As if to reserve the right not to be dragged into simplistic identity politics, the film refuses to tell us which man is the biological father of the baby born at the end of the story.

After this relatively optimistic comedy, *La haine* definitely comes as a shock. In this 1995 film noir, the multiracial trio provides a grim depiction of today's *banlieues*, and a decidedly tragic tone has replaced the lightheartedness of *Métisse*. Yet it is significant that the same techniques of representation of race and ethnicity reappear, the main characters forming an inseparable entity. Here, the role of the hero is divided between three members of a multiracial trio, this time, a blanc-black-Beur team of disillusioned young males from the same banlieue.

Since the beginning of the 1980s, films have not only participated in the representation of ethnic communities, they have also increasingly reflected an evolution in the hegemonic imaging of different races. Black and white binary oppositions are slowly losing their status of obvious relevance. They are being displaced by more up-to-date representations of complex, hybrid, and multifaceted identities. But as the violence and tragic hopelessness of *La haine* demonstrates, this is no reason to rejoice hastily. In this case, hybridity and multicultural relationships do not necessarily indicate progress. But the principle of the trio forces the story and the audience to go beyond binary oppositions between whiteness and otherness, between colonizer and colonized. In other words, the reappropriation of stereotypes by postcolonial subjects must take into account the increasing complexity of the representations that they are up against. Otherwise, they risk, like Rachid in *L'oeil au beur~~re~~ noir* to design a system that will backfire as soon as a third (black) character is inserted between the white woman and the Beur character.

L'oeil au beur~~re~~ noir is a mainstream comedy about a young white bourgeois woman, Virginie (Julie Jezequel) and two young men: Rachid (Smaïn), a Beur who lives in a typical housing project and whose white friends are "loubards" (thugs) and thieves, and Denis (Bernard Legitimus), a middle-class black artist who has to move out of his apartment unexpectedly. Throughout the movie, the two men are completely absorbed by a double and impossible quest: find an apartment and seduce the heroine. The film is obviously obsessed with a desire to explore the ambivalence of the representation of identity. The logic of the plot seems to suspect that it is impossible to construct a "Beur" or "black" identity, and it examines the possibility of creating an alliance between two nonrepresentative characters while at the same time devoting much energy to the reappropriation of stereotypes. Nothing prepares the "Beur" and the "noir" to cohabit harmoniously or even peacefully within this movie. In fact, nothing authorizes me to even suggest that there is such as thing as "a" Beur and "a" black character, let alone a relationship based on such terms between them. The ambivalence of the tandem is already made clear in the title of the movie.

Like the ambiguous and puzzling "beur~~re~~ noir" of the title, whatever is "Beur" about this movie is never autonomous but always attached to other connotations, other communities, other problems. If we look for a forceful affirmation of Beur culture, we find that it is always undermined by the movie's disrespectful tone and strong element of derision. The title suggests that the film will not decide whether or not it wants to be identified as a Beur movie. On the poster that is also the cover of the video tape, the presence of a Beur entity is visible only because the last syllable of *beurre* has been crossed out: we see four young men sitting on a public bench, looking at a young woman walking by. Above their heads, on the brick wall behind them, we can read: "L'oeil au beurre noir" painted in big clumsy red letters, like graffiti. The last syllable of the word "beurre" is crossed out by a superimposed white x. The word "Beur" appears in the title as the result of the fictional intervention of an anonymous hand that introduces a double entendre in the set phrase. The pun itself is not brilliantly original, but it is significant that the revelation of a Beur factor within the title should be the result of an act of tampering that some authority pretends to have overlooked, rather than a deliberate decision to take liberties with the spelling or the traditional association of words (as simply calling the movie *L'oeil au beur noir* would). The extra mark that both erases and preserves the end of the word "beurre" is emblematic of the film's ambivalence toward what could be a solemn affirmation of Beur culture. The pun does not go all the way; it points to certain intertextual references but denies the importance of, rather than celebrates, a hypothetical Beur identity. Implicitly, the title responds to those critics and journalists who have been eager to hail the birth of a "beuritude," perhaps because it was more convenient to remember familiar stories and conjure up recognized intellectual figures (Senghor, Césaire) than to examine the Beurs' ambivalence toward identity and community culture.[3]

The poster of *L'oeil au beur~~re~~ noir* is not the only example of facetiousness in the genre of recent French cinema posters. Jean-Luc Godard has been known to indulge in similarly self-parodic experiments. The advertising campaign that launched *Hélas pour moi*, for example, played with the director's amused discovery that "there is God in Godard and Dieu in Depardieu." But even if the intention is obviously ironic, what is being parodied is a megalomaniacal statement, whereas Serge Meynard's decision to let the title of the movie look like scribbled-over graffiti, a sloppy version of what was not even a slick design to begin with, is a more humble allusion to his film's lack of reference and origin. The graffiti also refuses to take sides, neither adhering wholeheartedly to a supposedly new Beur identity nor denying altogether the possibility of having something to do with the Beurs.

The association between "butter" and beur is almost a mockery of more conventional political gestures. I wonder if, in 1987, it did not sound like a specific reference to recently heard slogans since "blacks, blancs, beurs" was the rallying cry of the militants who participated in the 1984 march (Convergence), the second "marche des Beurs."[4] The allusion to the "beur(e) noir"[5] is the opposite of a serious declaration, and the title as a whole, with its reference to a form of latent violence and unmotivated threat (who will have "a black eye"?) remains unexplained. Yet the chance encounter between *verlan* (a politically charged slang) and butter (arguably a most down-to-earth and apolitical matter) is at the same time completely meaningless, obvious (it is not even a good pun), and yet a tentative sign of recognition.[6] In 1990, Azouz Begag's seems to remember the pun in his "Lexique des idées arrêtées sur des gens qui bougent . . . dans le désordre" (Dictionary of fixed ideas about people who move about . . . in no particular order):

Beur: mot désignant une substance alimentaire grasse et onctueuse (voir Petit Robert). De plus en plus écrit de cette façon par les journalistes (grosse faute d'orthographe! cf. *La Disparition* de G. Perec). Voudrait maintenant désigner une population issue de l'immigration maghrébine . . . on a eu *Pain et Chocolat* . . . manquait le Beur. Décidément, l'immigration ça se mange bien au petit déjeuner! (Begag 1990, 10–11)

[Beur: the word refers to a greasy and soft edible matter (see Petit Robert). More and more often spelled without an "e" by journalists (serious spelling error! cf. Georges Perec's *A Void*). Now supposedly refers to the children of Maghrebi immigrants . . . After *Bread and Chocolate* . . . all we needed was butter. Apparently, one can have immigrants for breakfast.]

The problematizing of a Beur community is not the only instance of ambivalent positioning in *L'oeil au beur~~re~~ noir*. The dislocation of the title phrase also functions like a prediction at the level of the plot: it announces that the solidarity that will slowly develop between the Beur and the black characters will owe as much to chance and necessity as to a supposedly shared minority status. No theory of race and culture will come to the heroes' rescue. Once the spectator realizes that the "beur~~re~~ noir" of the title means more than the sum of the literal meaning of the words, he or she may imagine new forms of multiculturalism. The original linguistic arbitrariness of the set phrase becomes an apt metaphor to express the cohabitation between Beurs and blacks in those far-off banlieues or cités. The alliance between the black and the Beur is not forced into the narrative as a form of cosmic destiny, as in Stanley Kramer's *The Defiant Ones* (1958), where two prisoners are handcuffed to each other and have to learn to accept their hybrid and collective self.[7] If a culture is represented in this movie, it may be close to what the press and the media are beginning to call "la culture des banlieues," a patchwork of different cultures, that unfortunately may end up functioning more like a Benetton ad (at best a mere juxtaposition of communities, at worst some sordid untold tale about the meaningfulness of the relationship) if a new discourse does not emerge soon. "La culture des banlieues" is at the same time an interestingly de-ethnicized and de-essentialized paradigm of coalition between communities and a reassuringly reuniversalized entity for the dominant culture, the Republic that seems to welcome the reluctance with which some Beurs refuse to embrace a

Beur identity. In the past few years, the media have seemed to consider it reasonable, intelligent, and sophisticated to side with those representatives of the Beur (non)-community who emphatically declare there is no such thing as Beur culture. Or, to reformulate, a new and powerful stereotype is slowly emerging.

A special issue of *Le Nouvel observateur* (1993) was thus entitled "Les Beurs tels qu'ils se voient" (The Beurs as they see themselves). The title hesitates between a desire to be catchy and a determination to be moderate in its sensationalism, but it certainly implies that there *is* such as thing as "les Beurs" and that they have a self-image. Strangely enough, that statement was proposed only to be immediately withdrawn by the conclusion of a (reassuring?) series of interviews with Beur celebrities. The question was: "Y a-t-il une culture beur? Smaïn, Mehdi Charef, Amina . . . Ils occupent la scène artistique. Veulent-ils pour autant revendiquer leur identité? Débat." (Is there such a thing as a beur culture? Smaïn, Mehdi Charef, Amina . . . they are in the limelight. Still, do they want to claim their identity? A debate.) Why "still"? And at the end of this so-called debate, François Reynart concluded:

> Acceptons l'idée qu'il n'y a pas de "culture beur" en tant que telle, en France. Certes, il existe une culture des banlieues, le rap et le verlan, mais elle appartient à tous les habitants des cités, où vivent autant de blancs et blacks que de beurs. (Reynart 1993, 34)
>
> [Let us accept that there is no Beur culture per se in France. There is indeed a banlieue culture, rap, and verlan, but it belongs to all the inhabitants of the housing estate populated by as many whites as blacks and Beurs.]

Interestingly enough, in this story, Smaïn occupies a rather ambiguous place. On the one hand, his popularity as an actor and performer is such that it was apparently unthinkable for *Le Nouvel observateur* not to include him as a guest of honor even in the title. Not only is Smaïn one of the most prominent artists among those identified as the children of immigrants from North Africa, but his work is related to his ethnic and cultural background. The parts that he has accepted so far and the texts he writes for his shows are often directly inspired by the adventures of the first generation of immigrants and their children's predicaments. He often attacks French xenophobia and racism, and he portrays older Arabs with more tenderness and complicity than most Beur writers ("Le président Beur," "T'en veux?" [1990])

Consequently, his absence from such a "debate" about Beurs would have stood out as a glaring absence, but only because we have already internalized a mental list of so-called Beur artists. And when reading *Le nouvel obvervateur*, it quickly becomes obvious that this preestablished list exists independently from how Beurs see themselves. In spite of the well-intentioned desire to let

Beurs define their own image ("comment ils se voient"), Smaïn's refusal to participate in the debate is not respected. After citing a few sociologists and other artists whose position is neatly categorized as either for or against the use of the word "Beur," the author must explain:

> Reste Smaïn. Lui fait bande à part, parce qu'il préfère, fait-il dire "ne pas figurer dans un dossier sur les beurs." On peut le comprendre, Smaïn. Il choisit d'être radical pour ne pas se retrouver dans un ghetto. Il n'a pas envie non plus d'être à la France des années 90 ce que Sidney Poitier fut à l'Amérique des années 50—le cache-misère commode d'une réelle discrimination. (34)

> [As for Smaïn, he chooses to remain on the outside because, according to the message that he sent us, "he would rather not feature in a story on Beurs." His position is understandable. He chooses a radical way out of the ghetto. He does not want to be the French Sidney Poitier of the 1990s and become what his black counterpart was in the America of the 1950s: a convenient decoy hiding real discrimination.]

What I find striking in the journalist's interpretation is that Smaïn's absence is never authorized. He is quoted as having someone else say that he has nothing to say, and yet this third-degree quotation is abundantly commented upon and reappropriated. Not only is Smaïn's decision "de ne pas figurer" (not to be present) completely dismissed, but his difficult desire for what I call "*departenance*" is heard as a transparent, unambiguous statement.[8] Someone who has made a very clear choice not to be cited within a certain context finds that his silence reverberates in an echo chamber and that his absence has turned him into a public performer as surely as if he had been pushed onto a balcony in front of a crowd. The moment is a remarkable instance of ventriloquism and puppet-master string pulling. Smaïn does not say anything, yet "on peut [. . .] comprendre" (we understand) that he wants to be "radical" (whatever radical means here), he embraces hegemonic myths about ethnicity (community equals ghetto), and he is afraid of being identified with Sidney Poitier. Naturally, I am not saying that it would be impossible for Smaïn to actually endorse this image of himself, but I find the assumption rather annoyingly hasty. The reason that certain Beurs refuse to be associated with "Beur culture" may result precisely from the media's tendency to carve an undesirable mold within which they are then forced to cast themselves. And the press then praises them, rather hypocritically, for their pro-integration stance. In the end, two groups repeat apparently the same thing: they object to the very idea of Beur culture. The repetition is of course motivated by very different reasons, but this profound difference ends up sounding like a happy consensus. Whenever the media suffer from a "Beur" attack, it really does not matter that each Beur may have a different reason for not wanting to be associated with the word, because the foregone conclusion is that a Beur culture cannot exist in France because it would embody an Anglo-Saxon vision and because French Beurs (unanimously?) object to the model.

In Stéphane Bouquet's review of Malik Chibane's 1993 *Hexagone*, he seems happy to let the director confirm that the question of his relationship to his community is a rhetorical one:

Malik Chibane se voit-il en porte-drapeau du cinéma beur? «Le cinéma beur fait référence à une grille de lecture, à une tradition communautaire plutôt anglo-saxonne, ça véhicule un peu un côté ghetto, et la société française fonctionne avant tout sur l'idée d'intégration. Il y a peut-être une fibre, une sensibilité beur, mais cette sensibilité est française aussi, puisqu'ils veulent ça, être français. Après tout, Pagnol a surtout filmé le sud de la France. Chacun a son propre univers.» (Bouquet 1994, 11)

[Does Malik Chibane see himself as a spokesperson for Beur cinema? "The phrase «Cinéma beur» implies a certain interpretative grid, a rather Anglo-Saxon tradition of communities. It tends to evoke images of the ghetto, and the French are primarily interested in integration. There may be a Beur angle or sensitivity, but that sensitivity is also French, because they want to be French. After all, Pagnol filmed mostly the south of France. We each have our universe."]

Chibane's remarks are not altogether convincing because his desire to avoid the "community" model is finally expressed in a rather paradoxical way: if the reference for his definition of identity within France is Marcel Pagnol's "universe," not only is the model of the community still present but it is, precisely, universalized. Pagnol's cinema is not seen for what it was: the portrait of a culture that perceived itself as different, recognizable, and that did not wish to lose its regional perspective. I am not so certain that what is culturally interesting about Pagnol's work was his desire for "*intégration.*" In Pagnol's trilogy, foreigners are not welcome. In *Jean de Florette*, the stranger is mercilessly excluded and dies. In the trilogy (*Fanny*, *Marius*, *César*), Mr. Brun is mocked and teased (after all, he is from Lyons!).[9] And by identifying Pagnol's "universe" as southern France, Chibane also dismisses crucial historical and sociological differences between turn-of-the-century southern French culture and Beurs. The reason why it is difficult to describe what the Beurs share is precisely that they cannot be territorialized. No geographical area can be said to be a Beur domain except for limited, fragmented, and stereotypical micro-spaces such as certain neighborhoods, the cités and their stairways and basements. The problem is that even such places, in their diversity, have become stereotypes as if all cités were alike, all banlieues comparable.

It is true that Chibane's perception of a French-Beur or Beur-French "sensitivity" has its advantages. For example, he is able to provide a very diverse and heterogeneous portrait of several Beur characters. Unlike Mehdi Charef's *Le thé au harem d'Archimède* and Abdelkrim Bahloul's *Le thé à la menthe* (criticized for their representations of the Beur hero as predictable delinquent), Chibane's *Hexagone* is a unique attempt to present a whole gallery of portraits: Slimane (Jalil Naciri), unemployed and depressed by his unsuccessful job search; Nacera (Faiza Kaddour), a young woman described by critics as "in search of her independence; Samy (Farid Abdedou), who dies of an overdose at the end of the film; Ali the intellectual (Karim Chakir); and Staf (Hakim Sarahoui), called "*le sapeur*" (the Dapper Dude) because clothes are his only passion. But this commendable effort at counteracting the simplification of the Beur-as-young-delinquent image does not successfully solve the problem of stereotyping. The multiplication of images and the representation of diversity within a community misses its goal because it fights one manifestation of a larger stereotyping system and not its actual process of fabrication. It is true that the strength of stereotypical images often comes from their uniqueness, because uniqueness begs for simple equations (community $x =$ delinquency), but the grammar or syntax of the stereotype can survive even if plurality is introduced. "All Arabs are . . ." can be followed by several adjectives or nouns, even contradictory sets of words. When the grammar of stereotyping is combined with diversity, a list results that adds the force of a litany to the rhetoric of formulas adopted by stereotypes. Abbas Fadhel wonders if it is fair or even an improvement to "enfermer les Arabes du cinéma dans le tiercé suspect victime-délinquant-flic" (to lock Arab film characters into the suspicious victim-delinquent-cop trio) (1990, 143–44). It may be that Chibane's decision to multiply roles will be translated as a stereotypical list. Beur intellectuals, Beur junkies, unemployed Beurs, and Beur women (the so-called "Beurettes") are not necessarily free from stereotyping as long as the grammar that produces them as a predictable and recognizable list is not questioned.

L'oeil au beur~~re~~ noir attacks the syntax of stereotyping rather than its manifestation at the level of the representation of characters. The question asked by all the characters is not how Beurs or blacks will achieve integration but how French society, in which they are already active participants, describes them. In a sense, integration is not even an issue—it already exists, and the current debate about whether it is possible or not is implicitly criticized as a rearguard and anachronistic preoccupation. *How* French language and culture integrate the presence of Beurs and blacks in their images, metaphors, and rhetoric is, however, the slightly different issue that Meynard explores. In this film, Smaïn/Rachid is neither the token minority, the unique representative of a hypothetical Beur community, nor a character whose position as a Beur is completely erased. For him, being Beur means being confronted by the grammar of the list and repetitions, and the film is a very specific case study. *L'oeil au beur~~re~~ noir* is not about identity, nor even about stereotypes in general, but about three characters who learn how to analyze and reappropriate the power of two very specific stereotypical statements that can either ruin their lives or allow them to fight back: "I will not rent to a foreigner" and "*'Insécurité'* [a right-wing buzzword] is due to the presence of immigrants."

An interesting rhetorical and discursive parallel is added to a rather conventional set of situations. The film suggests that the two heroes will never be in a position to sign a lease because they are the victims of the endless and unstoppable repetition of maddening racist stereotypes that supposedly disqualify them as tenants. But through a careful rotation of scenes, the movie also shows that the way in which Rachid and Denis endeavor to fight the system is also a form of systematic repetition, a deliberate and questionable tactic called the "Rachid system."

The intolerable effect of repetition on people's lives is the point of the very first scene of the movie. A series of leitmotivs that will accompany the black hero in his endless quest for an apartment is immediately presented as a given. The prospect of homelessness is alluded to discreetly. (The very first image is a close-up on a piece of cardboard from under which emerges an old man who obviously spent the night there.) A little further away, prospective tenants, standing in a ridiculously long line, are shown to be alienated from each other, the scarcity of places to rent creating an atmosphere of fierce competition. There is hardly any communication or solidarity among the individuals that the camera observes dispassionately, as if they were some exotic spectacle. Moving slowly from the end of the line to the front, the camera shares its powerful gaze and freedom with the spectators, allowing us to cut in line and putting us at a distance from the immobilized human beings. It is clear that we are not part of the line, that what we see is not limited to the back of the person ahead of us, and that we have the immense privilege of actually entering the apartment without waiting in line. When the door of the apartment is finally revealed at the end of a comically long pan, we realize that our hero (Denis Saint-Rose, a Caribbean painter) is first in line, a few remarks and his half-asleep silhouette indicating that he must have spent the night on the street to be there first. His pole position, however, cannot protect him from the barrage of stereotypes that greet him inside: the look of intense surprise on the renter's face, who apparently cannot reconcile Saint-Rose's face with the "French" name she reads on her list, and the subsequent refrain of lame and contradictory excuses, all revolving around some version of the implausible "the place has already been rented."

From an ideological point of view, the episode is so simple in its violence that there is little left to say. And from a narrative point of view, this scene is a bit of a paradox. It is simultaneously a first scene and an "always already" scene that insists on presenting itself as such. By definition, a first scene is not supposed to be a repetition—we perceive it as unique and original—but this scene must point to its repetitive nature to make the spectator aware that it is out of the question to interpret the incident as unique, exceptional, or self-contained. In other words, the film starts off with a denaturalization of stereotypically repetitive situations. The spectator discovers a new situation, a new hero, a new story, yet the point of the confrontation is to show us just how much individuals suffer from the relentless repetition of unformulated assumptions: Saint-Rose is systematically turned down by landlords because he is black. His story is reduced to a minimalist statement. For him, no first time is ever possible because he is always greeted by the same implicit statement. In spite of his efforts to play the game of the bourgeoisie (he arrives first, he is impeccably dressed, his exquisitely old-fashioned manners betray an exaggerated degree of formality), the very first second of encounter with the real-estate agent is always determinate, a premature closure.

The originality of the movie lies in the suggestion that the infuriating episode is also a crisis for storytelling. If everything becomes predictable, how does one tell a new story? How does one find an apartment when the encounter with the agent is an endless list of similar and predictable microdialogues that get repeated ad nauseam? Consequently, how does one make a film when a first episode cannot exist because it is the repetition of the last scene and the rehearsal of the next scene. The beginning of the movie establishes very quickly that some individuals suffer from the relentless repetition of stereotypes and immediately makes it every spectator's problem by suggesting that we will be deprived of stories if repetition continues to dominate our culture. Even if we do not identify with the character (that is, regardless of our identity), the black character's problem becomes ours in our capacity of audience waiting for a story.

The very next scene is apparently completely unrelated, and in this unrelatedness (and therefore unpredictability) lies the clue to the overall organization of the movie. When repetition threatens to kill stories, one has to reappropriate the power of lists and repetitions by depriving the other (us, the spectator, the maker of stereotypes) of their stereotyping grammar. Surprises (one of the conditions of storytelling) have to be stolen from the dominant discourse to which or at which lists will be repeated and thrown back from a completely unexpected position. The second scene of the movie will eventually appear to the spectator as a symmetrical version of the first one but initially we are under the impression that the first episode is finished and that an unrelated narrative has started. Exit the black character and his unsuccessful attempts at renting a place, his long wait and repetitive failures. This time, everything happens very fast. Rachid is sitting on his moped (the valiant steed of the modern knight), looking at women walking on the street. Suddenly, he notices that two punks, are harassing a vulnerable-looking young woman whom they terrorize and trap inside a telephone booth. A Zorro-like Rachid rushes to her rescue and courageously challenges the two punks who turn against him, yelling racial slurs and trying to hit him. The rest is easy to guess: Rachid defeats his unworthy opponents (kicking one of them in the balls), grabs the hand of his pathetic victim, who by now is sobbing and screaming, drags her out of harm's way, allows her a second to recover from the shock, and proceeds to deliver the punch line: "Un Arabe sauve une jeune fille agressée par deux blancs. C'est le monde à l'envers!" ("An Arab saves a young woman from her two white assailants. What is wrong with this picture?") After an exchange of niceties, Rachid suggests a drink. The young woman says she lives next door and invites him in. The camera follows them to the door of the building, but this time it does not have more power than the characters it follows. The couple disappears behind a closed door, and the camera does not intrude on their privacy. We are left outside, reduced to guessing whether Rachid gets what we think he wants. Given what we will find out about Rachid's propensity to make up stories, we will never know for sure what happens inside.)

The problem is, of course, that the camera has not really lost its powers to cut in line and enter apartments. Like Rachid, it is lying to us, pretending not to know what is really going on. For just as the spectator is beginning to think that this second episode is a rather moralizing bit of poetic and misogynistic justice (the minority knight in his shining armor has defeated the forces of evil and racism and he gets the woman as prize), just as we are beginning to wonder if the film was simply going to trade off women for minorities, the door reopens, and the camera, which has not moved at all, finally and reluctantly gives us the key to the whole episode. Rachid, standing with the door behind him, remains immobile for an inexplicably long time, a look of deep concern on his face, while the camera, from across the street, moves to the right until we realize that the two punks are still there, on the pavement, waiting for him to come out. When the camera has completed its rotation, the front of the screen is occupied by the back of the two punks. Their point of view becomes the spectator's reference; we now see Rachid from the same angle as they do. If I suggest that the camera lies to us (rather than simply maintaining a element of surprise), it is because the long seconds during which Rachid seems to hesitate before finally crossing the street toward the two punks are retrospectively unjustifiable, for suddenly a brutal anticlimax relieves us of our fear of a second street fight. In a childish, whining voice, one of the punks complains to Rachid that he should really be more careful next time and not kick him so hard because he broke his cup, and by the way did he sleep with her?

In other words, and in spite of appearances, this second scene is quite similar to the first one in that it is based on the repetition of a stereotype. Only this time, the stereotype is used by the person who would otherwise suffer from anti-Arab prejudices. Playing on the implicit "All Arabs are . . . ," Rachid uses racist fears and anti-immigrant hostility to win the woman's sympathy. He uses what he knows to be his otherness as a trump card in a game of mirror strategies that nicely complements the different tactics used by his future friend and rival, Denis Saint-Rose. Whereas the film gives the black character a name that entraps the agent into acknowledging her prejudices against him, the Beur character loudly presents himself as an Arab even before introducing himself as Rachid. Whereas Saint-Rose seems to hope that his "Frenchness" (which apparently includes a class element as shown by his use of formality) will be more significant than his skin color, Rachid's identity as an excluded and supposedly non-French minority is deployed cynically in an attempt to seduce the woman. When the two white men pretend to attack him, they make sure to insult him as an Arab, and when Rachid comments on the situation, he also takes great care to insist on the "whiteness" of the two offenders and on his own "Arabité" (not "beuritude").

Their script was obviously written carefully, memorized, and always subject to renegotiated alteration, as we will see. In other words, the grammar of lists and repetitions is also at work in this second scene, although the camera took great pains to make us believe otherwise. What seemed like an exceptional scene (as the woman puts it: "il ne m'arrive jamais rien" [nothing ever happens to me]), a one-of-a-kind incident ("le monde à l'envers" [the world upside-down]) is now revealed to be a well-rehearsed routine, a scenario, a film within the film written and directed by Rachid and his two accomplices. As the infamous trio retreats to a public restroom, they squabble about who will be the next victim and who will sleep with her this time, it becomes obvious to the audience that this was no trial run, that many women have been duped and that, as spectators, we have been taken in, too. We have been deceived by the trio and their manipulation of repetition. In a sense, we are in the same position as the woman until it is too late. Only after Rachid comes out of her apartment again do we realize that our fear, anger, or frustration (the poor woman, poor Rachid) were unnecessary. At one point, the camera shows us the woman's point of view, trapped inside the telephone booth by the two thugs (complete with leather jackets and bandannas), whose threatening faces look like distorted masks as they press their lips to the glass windows. Just like her, we were the victims of a hoax and of our lack of competence as interpreters. We did not recognize that the scenario was a bit too perfect, that the terrifying images of threatening punks were a visual quote, and that the situation itself was a stereotypical narrative. The episode suggests that there is a price to pay for our inability to identify repetition (including the repetition of stereotypes). If we fail to suspect that the whole scenario may be a sort of quotation, we are, just like the woman, at the mercy of an unscrupulous stereotype thief. We cannot escape what can be stereotyped in *our* identity (whether our ethnic origin or gender).

But the theft of stereotypes is not an infallible game: a first element of disorder sneaks into the well-oiled routine when one of the white men (the one whom Rachid pretends to kick in the balls during the fight) is suddenly overwhelmed by a rush of inspiration. He wants to rewrite the script and suggests improving the dialogue by adding what he thinks will be a realistic detail, the finishing touch: "Et si je disais, en m'écroulant, «Ah, les Arabes, c'est des fourbes!»" [And what if I said, as I collapse, "Oh, Arabs! They are all weasels"]. To which Rachid, who was about to leave the room and go back to the street, very quickly and seriously retorts: "Oui mais pas comme ça, parce que là, tu vois, tu me fais peur" [Okay, but not like that: you see, now you're scaring me]. This first element of discord among the three friends is an intriguing moment because Rachid's fear remains mostly unformulated. It is not clear why this addition to the scenario is more threatening than the rest of the prepared dialogue. (Why, for example, does Rachid not feel threatened by some unambiguously violent racial slurs in the original scene? The punk calls Smaïn a "*crouille*," arguably one of the most virulent anti-Arab insults, and declares that hunting season is open.) For the first time, he sounds earnest and seriously concerned. His fear is motivated by something he does not explain. Apparently, he does not object to the content of the sentence, but to something indescribable in the way in which his friend pronounced it: The "Oui, mais pas comme ça" opens up the possibility of a crack in the Rachid system. Suddenly, even in the rehearsed exchange, something invisible and mysterious becomes threatening that cannot be contained or exorcised by the principle of repetition. Even if both men agree to the formulation, there is a little something that escapes their control and Rachid's "pas comme ça" points to the risky nature of their game of make-believe. Even if Rachid controls the principle of repetition, thus becoming the master of the stereotype, the possibility of drifting into real violence against himself as an Arab is not so far away, hidden in the potential difference between two apparently identical statements. As it turns out, Rachid's warning, "oui, mais pas comme ça" is prophetic, a harbinger of impending catastrophes.

The next attempt at using the aggressor-savior scenario in the hope of impressing and seducing Virginie, who becomes one of the film's main characters, fails miserably and causes a series of grotesque misunderstandings as well as the implosion of the Rachid system. What should have been a simple repetition of the previous scene does not work. Nothing happens as planned and the spectator's superiority (we think that, this time, we know what is going to happen) is as shattered as Rachid's confidence in the iterativity of the system. The first difference is that Virginie, when pushed around and harassed by the two brothers, does not seem paralyzed with fear. Unlike the first victim, she jokes with them, and even before the miraculous intervention of her savior, does not look impressed. The second difference is that when Rachid pounces down on the two would-be aggressors, a red car suddenly appears out of nowhere and screeches to a halt in the middle of the staged fight. To everyone's surprise (the spectator's included), Denis Saint-Rose makes a spectacular entrance, adding a completely unexpected twist to the Rachid system: his own version of the chivalric knight. Obviously, the original script does not easily accommodate the new part. This is a case of too many saviors spoiling the cultural broth. Rachid-Zorro gets hit by Denis before being given a chance to explain "Mais je la sauvais moi" ("But I was saving her"), the strange imperfect tense confirming that the "saving" in question was a premeditated and orchestrated intervention. Ironically, he is now the victim of a bad reader of scenarios so that in order to save what appearances he can, he cannot go through the prearranged moves (the fake kick-in-the-balls trick) and must comply with Denis's request to imitate his own moves. The two white men get rather badly beat up as the result of the unexpected intervention of noise in the Rachid system. Once the Beur, the black, and the woman have left the scene, one of white men mutters, from under a car, as though for his own benefit: "Ah, les Arabes, c'est des fourbes" ("Arabs! They are all weasels") to which his brother adds, "Ouais, et les noirs aussi" ("Right! Not to mention blacks!"). At one level, the announced punch line is amusing because it now functions as perfectly well-timed line in spite of the thug's intention and because it is true that the two idiots are indeed the relatively innocent victims of a misunderstanding in this case. As Rachid had anticipated, however, their eagerness to repeat stereotypes drifts dangerously because it instantly imposes itself as an explanation of the situation, relegating another quite plausible truth in the background. Rather than voicing their understandable resentment at having been betrayed by their friend Rachid, who sacrificed them to his scenario, they stupidly resort to the prepared statement about Arabs in general, making it even worse by their inclusion of blacks.

In fact, their analysis is completely off the mark as the new, apparently multicultural team that has suddenly formed will not function easily according to gender or ethnic categories. From the very first meeting, the Beur, the black, and the woman form a tongue-in-cheek variation of a thousand Starsky-and-Hutch routines.[10] Their encounter inaugurates a whole series of misplaced quotations, ironic redoublings that end up completely discrediting the very principle of repetition. Deprived of his original script, Rachid is forced to improvise, and he does not prove very successful at patching up his secondhand stereotypical narrative. If we examine the reason why his system collapses once Denis intervenes, we realize that the film is slowly making the point that lists, repetitions, and therefore stereotypes can be defeated by the combination of two factors: the presence of noise in the stereotypical system and the presence of a good reader. Not only is it a pessimistic point of view and a mistake to imagine that we live in a world where there is no resistance to stereotypes, but it is an even more serious mistake to underestimate the power of readers to see through the logic of lists and repetitions.

That there is spontaneous resistance to, for example, street violence against a woman is in itself an answer to the stereotypical "nobody ever does anything." Denis ruins the scenario because the Rachid system is predicated on the assumption that only one actor (himself) will interfere. The scenario includes the prediction that everyone else will be indifferent to the plight of a young woman bullied by two thugs. The noise in this system is the element of generosity and relative disinterestedness in Denis's impulse, even if he soon jumps on the "drague" (Don Juan–esque) bandwagon.

Denis also creates noise by refusing to play along with the binary logic (white versus Beur) and ethnic assumptions of the Rachid system's punch line. When Rachid, Denis, and Virginie meet in a café for the first time, Rachid and Denis vie for her attention and put her in the annoying position of having to decide who is the more clever suitor. Rachid's first attempt to strike up a dialogue with Virginie is a failure because Denis continues to mess with the script. Because he must slightly modify the original punch line ("Un Arabe sauve une jeune fille" becomes "Un noir et un Arabe sauvent une fille agressée par deux blancs c'est le monde en l'envers" [A black man and an Arab save a young woman, . . . what's wrong with this picture?]), Rachid is immediately challenged by Denis, who reacts strongly to his essentialist declarations. Denis objects to being brought into the system as "un noir," starting a grotesque and apparently irrelevant quarrel between the two men. Denis interrupts Rachid's pickup line with an unexpected, "Elle aurait été agressée par un beur je serais intervenu aussi" ("If she had been mugged by a Beur, I would have done something, too"), the meaning of which remains unclear: Does he object to Rachid's racialized discourse or to his implication that only white men can be aggressors? Rachid furiously retorts, "Et si ç'avait été un black?" ("What if he had been black?").

The scene slips dangerously close to first-degree racism again. Refusing to be involved in Rachid's theft of stereotypes, Denis sabotages the script, both of them temporarily losing track of their original goal. Virginie is forgotten, except by the camera focusing on her eyes, closely following the ideological ping-pong game. The two men are trapped in a hostile debate about ethnicity until Virginie herself intervenes, a straight-faced ironist who puts a sudden end to the argument by giving a name to the dynamic of the whole conversation. Having listened carefully to the silly inflation of the words such as "mug," "black," and "Beur" in the men's conversation, she suddenly interjects, "Un black tout seul c'est pas possible. Il faut vraiment qu'il y ait un Arabe qui l'entraîne pour que ça arrive . . . [dead silence, enjoyed by the woman who has suddenly won their undivided attention, and, after a pause] et vice-versa" (A black man on his own? That can't be. You really need a Beur to drag him into it . . . and vice versa).

Virginie is the good reader in this story, the reader who does not let repetitions fool her. And as the two men look hurt and surprised, confirming that the

Rachid system and its reappropriation of stereotypes had been engulfed in a sudden flare of first-degree racialization, she finally moves from the endless repetition of identical statements to a description of the type of language she has been using: "Non mais c'est une blague, c'est du deuxième degré" (Hey, just kidding, second-degree humor). The noise that she introduces in the system is a level of self-consciousness about the genre of discourse. Her comment is a form of interruption that announces her role as the much-needed competent reader, and her introduction of the notion of "second degree" not only gives a name to the whole series of episodes that have been unfolding before our eyes, it also makes a series of important points. Virginie's attention to degrees of meaning invites us to be more attentive to the ways in which statements are used and to the context. Her "Non mais c'est une blague" recalls Rachid's mysterious "pas comme ça" and his unformulated fear of falling into first-degree stereotypes. The fact that she has to reassure her shocked audience that it was a joke suggests that nothing in her use of stereotypes about "blacks" and "Beurs" makes them intrinsically funny. "Deuxième degré" is neither innocent nor harmless because it puts the Other at the mercy of whoever has the right and power to suddenly declare "c'est une blague." Her own use of "second degree" also demonstrates that the power of such tactics is unstable. In a sense, she does to Rachid what he did to the all the other women and what the film did to us by lying about what Rachid was up to.

If her statement about Beurs and blacks is misconstrued as first degree when it is, according to her "du deuxième degré," her own critical intervention is yet another level of interpretation—"third-degree reading." What the third-degree reader must do is remember quotations and expect repetitions and be able to start looking for meaning beyond the content of repeated statements. The third-degree reader is trained to see difference through sameness. Symmetrically, third-degree discourse, of which the film itself is an example, can be imagined as a series of self-conscious and ironic audiovisual echoes (rather than as a form of systematic but often unconscious intertextuality or intervisuality), as a constant and conscious reference to previous images or words. Third-degree discourse always suspects what has already been seen or said as a prepackaged sound bite or a visual quote that irony now displaces and modifies.

Third-degree discourse, in the movie, is on the side of Virginie, some narrative power or voice having evidently decided not to let her be the victim of a limited and sexist alternative. (Why should she choose either Rachid or Denis?) When the three of them meet in the café, the film portrays the female character as amused and entertained by the two men's performance. Not only does she listen carefully to what Rachid and Denis say, but she is able to take into account apparently irrelevant elements of the environment; she controls the frame of meaningfulness. Refusing to be controlled by the point of view of the camera (which focuses on Rachid, then on Denis, then on both), her eyes wander away from their table, apparently by chance, looking elsewhere for signs that the camera does not show us at first. Only later, as though reluctantly, does the camera follow her gaze, moving away from Rachid, distracted by other resonances, other noises, until the whole café starts functioning like an echo chamber, providing Virginie and the spectator with third-degree grids of interpretation. When Rachid makes the mistake of quoting Marcel Carné's 1938 *Quai des brumes*, the special bond that he tries to establish between Virginie and himself is shattered. Appropriating the lines of a famous Don Juan (Jean Gabin) from such a famous movie might be a blunder in any case (since the female character seems sensitive to the negative power of repetitions) but he rather poorly chooses his reference. The arch-famous "T'as de beaux yeux tu sais" ("You've got great eyes, kid") is such a cult pickup line as to have become exclusively ironical especially among young people. At best, the quote might function as a secondhand statement, dwarfing Rachid in his appeal to supposedly timeless, classical, monumental figures. And for the spectator, the sentence is both symbolically and a literally second degree, a double repetition since we know that it is part of the Rachid system. (We have heard it before, when the three accomplices were rehearsing their lines in the public bathroom.) But the camera shows that Rachid's attempt to appropriate another kind of stereotype is defeated by his inability to eliminate undesirable redoublings from his own voice. The camera pivots to an another table in the café where an older man is sitting alone, slouched over his food, looking at no one in particular, using his fingers to push bits of food into his mouth without removing his cigarette. Trembling, mumbling to himself, a picture of senility and alienation, the old man apparently repeats Rachid's words in a much more convincing imitation of Gabin's rough tone "T'as d'beaux yeux tu sais, embrasse-moi." The ridiculous echo emphasizes the stereoypical nature of Rachid's chosen sound bite and proposes to the spectator and to the trio a nasty version of Rachid himself, a portrait of the hustler as aging Don Juan, doomed to the ironic repetition of once-successful lines.

That portrait, in the end, is the film's most optimistic contribution. In a world governed by the tyranny of repetition, only the first two episodes of the movie would get endlessly repeated. If nothing more was added to this pattern, the film would confirm that people's identities are always governed by what others consider meaningful about them (e.g., gender, ethnicity, or class). Throughout the movie, Virginie would be only "a woman," Denis "a black man," Rachid, "a Beur." And if the film's only contribution was to suggest that negative stereotypes can be counteracted by other stereotypes, I would not have found its discourse powerfully seductive. What occurs, however, after the two initial scenes is a more interesting series of experiments, and the tentative invention of third-degree reading. If the first scene represents the first degree of stereotypes based on the harmful power of their literal meaning, Rachid's reappropriation of anti-Arab prejudices is a form of second-degree that still implies a gullible reader—someone has to be taken in by the reappropriation of stereotypes. What the rest of the movie demonstrates, however, is that we are not reduced to this alternative. Between the three main characters, a new form of relationship develops as they become an interestingly conflictual trio. Both of the heroes are quite aware of the existence of stereotypes and of their double-edged nature, but they also know that the other members of the team share their knowledge. This complicity enables them to not only take into account the existence of ethnic origin or gender but also to treat these elements with a tactically effective ironic distance. A third-degree discourse emerges, and we are invited to respond with a third-degree reading that transcends the repetitive nature of stereotypes, whether used by malicious real-estate agents or clever poachers. "Third degree," in this sense, does not and should not refer to any content in particular, but the phrase is supposed to generate a number of echoes, perhaps of all the third parties that provoke a dialect with our binary world. A third-degree reading would be the kind of skill achieved by a hybrid "*tiers instruit*" as described by Michel Serres in what Homi Bhabha calls a third space, and it also evokes what has been called "third cinema," as long as we carefully maintain the distinction between third cinema and third-world cinema (Serres 1990; Bhabha 1994; Pines and Willemen 1989).[11]

What we discover, as the story unfolds, is that the so-called Rachid system, based on the belief that repetition is a matter of rehearsed scenarios, is far from infallible. Controlling the repetition of situations is not always possible when one tries to reappropriate stereotypes, and this may be one of the most optimistic statements of the movie, as we are led to suspect that repetition may be impossible even in the case of the first-degree stereotype. In the real world of narratives and stereotypes, the same causes will not always produce the same effects because the Rachid system cannot work without a naive misinterpreter. The Rachid system would only work in a noiseless system (where stereotypes could not be opposed), in a universe where every ideological variable is predictable, and that is not the case. Rather than insisting that the repetition of stereotypes is morally undesirable and that the stereotype thief is just as bankrupt because his strategy is guilty of the same shortcomings as first-degree stereotyping, the film suggests that the Rachid system is threatened by its own pessimistic belief in the absolute power of repetition. There will always be an element of resistance in the world of repetition, and the stereotype thief will be betrayed by his lack of control over repetition.

Chapter 4

Stereotypes as Gifts

From Baudelaire to *Banlieues*

"Oh, le pauvre malheureux!"

Si Bachir fit connaissance avec la France à l'âge de soixante-treize ans. Il arrivait tout droit d'un gros village saharien où l'on commençait à construire des HLM qui ressemblaient comme des frères à ceux qu'il découvrit à sa descente d'avion. Là-dessus, il ne fut pas dépaysé!

Si Bachir était venu faire soigner ses yeux. Il passa donc plusieurs mois chez son fils établi à Roubaix. La rue de l'Alma, où habitait la famille L., était à cette époque-là l'une des rues les plus animées de la ville. La crise n'avait pas encore ruiné le petit commerce et personne n'avait besoin de s'angoisser en recomptant, chaque quinzaine, les chômeurs qui pointaient à l'ANPE. Bref, le ciel n'était pas encore tombé sur la tête des Roubaisiens!

Commerçant lui-même, Si Bachir eut tôt fait de connaître les profits et pertes de ses confrères du quartier. Les petits-commerçants de France avaient les mêmes problèmes que n'importe quel petit-commerçant de son pays. Cette constatation rassura Si Bachir.

"Oh, the poor old man!"

by Marie Féraud, translated by Colin Davis[1]

Si Bachir became acquainted with France when he was seventy-three years old. He came straight from a large village in the Sahara where they had begun to build high-rise flats just like the ones he saw as he got out of the plane. On that point at least, he felt quite at home!

Si Bachir had come for treatment on his eyes. So he stayed for several months with his son who was living in Roubaix. Alma Street, where the L. family lived, was at that time one of the busiest streets in the town. The recession had not yet ruined the small shopkeepers, and no one needed to worry as they counted, each fortnight, the unemployed who came to sign on at the Employment Exchange. In short, the sky had not yet fallen in on the people of Roubaix!

As a shopkeeper himself, Si Bachir soon got to know about the profits and losses of his colleagues in the area. The shopkeepers of France had the same problems as any shopkeeper in his own country. This observation reassured Si Bachir.

One of Si Bachir's great pleasures was

Un grand plaisir de Si Bachir était de s'installer sur une chaise devant la maison de son fils et de regarder les gens passer dans la rue.

C'est ainsi que "Oh, le pauvre malheureux" se produisit—"Oh, le pauvre malheureux!" est le nom que toute la famille donna, par la suite, à l'aventure qui arriva à Si Bachir, ce jour-là.

Il devait être six heures du soir. Si Bachir était à son poste d'observation depuis une heure ou deux. Il avait échangé toutes sortes de salutations avec des parents et des voisins. Son petit-fils lui avait apporté un café vers cinq heures, et il se rappellera plus tard la réflexion qui lui vint à propos de tous ces chiens tenus en laisse:

"Qu'est-ce qu'un pays où on promène les chiens en laisse?"

Cette réflexion en avait amené d'autres. Si Bachir aimait philosopher. Et quand il philosophait tout seul, il prenait une certaine position: la tête courbée vers le sol, les yeux fermés, un coude appuyé sur ses genoux, une main se tenant le front, l'autre, paume en l'air, posée simplement sur les genoux. Dans cette attitude, Si Bachir pouvait philosopher des heures entières.

Il réfléchissait depuis un bon moment déjà, quand, sentant que quelqu'un venait de s'arrêter à sa hauteur, Si Bachir ouvrit les yeux. Son regard tomba sur une paire de pantoufles puis, remontant lentement, découvrit une vieille dame qui s'exclamait d'un air de profonde pitié:

"Oh, le pauvre malheureux!"

Et de glisser avec un bon sourire une pièce de vingt centimes dans la main de Si Bachir pétrifié.

Jamais! Non, jamais de sa vie, Si Bachir ne ressentit pareille émotion! Une tempête lui révolutionna la tête. L'humiliation l'étouffait. Comment! Lui, Si Bachir Laamari, commerçant honorable de Biskra, qui venait de dépenser près de trois mil-

to make himself comfortable in a chair in front of his son's house and to watch the people who passed in the street.

That is how "Oh, the poor old man!" happened—"Oh, the poor old man!" is how the entire family later referred to the incident that befell Si Bachir on that day.

It must have been six o'clock in the evening. Si Bachir had been at his lookout post for an hour or two. He had exchanged greetings with relatives and neighbors. His grandson had brought him coffee at around five o'clock, and later he will remember what he had been thinking regarding all the dogs kept on leads: "What sort of country is it where dogs are kept on leads?"

This thought had been followed by others. Si Bachir loved to philosophize. And when he philosophized on his own, he used to adopt a certain posture: his head bent toward the ground, his eyes closed, one elbow leaning on his knees, one hand against his forehead, the other, palm upward, resting simply on his knees. In this position, Si Bachir could philosophize for hours on end.

He had been thinking for quite a while when, sensing that someone had just stopped beside him, Si Bachir opened his eyes. His gaze fell on a pair of slippers then, slowly rising, it alighted on an old lady exclaiming with an expression of profound pity: "Oh, the poor old man!"

And, smiling kindly, she slipped a twenty-centime coin into the hand of the stunned Si Bachir.

Never! No, never in his life had Si Bachir felt like this! A tempest spun around his head. He was stifled by humiliation. What! Him, Si Bachir Laamari, respectable shopkeeper from Biskra, who had just spent nearly thirty thousand francs on his journey, on his eyes, presents for the family . . . being described as a "poor old man!"!!!

lions de centimes pour son voyage, pour ses yeux, les cadeaux à la famille . . . se faire traiter de "pauvre malheureux!"!!!

La pièce de vingt centimes lui brûla la main.

Il ouvrit la bouche . . . Aucun son n'en sortit.

"Pourquoi tu me fais la charité? cria en silence Si Bachir. J'ai des sous, j'ai une maison, un commerce, j'ai mes enfants . . ."

Mais la voix de sa conscience lui intima de se taire.

"Tu es obligé d'accepter la pièce, disait-elle. Tu ne peux pas faire autrement. C'est une vieille femme et elle croit que tu lui demandes la charité. Elle n'a peut-être que ça à donner . . . Si tu te mets à crier, une autre fois, quand un pauvre malheureux lui demandera vingt centimes, elle va dire: "J'ai donné à l'autre et il a commencé à m'engueuler. C'est pas la peine de donner à celui-là."

"Merci madame", gémit Si Bachir en ravalant sa fierté.

Mais depuis ce jour-là et jusqu'à son départ, jamais plus Si Bachir ne philosopha devant sa porte.

The twenty-centime coin scorched his hand.

He opened his mouth. . . . No sound came out.

"Why are you treating me like a charity case?" Si Bachir cried in silence. "I have money, I have a house, a business, I have my children. . . ."

But the voice of his conscience told him to remain silent.

"You must accept the coin," it told him. "You have no choice. She is an old woman and she thinks you are asking for charity. Perhaps that is all she has to give. . . . If you object, next time, when a poor old man asks her for twenty centimes, she will say, 'I gave once before and the man insulted me. It's not worth giving to this one.'"

"Thank you, Madame," Si Bachir moaned, swallowing his pride.

But from that day until he left France, never again did Si Bachir philosophize in front of the door.

In spite of, or perhaps because of, the Beur character's mitigated success, the previous chapter ended on an optimistic note. The stereotype thief does not have to worry—his successful tactics of reappropriation do not turn him into a stereotyper. Flipping the mirror over and handing it to those who would like to force him into the narrow confines of ethnic generalizations is a potentially dangerous form of repetition, but neither the stereotype thief nor stereotyping fictions can hope to completely control the chain of repetitions. The final word of stereotyping can never be uttered. In this chapter, this optimistic certainty is tempered by the knowledge that it is never simple, even in a fictional discourse, to oppose the stereotyper and the stereotyped, nor to distribute good and bad moral points when it comes to the use and abuse of ethnic images. In the films and short stories or novels that I have discussed until now, it is usually clear who is the victim of stereotyping. As we have seen, most culturally hybrid subjects are well versed in the art of using stereotypes and quite capable of returning negative pictures to the sender, but just as obviously, the reader or viewer is certainly aware that the danger of suffering from internalization is always present. As a result, when, within the economy of a film such as *L'oeil au beur~~re~~ noir* or within a short scene such as Smaïn's "Le président Beur," it is significant that the fictional distribution of roles should be relatively clear. The subject who is responsible for the gesture of reappropriation is also the stereotyped Other who manages to win some sort of symbolic battle. As readers, we may share a feeling of triumph and just vindication. We are at least expected to side with the clearly identified hero. As for the realization that no stereotype thief is capable of falling prey to the liberator-turned-dictator syndrome, it may even enhance a moment of exorcism and build an element of safety and relief into the mechanism. The stereotype thief takes advantage of the cynicism and ignorance displayed by those who would like to typecast him. In this chapter, the reappropriation of stereotype is a much more ambiguous episode, and it would be very difficult to ascertain who wins anything at the end of the encounter between two differently empowered or disenfranchised individuals. The tactics used in the two texts I will analyze involve an element of loss and renunciation, and the ends of the stories do not provide any cathartic satisfaction. Rather, they end on sweet and sour notes of victory and defeat for everyone, including the reader. They leave us in a strangely undecidable mood and with a rather ambiguous proposal. It may be that certain contexts demand that we refrain willingly from intervening, even though it is quite clear that the stereotype could be stopped, challenged, or at least addressed. Another story from Marie Féraud's collection will serve as a point of departure and lead us to reconsider the fraught relationship between what is given and what is taken when the matter exchanged between two subjects is the mutual negotiation of the representation of their physical appearances. In other words, while the previous chapters analyzed different interventionist strategies, I will here attempt to disentangle the complicated web of reasons that could explain and even justify certain moments of silence.

So let us look at two very different texts: Baudelaire's prose poem "La fausse monnaie" (Counterfeit money), and another Marie Féraud's short story, "Oh, le pauvre malheureux!" (Oh, the poor old man!), published in the same collection as "Les Ray-Ban." Each of the narratives tells the story of an encounter between the narrator and a silent or silenced other and constitutes an invitation to test our own stereotyping reflexes. Between the two texts, interesting crisscrossing patterns and echoes will emerge as soon as we look at what positions are respectively occupied by the narrator and the silent Other. It is well worth considering such differences as a symptom of how the two stories differ in their dealing with stereotypes. For students of literatures in French, this invitation to compare Baudelaire's poem and Marie Féraud's short story already introduces a discrepancy, an imbalance between the two objects of study. A difference in value is created due to the fact that the canon does not equally recognize the two textual samples. "La fausse monnaie" is immediately identifiable as one of Baudelaire's prose poems, but "Oh, le pauvre malheureux!" is not entitled to the same instant recognition; its literary and cultural value is not immediately apparent.[2] Féraud's multidisciplinary position is familiar to us by now, but if I wanted to describe the text for hypothetical students, I would probably have to present "Oh, le pauvre malheureux!" as a little-known text written by a little-known sociologist. While "La fausse monnaie" is anthologized and likely to be studied in many universities, there is little chance of seeing Marie Féraud's story in a textbook. Nor would I necessarily want to argue that the situation must change. Rather, I would like to speculate on this difference of literary and cultural value between the two texts. I suggest that the different types of legitimacy enjoyed by "La fausse monnaie" and "Oh, le pauvre malheureux!" respectively are worth exploring as a metaphor for the dialogue created by an encounter between hegemony and relative powerlessness in the two stories. Stereotypes are also a product of sometimes unconscious expectations of value. And moments of comparison and translation are particularly well adapted to research on stereotyping as they require the putting in perspective of our assumptions about the texts or human beings we are in the process of interpreting and constructing.

In "Oh, le pauvre malheureux!" no theft occurs and the characters are not young adolescents in the process of reinventing norms and subversiveness. This time, the text focuses on the encounter between a Maghrebi character and an old woman. The encounter is clearly marked by the specific historical context in which it takes place, and it is worth remembering how this collection of stories fits in its generation of Parisian literary productions. *Histoires Maghrébines* came out two years after the first "marche des Beurs," a moment when the debate about immigration and French nationality was framed in a way that has already evolved considerably. Questions about national and ethnic identities were bound to force the French to reflect on the nature of the link between identity and visible ethnicities. In 1983, the focus was on racism and integration, rather than, for example, on illegal immigration and deportations, as has more recently been the case. Today's recognizable vocabulary is part of a context-specific jargon used by politicians and journalists alike, and the fact that key words have changed is an indication that the issues are no longer the same. For better or worse, in the middle of the 1980s, the sons and daughters of Maghrebi immigrants were in the limelight. They were much more often portrayed and talked about than today when the media focus more systematically on the new arrivals and especially on the illegal immigrants from Mali, Senegal, or Zaire for example. The Beurs have been displaced by "*les sans-papiers*" (undocumented immigrants, literally "paperless"), and integration is less often mentioned than "*reconduites à la frontière*" (deportations) or chartered flights hired by the French government to fly illegal aliens back to their countries. From a literary perspective, Féraud's text coincides with the emergence of what has been called, more or less tentatively, the Beur novel. The best-known and most often studied Beur novels date from that period, and most Beur writers' novelistic production is neatly concentrated in the 1980s (Hargreaves 1991; Laronde 1993). Mehdi Charef, Azouz Begag, and Farida Belghoul's work, to name but three of the most famous novelists whose texts are discussed in this book, are contemporaries of *Histoires Maghrébines*. The issues dealt with in "Oh, le pauvre malheureux!" are more similar to those addressed in Azouz Begag's *Béni ou le paradis privé* than in Van Cauwelaert's *Un aller simple*, for example.[3]

"Oh, le pauvre malheureux!" offers an original viewpoint for one interested in how stereotypes work because the story is both informed by its immediate context and intriguingly different from other texts. Rather than focusing on a fashionable Beur youngster, Féraud concentrates on two older characters and especially on a hero whose physical appearance is the subject of much speculation. The relationship between speculation, identity, and stereotype is the ground on which we can articulate the comparison between Baudelaire's poem and Féraud's text.

Both in "La fausse monnaie" and in "Oh, le pauvre malheureux!" the reader is presented with a reflection on how to define what is valuable and with a debate on intellectual, human, and moral worth at the end of which the narrator of each story is able to draw different conclusions. A double speculation occurs: in the commercial sense of a calculated and risky investment where someone hopes to make a substantial profit, but also in the intellectual sense of meditating, pondering, deliberating. In both stories, the narrators seek an answer to the following questions: What is a gift, what is real charity, what is a real gift, and what is a fake gift? And they are just as equally fascinated by the issue of circulation and exchange: How does money change hands, what is the definition of charity, but also how do ideas and stereotypes circulate, especially ideas and stereotypes about "the poor" (the social Other in "La fausse monnaie" and the imagined social and ethnic Other in "Oh, le pauvre malheureux!")[4]

The second story, "Oh, le pauvre malheureux!" which is not worth much in terms of the literary canon, is paradoxically in a position to give something to the other text, to enrich the prose poem, by adding to its meaning a level of complexity that it cannot otherwise acquire. More than a century later, the characters in Marie Féraud's story finish a transaction started in the poem where a dandy gives a beggar a counterfeit coin. The second text functions like a bit of small change finally given back, with interest. As the double meaning of the French phrase "rendre la monnaie de sa pièce" implies, what is returned also settles a moral debt, as if the second story managed to avenge the silent victim of a gross indelicacy.[5] The fact that the first coin given to the beggar was fake naturally complicates this settling of accounts. We find ourselves confronted with a situation in which money continues to be exchanged when the system normally attempts to stop all speculation by withdrawing the fake coins from circulation. This places this exchange on the margins of authorized markets, on the wrong side of cultural and financial legitimacy.

A gift and a speculation

Let me outline the elements of "Oh, le pauvre malheureux!" that allow it to function as an ironic and sarcastic distorting mirror, for it exposes and criticizes the ethical and aesthetic certitudes of the prose poem. The two texts display an uncanny symmetry: in both stories, a gift instantly provokes a serious moral crisis, one of the characters is forced to judge the act he has just witnessed and to draw from the episode a whole new set of rules about giving and receiving. In the prose poem, two dandies meet a beggar and both respond to his silent plea by giving him some money. But when the narrator learns that the impressively generous alms that his friend gave the poor man was in fact a counterfeit coin, the gift undergoes a metamorphosis, loses its status of gift. At the end of the story, the gift has become what the narrator calls a "*calcul inepte.*" The "ineptitude of the calculation," as Peggy Kamuf translates it, is motivated by the desire to "faire à la fois la charité et une bonne affaire" (to do a good deed while at the same time making a good deal) (137).[6] The episode also causes the narrator to speculate about the future consequences of his friend's gesture. Would the counterfeit coin continue to circulate, would the beggar benefit from the gift or would he get in trouble, what would happen to the coin itself? "Ne pouvait-elle pas se multiplier en pièces vraies? Ne pouvait-elle pas aussi le conduire en prison?" (136) (Might it not multiply into real coins? Could it not also lead him to prison?). The narrator also wonders if he should forgive his friend for his cynical economical and gratuitous joke.[7] The encounter between the rich and the poor thus becomes a pretext for a more general reflection on the art of giving, on what constitutes legitimate and illegitimate gifts.

Similarly, in Féraud's story, a crisis generated by a problematic gift is immediately followed by long discursive and ideological speculation. In this text, an old woman makes a rather serious error: she takes the hero of the story for a beggar when in reality Si Bachir is a rich merchant from North Africa who is visiting his relatives. Because Si Bachir is sitting outside, she thinks that he wants her to give him money. When she does so, she gives him a twenty-centime coin, which the hero will later call "une misère" (22), a pittance, peanuts, next to nothing. Si Bachir's conclusions about this event provide an ironic echo to the "morale désagréable" (unpleasant lesson) that Baudelaire's characters search for.[8]

The two main characters of the poem and of the short story are themselves symmetrical: the narrator of the poem is described as a compulsive philosopher, gifted by Mother Nature with a "misérable cerveau, toujours occupé à chercher midi à quatorze heures" (136) (miserable brain, always concerned with looking for noon at two o'clock) while Si Bachir, merchant and philosopher himself, devotes much of his time enjoying the great pleasure of "s'installer sur une chaise devant la maison de son fils" (making himself comfortable in a chair in front of his son's house) in order to "philosopher tout seul pendant des heures" (22) ("philosophize for hours on end"). And yet, this apparent similarity between Baudelaire's narrator and Si Bachir is deceptive: like a real coin and its fake counterpart, the two characters resemble each other but occupy completely distinct functions in the economy of an encounter with otherness. In the prose poem, the philosopher is the person who gives to the poor, in the second story, the philosopher is the one who receives a gift. At least, this is what is suggested by a first thematic reading, which will precisely be modified by a close analysis of how each gift is defined and of how each act of receiving is conceived and narrated. The comparison between the poem and the short story results in a reevaluation of what the Baudelairian narrator concludes. The second story will eventually enable us to reinterpret the prose poem and to propose that the first text made a serious mistake in the attribution of roles: the giver and the receiver are not who they appear to be at first. The cynical dandy who thinks he knows when to give and forgive never doubts for a minute that he knows what "giving" means. While the second text, by questioning simple interpretations of who gives and who receives, makes the point that the definition of generosity also hinges on the criteria one selects when determining not so much what is given and received but who is the giver and who is the receiver. In spite of superficial evidence to the contrary, I would therefore like to propose that in "Oh, le pauvre malheureux!" whatever gift there is emanates from Si Bachir and not from the old woman, from the apparent beggar and not from the supposedly generous passerby.

Giver and receiver: Role reversals

The logic of the text originally misleads the reader by suggesting that the role of the giver is occupied by the old woman and that the role of the receiver is imposed on the rich merchant and philosopher. But as the story unfolds, we realize that the interest of the episode lies in the imaginative way in which Si Bachir deals with the unwelcome gift. For not only is the gift a pittance that the rich merchant does not need and does not want, but we will see that it is also corrupted and poisoned by ideological and racist assumptions about the Maghrebi. As a result, the most significant consequence of the exchange is that Si Bachir is forced to redefine his own position: the reluctant receiver becomes a giver by rapidly improvising a coherent set of ethical rules governing the art of responsible giving.

The violence of the situation comes from the fact that both givers and receivers end up being forced into their positions as the result of an original error of interpretation that, I suggest, has everything to do with Si Bachir's physical appearance. The old woman's benevolence is in fact a grave insult. Her generous intention is coupled with such suspicious interpretive reflexes that her gift is akin to a form of racist violence. And while her gift is exposed as a form of abuse, the generosity of the story as a whole consists in a refusal to reciprocate and to be caught in a logic of retaliation.

Si Bachir never corrects the old woman's mistake. The misunderstanding lasts longer than the exchange between the two characters and lives on to tell the tale, to present us with new interpretations and new responsibilities as readers and citizens. Si Bachir, throughout the story, mostly remains strangely silent. From that point of view, he is quite similar to the the beggar in the prose poem. Like Si Bachir, Baudelaire's pauper is both eloquent and dumb. The beggar's eyes are full of "éloquence muette" (mute eloquence) while Si Bachir is silenced by the intensity of his feelings: "L'humiliation l'étouffait. . . . Il ouvrit la bouche . . . Aucun son n'en sortit" (22) [He was stifled by humiliation. . . . He opened his mouth . . . No sound came out]. Finally, Si Bachir "cria en silence": silently, he cried, not his gratitude, but his indignation.

Si Bachir's silence, however, cannot be read as a form of passivity or quiet acceptance. In fact, the moment of silence is a turning point; it is in the middle of Si Bachir's silence that a radical role reversal suddenly occurs. Unbeknownst to the old woman, Si Bachir changes places with her. Suddenly, the giver becomes the receiver and the receiver becomes the giver. The whole situation is turned upside-down at the very moment when the North African shopkeeper, while remaining silent, makes a choice. At first, he cannot speak because he is gagged by the force of his indignation and an intense feeling of humiliation, but gradually his silence takes on a different meaning, becoming a personal intervention and a strategic decision not to confront the old woman.

Mais la voix de sa conscience lui intima de se taire: "Tu es obligé d'accepter la pièce. . . . Si tu te mets à crier, une autre fois, quand un pauvre malheureux lui demandera vingt centimes, elle va dire: 'J'ai donné à l'autre et il a commencé à m'engueuler. C'est pas la peine de donner à celui-là.'" (23)

[But the voice of his conscience told him to remain silent. "You must accept the coin," it told him. "You have no choice. She is an old woman and she thinks you are asking for charity. Perhaps that is all she has to give . . . . If you object, next time, when a poor old man asks her for twenty centimes, she will say, 'I gave once before and the man insulted me. It's not worth giving to this one.'"

At this juncture, the rich merchant becomes the generous giver of alms. But he does not give the old woman some of his money or power. His gift is, at the same time, a nonviolent reversal of an ideologically violent situation and an implicit comment on the way in which the poem deals with the encounter between the dandy and his other, the rich and the poor, the dominant and the dominated. By defusing the potential violence of a confrontation, the North African merchant gives the old woman a magnificent present.

But what exactly does the merchant give his white benefactor? The silence that "stifles" Si Bachir's voice is the textual sign that what he forces himself to give the old lady is the very identity she imposes on him. One word from him would dispel the myth, but he refuses to say that word. Si Bachir gives her the right to treat him like a beggar, like the necessarily indigent Arab immigrant that the French media tend to capitalize on. The rich North African merchant agrees to let the old woman's narrative become some kind of historical truth. He himself accepts the role of a "pauvre malheureux."

The originality of this misunderstanding is that Si Bachir manages to make a gift from a position that he does not really occupy; he gives as a poor Arab immigrant. And not only, as in a typically Lacanian scenario, does he give what he does not have, but he also gives as what he is not: a stereotyped ethnic Other, the caricature of the excluded marginal. If Lacan is right to suggest that "l'amour, c'est donner ce qu'on n'a pas," Si Bachir's silence is an act of love: his gift consists in an absence of words and explanation.[9] He gives the fact that he does not say what he wants to say, he gives his refusal to share what he knows, he gives by refusing to give what he could easily give: a little of his own power or his knowledge of the situation. This gift of what he does not have is a lot more generous than it seems, not because it is more authentic or more altruistic, not because more purity is involved. Quite the opposite, this gift, just like Baudelaire's counterfeit coin, belongs to the category of fake currency.

For what the shopkeeper gives away is his own identity and his dignity. And if that renunciation was not painful enough, he adds political injury to personal self-abuse: he takes on the enormous responsibility of giving a pathetic and pitiful image not only of himself but also of all the bodies that look like his in the eyes of white French people. In other words, the old woman receives the gift of a stereotype. She is given the latitude to continue to interpret every North African–looking body sitting outside on the street as a beggar asking for public charity. Obviously, the shopkeeper's gift entails the extremely dangerous consequence of complicity. By allowing the old woman to go away with a reinforced stereotype about Arabs, Si Bachir also sides with her and suggests that it is acceptable to make that kind of mistake. His generosity is politically and ideologically impure, contaminated by the stereotype behind the woman's reaction. And, as a visitor who will soon leave this symbolic "rue de France" to go back to his country of origin, he takes on the responsibility of exposing other more permanent immigrants to the same type of humiliation. In the old woman's logic, he is at best the exception to the rule: a rich Arab in a French *banlieue*. And yet, he accepts the fictional marks of what Gayatri Spivak calls a strategic essence. He accepts being treated as typical even though one word from him could make the point that the community defined as "pauvres malheureux" is an imaginary construct, a fallacy. Si Bachir knows better than anyone else that even if one could verify the truth of stereotypes (all Arab-looking middle-aged males are unqualified and probably unemployed workers who live off public charity) he would be the counterexample that sabotages racist demonstrations.

I suggest that there is an element of theoretical treason in Si Bachir's generosity because it is based on the acceptance of the status quo, and because it entails a strong dose of resignation to currently accepted racist imageries. All things considered, this gift is a triple form of treason: Si Bachir betrays himself, betrays the old woman, and betrays the others who look like him and whom he has been forced to represent. Si Bachir betrays himself as a rich shopkeeper and philosopher, but he also betrays the old woman because he treats her like a rather stupid, slightly pathetic, and terminally uneducable human being. By refusing to speak to the old woman, Si Bachir treats her with the same condescending contempt as the narrator and his friend treat the poor beggar in Baudelaire's poem. Once again, the poem's ideology is implicitly criticized and receives a sort of implicit philosophical change. And finally, Si Bachir also betrays those very people he pretends to protect by preserving the possibility of future alms, for he unilaterally imposes the vision of a typical beggar who happens to look like him.

Si Bachir's gift consists in authorizing future discourses about himself as Other. His resignation amounts to a refusal to withdraw from circulation a narrative that he identifies as bankrupt, false, counterfeited. He will not intervene and will allow the circulation of a discourse on Maghrebi immigrants that, in any other situation, he would want to denounce and oppose.

Treason itself, however, can function as a form of sublime generosity. What happens between Si Bachir and the old woman is a type of exchange similar to smuggling. Discourse is smuggled, and this form of contraband resembles what the Algerians know as "*trabendo*."[10] Trabendo is a practice that consists in bringing back from Europe, and from France in particular, merchandise that will then be sold on the black market. In Féraud's story, Si Bachir operates like a customs agent who would refuse to intervene, who would pretend not to notice that the suitcases of a given passenger are disproportionately bulky. In a similar manner, Si Bachir refuses to see that an enormous symbolic object is being smuggled right under his nose. As "poor old man," Si Bachir authorizes the circulation of a caricatural stereotype. His own symbolic borders are made permeable to the passage of a narrative that he is entitled to stop. What he allows to go through the net of his own indignation is a description of himself that is so far from plausible that allowing it to pass by him without comment is an insult to his own intelligence. Si Bachir must be blind if he allows this old female traveler to smuggle such an enormity. The enormous parcel in question goes beyond the limits of relative interpretation and cultural ignorance. The old lady is allowed to pay him with a blatantly fake coin. She is allowed to go unchallenged in spite of the obvious error, in spite of her ridiculous gesture.

We must suppose that the old woman acts in good faith, and the narrative assumes that she has read a whole series of clues before reaching the conclusion that the person sitting in front of her deserved her pity and generosity. She had apparently read signs before deciding that she was in the presence of otherness, that she was confronted with a "pauvre malheureux." And here is where the main difference between the poem and the short story lies, here is what distinguishes Baudelaire and Féraud: The poem never tells us what the beggar thinks or feels when he meets the two friends. That encounter is told exclusively from the position of the relatively well-off and relatively powerful dandy. The poem as a whole never doubts that the other character, the one who never speaks, is indeed a beggar asking for charity, and, if I had not read "Oh, le pauvre malheureux!" I suppose it would have never occurred to me to question the two friends' reading of this other body. What happens in Féraud's text is that the so-called poor old man disappears behind a completely implausible reading, vanishes behind a racist stereotype. The encounter causes the Other to disappear and to be replaced by a fictional invention. What the old woman sees is an Arab sitting in front of the door in the position that could remind an art historian of Rodin's statue of the Thinker. Instead, the old woman jumps to the conclusion that this has to be a poor immigrant, a beggar. This incongruous equation, the good faith with which the old woman makes her irredeemable mistake, the jumping to conclusions and invocation of grossly incorrect stereotypes, all these erroneous interpretations are given away to the old woman as presents when Si Bachir understands what is going through her mind. Si Bachir gives the old woman the gift of her own mistake. He gives her the right to use stereotypes, caricatures, obviously idiotic narratives and get away with it. When he refrains from correcting her, he refuses to force her to open her eyes to a reality she does not see. As for him, he keeps both his mouth and his eyes shut. He goes along with the old woman's interpretation rather than simply stating that she is wrong and that he is a rich philosopher.

Rich people's eyes

Given the emphasis on smuggling and illegal resemblances in the poem and in the short story, it is no coincidence that literal and metaphorical blindness and insight play such important roles in both texts. Si Bachir, for example, seems to equate gifts with the act of closing one's eyes. In fact, the whole episode of "Oh, le pauvre malheureux!" makes the point that there is a direct correlation between how one defines giving and how one looks. By suggesting that generosity is one specific subcategory of the gaze, the story offers an ironic criticism of the prose-poem narrator's paradoxical blindness. What is paradoxical about his specific type of blindness is that, like many of the heroes of Baudelaire's prose poems, the dandy is an obsessive observer, fascinated with eyesight (and insight), he is constantly scrutinizing others' eyes.[11]

Not only does the narrator spend most of his time looking around him, but he also analyzes and decrypts what he thinks others see. We could summarize "La fausse monnnaie" as a double reading of two pairs of eyes. First, the dandy reads the beggars' eyes, and then he reads his friends' eyes as he tries to find there an explanation to what seems an incredible error of interpretation. The narrator reads people's eyes like simple and decipherable texts. In the beggar's eyes, he reads "l'éloquence muette de ses yeux suppliants, qui contiennent, pour l'homme sensible qui sait y lire, tant d'humilité et tant de reproches" (135) (the mute eloquence of those supplicating eyes that contain at once, for the sensitive man who knows how to read them, so much humility and so much reproach). As a "*homme sensible*" (sensitive man), he prides himself on being a good reader of eyes. And in a sense, one may congratulate the narrator for suggesting a way of reading otherness that bypasses language and the cultural patrimony inscribed in its metaphors and clichés. But having read "Oh, le pauvre malheureux!" we are offered a different vantage point. It becomes rather obvious that the narrator should not take much credit from the fact that he can read eyes, since what he finds there is but a caricature of what he thinks he already knows about poverty. What he thinks he has read is a stereotyped definition of otherness. And what is even more striking in this supposedly sensitive reading of the beggar's eyes is that the dandy never doubts that his interpretation is the correct one. For him, visual texts are simple, unsophisticated, eminently interpretable. The narrator seems convinced that the eyes' "mute eloquence" address him directly and have a clear and unambiguous message for the rich passerby. The poem downplays the element of encounter between two differences, one of which is relegated to the role of translated object of study.

We can now go back to the prose poem and wonder whether Baudelaire's narrator does not display ignorance and naïveté when he offers us his supposedly obvious reading of otherness. If Si Bachir's silence is any indication, it may very well be that the beggar's "mute eloquence" is a lot more ambivalent and complex than it seems. And even if we had not read Féraud's text, the suspicion that the narrator is wrong could dawn on readers who notice contradictory hints in the overall economy of the poem. At times, internal contradictions seem to disavow the main character. When he looks into his friend's face to find the solution to what he perceives as an enigmatic response (his companion does not seem aware that counterfeit money does not count as charity), he is satisfied that he has found an answer simply by interpreting the other's eyes. "Je le regardai dans le blanc des yeux et je fus épouvanté de voir que ses yeux brillaient d'une incontestable candeur" (137) (I looked him squarely in the eyes and I was appalled to see that his eyes shone with unquestionable candor). Arguably, the narrator's formulation is a rather unfortunate and self-accusatory choice of words. By using the set phrase "regarder quelqu'un dans le blanc des yeux" (look straight into someone's eyes) he opens himself up to sarcastic comments about the tautological presence of "whiteness" in his reading. I suppose that it is fair to be at least slightly amused by the fact that the narrator does not have to be too perceptive to find "candidness"—that is, etymological whiteness—if what he is looking at is the white part of his friend's eyes.

But the narrator's formulation also leads to more serious criticism of his perception of otherness. This narrator, who is a compulsive observer, who is constantly accusing others of being unable to look, is himself capable of only one type of gaze; he is a voyeur. And, as J. A. Hiddleston nicely puts it, "It is a voyeurism which might be thought of as the moral equivalent of that most poetic of all faculties, «voyance»" (1987, 33).

Si Bachir, on the other hand, never pretends that he can read anything in other people's eyes. Besides, he never claims that he can see very well, quite the opposite in fact: his eyes are diseased. His first trip to France, at the age of seventy-three, is not motivated by a desire to immigrate or to flee his country for political or economic reasons. Unlike most stereotypical figures of migrant workers, "Si Bachir était venu faire soigner ses yeux" (21) (Si Bachir had come for treatment on his eyes). And not only does he have bad eyes, but he does not use them much. Unlike the narrator of the prose poem who spends all his time interpreting others' gaze, he did not even see the old woman getting close to him. To explain his surprise, the text takes the trouble to inform us that when Si Bachir "philosophait tout seul" (philosophized on his own), he kept "his eyes closed" (22).[12] And when the old woman, who is about to make such a lasting impression, walks toward him, he does not see her: "sentant que quelqu'un venait de s'arrêter à sa hauteur, Si Bachir ouvrit les yeux" (22) (sensing that someone had just stopped beside him, Si Bachir opened his eyes). And even then, his eyes are not an instrument of reading, his visual perception is not described as a hermeneutic activity, as an active attempt to decipher. In the prose poem, the dandy's eyes "read" everybody else's eyes, whereas Si Bachir's eyes fall on what is in front of him, as though by chance. And what he looks at, when the old woman stops in front of him, are not her eyes but "une paire de pantoufles" (a pair of slippers), the emblematic reminder that this human is marginalized by social codes, and that the distinction between inside and outside, private and public no longer operates strictly. Then and only then, his gaze "remontant lentement, découvrit une vieille dame qui s'exclamait d'un air de profonde pitié" (22) (slowly rising, it alighted on an old lady exclaiming with an expression of profound pity). In an ironic reversal spanning a whole century, we now perceive the encounter from the point of view of the poor, of the beggar whose position is interpreted by supposedly more sophisticated readers of eyes.

To the tautological reading of the voyeuristic narrator who cannot tell the difference between candidness and whiteness, Si Bachir opposes another way of seeing and another formulation. Instead of looking at people "dans le blanc des yeux," Si Bachir suggests that we should learn the great art of not being "*regardant*": to be *regardant* in French has everything to do with watching and looking, but it is mostly applied to individuals who are careful with their money, who carefully watch any expenditure, who therefore are bound to set limits to gifts. Here, Si Bachir chooses not to be *regardant* both in the literal and in the figurative sense of the word. He refuses to see, refuses to be placed in the position of some sort of symbolic antitrabendo border police, and he accepts the unreasonableness of limitless gifts. He also keeps his eyes shut to the fact that his gift is not pure and that he simply cannot claim for himself the position of the generous and powerful donor. He is aware that the type of generosity to which he finally resigns himself is simply good and that its consequences could be undesirable or at the very least uncontrollable.

Conclusion

In Baudelaire's poem, the narrator explains that an "event" has occurred in the life of the poor beggar. Similarly, the meeting with the old white woman represents an "event" for Si Bachir. The reading of the two texts in parallel enables the reader to write a different and perhaps less stereotypical narrative of what constitutes that event. What happens in "Oh, le pauvre malheureux!" is a form of undecidable transaction/gift that is reminiscent of Marcel Mauss's potlatch, but with a difference. What we have here is a reverse potlatch. The principle of the potlatch has been described by Mauss, but I am more influenced by later narrativization and social analyses of the phenomenon, especially the work done by Franz Boas and Michel de Certeau. When De Certeau, for example, defines the potlatch as a series of "générosités à charge de revanche" (1980, 71) (generosities for which one expects a return [1984, 26]), he highlights a system of transaction that our current world order, obsessed with the myth of economic growth and capital gain, may consider illogical and paradoxical: the idea is that one gives back more than one has received. In the process, a dynamic process of one-upmanship is started which, in a sense, provokes a constant disequilibrium, a constant debt, a constant crisis of what is owed and circulated. As Franz Boas puts it in his *Fifth Report on the North-Western Tribes of Canada*:

> Le système économique des Indiens de la colonie Britannique est largement basé sur le crédit tout autant que celui des peuples civilisés. Dans toutes ses entreprises, l'Indien se fie à l'aide de ses amis. Il promet de les payer pour cette aide à une date ultérieure. Si cette aide fournie consiste en choses de valeur . . . il promet de rendre la valeur du prêt avec intérêt. . . . Contracter des dettes d'un côté, payer des dettes de l'autre côté, c'est le potlatch. Ce système économique s'est développé à un tel point que le capital possédé par tous les individus associés de la tribu excède de beaucoup la quantité de valeurs disponibles qui existe; autrement dit, les conditions sont tout à fait analogues à celles qui prévalent dans notre société à nous: si nous désirions nous faire payer toutes nos créances, nous trouverions qu'il n'y a à aucun degré assez d'argent, en fait, pour les payer. Le résultat d'une tentative de tous les créanciers de se faire rembourser leurs prêts, c'est une panique désatreuse dont la communauté met longtemps à se guérir.[13]

> [The economic system of the Indians from the British colony is as largely based on credit as that of civilized peoples. For each project, the Indian relies on his friends. He promises to pay them back later. If the help consists of valuables . . . he promises to give the valuable back with interest. . . . Incur a debt on one side, pay the debt on the other, that is the potlatch. That economy system develops to the extent that the capital owned by all the individuals who are related to the tribe is far greater than the quantity of available resources; in other words, the system is quite similar to what happens in our own society: should we wish all our creditors to reimburse us, we would discover that there is not enough available money to pay us back.]

In Féraud's story, what is officially given diminishes, vanishing like some symbolic Cheshire cat, shrinking like Balzac's magic skin (Balzac 1915). From Baudelaire's forged coin, already a fake gift, a spurious example of generosity, we move on to a twenty-centime coin, which could only be considered a gift if the sum was indeed incommensurable for the old woman. By appearing to give more than conventions would lead us to expect, Baudelaire's dandy created an "event" both for the old beggar and for his friend who then started to speculate. The intellectual and fictive or poetic speculation went much further than his actual gesture, as if his fake generosity had indeed yielded an unexpectedly high return. In Féraud's story, on the other hand, what happens is a sort of nonevent. The reverse potlatch is started by the fact that what is given is much less than what was expected and actually occurs when the surprise caused by the disappointing sum creates a second nonevent: the recipient of the nongift refuses to publicize the double mistake (not only is he not a beggar, but even if he were it is clear that twenty cents would have been an insulting gift). And then he gives back even less than the nothing he was given: he gives back a moment of fake gratitude, a simulacrum, a hypocritical thank-you that, in a sense, is also a forged coin. He never gives the old woman the result of his analysis, keeping it to and for himself. His own fictional constructions, his hypotheses, are his own; they are not shared. The old woman is excluded from the deliberation that goes on in Si Bachir's mind, and, perhaps more important, she is excluded from the future scenarios that he has imagined as the consequences of his decision. For example, the old woman can draw no satisfaction from the fact that her twenty centimes have a future. She does not know that she is now more likely to give a beggar a little sum of money that she may otherwise have decided not to give. Or, to put it differently, the twenty centimes are the investment that Si Bachir has made in another unknown person by insuring that the old woman will not be hostile to a beggar. The sad logic of the gift of the stereotype is a resignation to the idea that the less one gives, the more one gives. And Marie Féraud's text as a whole is also resigned to the systematic asymmetry between who gives and who receives. The philosopher asks of himself much more than what he demands of this other subject, and yet it is the other subject who keeps the benefit of the doubt, who remains the giver in the story.[14]

In the poem, the narrator thought he had learned a crucial lesson. "On n'est jamais excusable d'être méchant mais il y a quelque mérite à savoir qu'on l'est; et le plus irréparable des vices est de faire le mal par bêtise" (49) (To be mean is never excusable, but there is some merit in knowing that one is; the most irreparable of vices is to do evil out of stupidity). At the end of the encounter, the narrator thus refuses to forgive his friend because he has failed to demonstrate that he knows how to give. There is no possible redeeming aspect to what he did. After reading the two narratives, however, it is possible to see "Oh, le pauvre malheureux!" as this redemption that Baudelaire's narrator thinks impossible. After all, the refusal to forgive could easily turn against the narrator himself. By deciding that he will not forgive the narrator for being malicious out of ignorance or stupidity, he implicitly condemns himself for all the occasions when he harmed someone without being aware of it. A reading of "Oh, le pauvre malheureux!" makes his peremptory judgment quite ironic by suggesting, precisely, that he may well be in the very position that he considers unforgivable and against which he stridently inveighs. Although the dandy sees himself as greatly sophisticated, although he prides himself on having redefined conventional definitions of bourgeois good and evil, his morality turns out to be a rather simplistic set of rules that condemn his own behavior and logic. For if the narrator is indeed in the process of making a mistake, if the poor man's eyes, which he believes to be so transparently interpretable, are in fact more ambiguous than he thinks, and if, like the old woman, he has just made a fool of himself as an interpreter, he could not forgive himself.

Si Bachir does not offer a whole new set of ethical rules; he does not present himself as a moralist who has discovered a new truth about stereotypes.

The solution he adopts cannot be applied to anyone else without theorizing the link thus created. He has not invented a new axiom or theorem. When he forgives the old woman for her insulting gift, when he even refrains from pointing out her mistake, the rich merchant implicitly asks for similar forgiveness should he find himself in the same situation (a hypothesis that his humility does not rule out). Whereas Baudelaire's narrator would like to recover a form of elitist innocence based on an unconventional and self-conscious knowledge of how to treat otherness, the humiliated merchant renounces innocence, both as a giver and as a receiver. For him, harming someone without knowing it will be excused under certain circumstances because gifts between differently knowledgeable subjects are incommensurable. Like debts, gifts are always infinite. Both the old woman's gift and the gift constituted by Si Bachir's reaction can never be judged according to a simple set of cultural rules because the consequences of each act have ramifications in a future chain reaction that no self-contained subject can ever hope to completely control.

In "La fausse monnaie" the dandy narrator wonders what happens when a cynic knowingly gives a counterfeit coin to a beggar. In "Oh, le pauvre malheureux!" the rich merchant takes the twenty-centime coin from an old lady and her insulting assumption that all Arabs are beggars. He accepts that he fits her stereotypical definition of the poor old Arab man. Both texts explore the delicate relationship between charity and stereotypes, but while Baudelaire's text presents us with the point of view of the giver, Féraud concentrates on the point of view of the receiver offended by the useless gift. Because the position of the actors are comparable, if dissimilar, a historical perspective crisscrosses our own position vis-à-vis the text and colors our own interpretations. Not only does second text thus provide us with an ironic vantage point from which to read the untold story in Baudelaire's prose poem, but the operation of rereading that occurs when the two texts are superimposed also yields a moral commentary.

A parallel reading of the two stories makes Baudelaire's narrator's judgment very ironic by suggesting that he may be in precisely the situation he denounces so virulently. The dandy's supposedly sophisticated set of ethics turns out to be a little simplistic and condemns itself. The second story, on the other hand, suggests that the alliance between giving and forging constitutes an adequate precaution against the danger of stereotyping. By forgiving the old woman's error, the rich merchant implicitly asks to be forgiven similar errors of interpretation: this guilty generosity certainly does not exonerate the producer of stereotypes, but it does provide an alternative to the dandy's rather scary self-righteousness.

Chapter 5

Disarming Stereotypes

Coline Serreau's *La crise*

For more than two decades, Coline Serreau has been humorously engaging gender and racial stereotypes. At first, toward the end of the vibrantly feminist 1970s, Serreau's public was typically limited to the militant audiences of Festivals de Films de Femmes (women's films festivals). In 1976, Serreau released *Mais qu'est-ce qu'elles veulent*? (What on earth do they want?) a series of interviews with and portraits of women that functions like a feminist documentary. As early as 1978, she started reflecting on the fictional potential of male and female role reversals in *Pourquoi pas* (Why not?). After a short incursion into the world of comedians and actors (*Qu'est-ce qu'on attend pour être heureux* [Why not be happy now?] in 1981), Serreau continued to explore stereotypical gender roles.[1] Her career took a decisive turn in 1985 when the success of *Trois hommes et un couffin* and of the American remake *Three Men and a Baby* turned her into a widely known and internationally appreciated director. The film not only received critical acclaim, but it is also remembered as the first film by a woman director to have attracted such enormous audiences. One narrative or legend emphasizes the fact that in France in 1985 *Trois hommes et un couffin* competed successfully against *Rambo* (just like *Germinal* was later said to have dethroned its supposedly natural American rival, Steven Spielberg's *Jurassic Park*). As is often the case, the episode of cultural and economic rivalry between French and American cinema was less than subtly settled by the production of a Hollywood remake that highlighted what was perhaps specifically French about Serreau's reappraisal of gender roles. In the meantime, she went on to direct two other films, focusing more and more explicitly not only on gender roles but also on the issues of racial and cultural stereotypes in contemporary France.[2] In 1989, the year *L'oeil au beur~~re~~ noir* also came out, Serreau released *Romuald et Juliette* (Romuald and Juliet), the optimistic and tongue-in-cheek story of an encounter between a white boss and his black, female employee. In 1992, in *La crise* (Crisis), Serreau continued her exploration of the fraught territory of multicultural and multiracial relationships. This time, she focused especially on the construction of the image of the Arab as a national phantasm. Her latest film, *La belle verte* (Green Planet, 1996), contains tender and compassionate yet blunt criticism of capitalism and consumerism, sexism and homophobia, racism and xenophobia in a refreshing science-fiction version of *Candide*. Aliens who visit France are astounded by the decidedly uncivilized state of Western societies, and their naive questions implicitly propose other models or relationships and principles of government. Once again, a comparable American film came out practically at the same moment and, this time, there was no miracle. *Independence Day* bulldozed its way up the charts, pushing its nationalist values and military logic, advocating individualism and turning the president of the United States into a universal gatekeeper. It could be argued that the ecological and political message of *La belle verte* is as unsophisticated as that of *Independence Day* when the aliens try to explain how they live on their planet—the positive utopia is perhaps not as convincing as their critique. But *Independence Day* is certainly not more complex, and it is a sign of the times that audiences preferred one type of naïveté over another. In October 1996, after two weeks in Paris, *La belle verte* had been seen by only a little over one hundred thousand people, which does not even come close to the twelve million viewers that *Trois Hommes et un couffin* had attracted.

Still, it is clear by now that Serreau's social comedies are eminently relevant to the preoccupations of a French public that she does not hesitate to mock and criticize gently. In *Romuald et Juliette* as well as in *La crise*, she taps the tradition of "café théâtre" that characterizes many of the recent French comic films, but it is quite clear that she is concerned with the same vexing social dilemmas that also inspired *banlieues-films*. Although Serreau's tone is incommensurable with that of *La haine*, for example, *La crise* also asks difficult and pointed questions about the potentially explosive use of stereotypes in a context where the very possibility of encounters between individuals is overdetermined by their racial and class identities.

Yet, as Ginette Vincendeau noticed when she reviewed the British release of *La crise*, Serreau's films are not taken very seriously. In 1982, when Jean Tulard published his *Dictionnaire du cinéma*, he included Serreau in the index of directors, but he was certainly not willing to sing her praises. At the time, he wrote that her work is "Un cinéma de femme sur les femmes, un peu schématique, mais lucide et souvent sans illusion" (A woman's cinema about women, a bit formulaic, but lucid and often disillusioned) (631). Because the dictionary was written when Serreau had directed only two films—*Mais qu'est-ce qu'elles veulent?* and *Pourquoi pas*—it is possible to assume that Tulard had simply failed to anticipate that Serreau was about to become the acclaimed director of *Trois hommes et un couffin*. After all, one could argue, he is not expected to be a prophet. Yet I suggest that the use of the word "*schématique*" (formulaic) was precisely a moment of prophecy, or better yet, a remarkable moment of intuition that I propose as a critical key to Serreau's latest comedies. In Tulard's entry, the word "*schématique*" obviously carried the derogatory connotation of simplicity understood as lack of nuance, lack of sophistication. The implicit value judgment obfuscated another level of the reference to schemes: that of patterns of thought and systems of ideological units that Serreau's films repeat, represent, in order to explore their cultural repercussions and exploit their comic potential. As early as 1982, Tulard had apparently suspected that Serreau's films would regularly engage the stereotypical, all the ready-made constructions of culture. But rather than identifying the *representation* of what is fixed, congealed, and stereotypically simplified as one of the recurrent elements in Serreau's cinema, critics continue to confuse her primary object of study with her work as a whole. Ginette Vincendeau regrets that critics tend to treat her films in a perfunctory way, and it is quite possible that Serreau's scrutiny of perfunctory forms of thinking has everything to do with the treatment her work receives. When reviewing *La crise,* for example, Martin Wagner repeats the gesture and regrets the "formulaic" quality of the film as a weakness (1994, 38). I would argue instead that Serreau's cinema has taken a chance and is now threatened by contamination between the "formulaic" and the representation of the formulaic, the "schematic" and the representation of schemes. Serreau thus becomes the victim of the insidious effect of stereotypes that we have already seen at work in previous chapters. Like Chaplin squirting too much oil into the assembly line, the excess of stereotypes (even if they are displaced, framed, stolen, or defamiliarized) affects the whole system of representation. Consequently, the racist and antiracist stereotypes scrutinized by Serreau seep into the texture of her films until an ambiguous space of representation obtains where the stereotypification of characters is the unavoidable consequence of the convincing embodiment of stereotypes.

Analyzing what is deliberately simplistic and minimalist about *La crise*, I thus argue that "le schématique" is not something that should be forgiven as a flaw but a personal cinematographic tactic that allows the director to make a powerful intervention as a cultural critic of France in the 1990s. In *Le thé au harem d'Archimède,* in Smaïn's skits, in *L'oeil au beur~~re~~ noir*, racial stereotypes are seen from the point of view of the victim of racist insinuations (the black, the Beur, the Arab). In *La crise*, a merciless camera focuses on how self-righteous antiracists as well as self-proclaimed racists construct different and incompatibly stereotypical images of Arabs.

A perfunctory or voluntarily schematic analysis of the use of ethnic stereotypes in *La crise* could result in the following formulation: *La crise* is the story of what happens when typically or stereotypically white French individuals meet typical or stereotypical ethnic Others. But the film suggests that this is only half of the story and that amalgamating otherness and ethnic difference is a lazy and facile reflex. Here, the very definition of ethnic otherness is put to the test when a white man (Victor) meets another white man (Michou). In other words, this is an analysis of the conflictual and problematic constructions of ethnic images and fantasies within one, diverse French culture rather than between French and non French cultures. Serreau refuses to treat the category of Frenchness as an unproblematic reference, as the neutral point of departure and the opposite of the immigrant.[3] While the representation of Frenchness is not as often scrutinized as that of the alien, the foreigner, the Arab,[4] Serreau's originality lies in taking the time to explore the ways definitions of "otherness" in France are directly related to the fact that the category of the "Français de souche" (French person of French origin) is also split by what the media have come to call the "fracture sociale" (social fracture). In *La crise*, an imaginary and abstract white community is irreparably fractured by class difference. In other words, not only do many white voices put forward different definitions of racism, antiracism, social harmony, and integration, but the film shows that the different definitions are also the site of a rivalry, or at least of a struggle, that normally tends to be swept under the carpet in the name of more spectacular confrontations between visibly different skin colors. Recognizable categories such as race and class are not treated as discrete objects of study in this film. Rather, Serreau suggests quite forcefully, it is practically impossible to talk about race from a position that is not already overdetermined by one's own class origin. She somewhat sadly implies that the reason why it is so difficult to talk about race and class without separating the issues is that it is even less plausible for interclass discussions to occur than for interracial relationships to develop. In *La crise*, the intersection between class and race is brought into relief by the arguably improbable encounter between Michou and Victor. Michou is a homeless sponger who normally lives in a poor suburb (Saint-Denis) but vacated his room in his brother's apartment when his sister-in-law came back home from the hospital, terminally ill with cancer. Victor, on the other hand, is a high-flying executive whose momentary "crisis" is an obviously reversible phenomenon.

Michou and Victor's budding relationship represents the intersection between two normally segregated universes and their partnership allows the director to present us with two quite different ways of deploying racial stereotypes. *La crise* refuses to fall into the trap of ascribing individual blame and of determining who is a racist and who is not, as if the work was done after one unique trophy of infamy has been awarded. Instead, the film is interested in confronting different types of racist stereotypes that may or may not coincide with racist social practices. Nowhere in the film is it suggested that an exclusively economic analysis could replace a gendered and political perspective as an overarching explanation. We are not expected, for example, to believe that it is generally plausible that working-class white French people and working-class foreigners or minorities will be natural allies and will miraculously get along just fine. That moribund left-wing stereotypical assumption has obviously not survived the fall of the Berlin Wall.[5] Viewers of *La crise* are expected to know that in 1992 a different horizon of verisimilitude can be found in a debate about minorities and social classes. Today the assumption, the preconceived suspicion, is not that there is solidarity (left-wing version) nor collusion (right-wing version) between all "banlieusards," as the inhabitants of the suburbs are called.[6] Instead, one plausible stereotype is that working-class people are more likely to be prejudiced against ethnic minorities because they share the same neighborhood, the same housing estates, and the same problems, whereas the rich live miles away in sheltered environments. In other words, the film looks at what happens when we refuse to separate and compartmentalize individuals and problems. If we agree that one of the lessons of postcolonialism is that it has forced the nations of the north to confront at home the same structures that were supposedly indigenous to the colonized countries, then *La crise* is an interesting depiction of the consequences of that "postcontact" moment.[7] Here, the emphasis is not on encounter with otherness but on living together permanently after the original colonial clash, not on brief and self-contained moments of confrontation but on long-term cohabitation, not on difference and foreignness but on how to manage conflicts in the midst of familiarity and sometimes even intimacy.

At one crucial turning point in the film, Isabelle, the upper-middle-class hero's sister, is invited to dinner by a socialist politician who wants her to design a publicity campaign for him. Isabelle and Victor go together. Michou tags along, as usual, but apparently, at one juncture that the camera does not choose to relate, it is decided that Michou will stay outside while the two other characters have dinner with their hosts. Only much later, when informed that Michou has been standing outside the gate for the best part of the evening, does the politician invite him in, curious to find out what this average Frenchman thinks about "*le racisme, ce fléau*" (the plague of racism). Michou then calmly delivers the following speech.

—Michou: "Ahhhhhhh ben, moi je pense que c'est beaucoup plus facile d'être contre le racisme quand on habite à Neuilly que quand on habite à Saint-Denis hein? Voyez moi par exemple je suis de Saint-Denis et je suis raciste et vous par exemple, ben vous habitez cette maison, et vous êtes pas raciste voyez?"

—Le député: "Franchement Michou, vous vous considérez comme raciste?"

—Michou: "Ah oui, franchement oui. Moi les étrangers je vis avec alors je peux pas les saquer voyez. Ils foutent rien, ils sont sales, ils nous piquent nos bagnoles, on leur file des appartements en priorité sur les Français, ils gagnent plus de fric que nous avec toutes les allocations qu'ils ont, dans les écoles nos mômes ils apprennent plus rien parce qu'il y a soixante-dix pour cent d'étrangers qui parlent pas un mot de français, ils nous font chier avec leur foulard et encore il faudrait qu'on paye pour leur construire des mosquées alors vous avez qu'à voir.

[—Michou: "Well, I think it is a lot easier to be against racism when you live in Neuilly (a very affluent neighborhood) than when you live in Saint-Denis (prototype of poor suburb), right? You see, for example, I am from Saint-Denis and I am a racist and you, for example, you live in this house and you're not a racist, see?"
—The Representative: "Seriously now, Michou, do you consider yourself racist?"
—Michou: "Seriously? Yes I do. I live with foreigners so I can't stand them, you see. They are lazy, dirty, they steal our cars, they get apartments before the French do, they make more money than we do with all the benefits they get, at school our kids don't learn anything anymore because there are 70 percent of foreigners who can't speak a word of French, we've got to put up with their fucking Islamic scarves, and on top of that, they want us to shell out to build mosques, you get the picture."]

As is always the case with the quoting of stereotypes, I isolate this passage at a very high price. What gets repeated here is a string of stereotypes that are so violent and painful that it is difficult to protect oneself from their sharp points. Hearing this, even on a screen, even (or perhaps especially) in Michou's mouth may hurt and alienate the audience. And quoting Michou out of the visual context is even more dangerous because I have only my own written text to contain this barrage of familiar horrors, with none of the more sophisticated tactics used in the film. And yet, *La crise* certainly does not set out to prove that racism might be more acceptable when it emanates from unprivileged people and never allows the reader to draw the deterministic conclusion that nothing can be done against racism unless one eliminates financial inequalities, as if racism was a disease caused by poverty.

Because the politician insists on imagining Michou as the representative of some monolithic France, he does not listen to the crucial distinctions that Michou introduces. When Michou compares Neuilly and Saint-Denis, he says nothing about being a racist but "être *contre* le racisme" (to be against racism): his emphasis is not on identity but on opinions. Only later, when the representative puts the word in his mouth, does he claim the unsavory title of "racist" individual. Naturally, the politician hastens to minimize the meaningful difference between "être contre/pour" (to be for/against) and "être/ne pas être raciste" (to be or not to be a racist) because his own form of racism is predicated on the reduction of antiracism to the proclamation of his own nonracism.

The film, however, also contains a warning: it refuses to take for granted the naive and condescending assumption that lines of solidarity are more easily drawn among classes and across ethnic groups than among ethnic groups and suggests that nothing will ever change unless the focus of our analysis of differences shifts from an analysis of foreignness to an analysis of sameness. What splits the category of Frenchness is here taken quite seriously as a problematic site of cultural struggle that has direct repercussions on racist practices.

On the one hand, while Michou and Victor perceive their positions as diametrically opposed (Michou is a racist, Victor is an antiracist), they are, in effect, perfectly symmetrical: one is a stereotypical racist, the other is a stereotypical antiracist. This symmetry is why it is necessary to quote Michou at length because his tirade is supposed to be an echo, a perfectly recognizable list of similar statements about foreigners, immigrants, and Arabs. Michou and Victor each want to impose their own version of sentences that are syntactically identical: the generative matrix is the familiar "All the [insert ethnic group (Arabes, étrangers, etc.)] are [insert adjective]." Of course, even though Michou and Victor share the syntax of stereotypes, they seem to disagree, but the film implies that here is a difference that does not make a difference.

The only radical difference between Michou and Victor that *does* make a difference is the ways in which they interact with Arabs or foreigners on a daily basis. Michou was brought up by his Arab sister-in-law, Djamila, whom he loves and protects; he would rather be homeless than see her go back to the hospital. He went to school with Farid and Mohammed—are they those foreign children who supposedly do not speak a word of French, who stopped Michou from learning anything at school?—and who are the very first people he invites when he has something to celebrate. Victor, on the other hand, does not know any Arab personally until he meets Djamila and Michou's friends. That chiasmatic structure (itself a stereotype) enables Serreau to scrutinize the extremely fine line that separates racist stereotypes from racist social practices, the violence of representations from the violence done by individuals to individuals. What is at stake when Michou and Victor confront their differences is the discrepancy between their own social practices and the values they both claim to defend. *La crise* suggests that it is possible for viewers to distinguish between, and denounce, the discrepancy between antiracist stereotypes and the ideal of nonracist practices. That warning would not be a very new take if it meant only exposing the hypocrisy of racist social practices hidden behind benevolent talk, but it is a much more controversial and original point to make if the logic is reversed to the extent that the film suggests that nonracist social practices accompanied by racist stereotypes may be, if not acceptable, at least a lesser and necessary evil.

The film also invites us to listen more carefully to what people say exactly. Slight differences in formulations are sometimes indicators of crucial political differences. Michou's series of impersonal action statements ("ils foutent rien, ils sont sales, ils nous piquent nos bagnoles" [they are lazy, dirty, they steal our cars]) should be a dead giveaway that he is not the individual author of the statements. The repetition of congealed xenophobic stereotypes is a ritual and has nothing to do with his own life. Should we miss this first grammatical hint, the allusion to "*nos voitures*" [our cars] and a little further on "*nos mômes*" (our kids) should comically reinforce that this is a phantasmagoric invention of the foreigner (as viewers, we know very well that Michou does not own a car and does not have children). The construction "*ils* nous piquent *nos* bagnoles" (*they* steal *our* cars) functions so well as a stereotype that no one bothers to ask if the story is relevant to Michou's life or if the use of "we" belongs to a completely different realm of discourse.

Racist stereotypes, racist social practices, antiracist stereotypes, and nonracist practices thus become the four corners of a dangerously unstable semiotic square that needs serious scrutiny as one inseparable set of symptoms. It is a delicate and highly risky ground to tread, and *La crise* draws much more daring conclusions than the light humorous tone and the happy ending might lead the viewer to suspect.

The film is able to experiment with the meeting between upper-middle-class and working-class stereotyping practices thanks to a very narrow window of fictional opportunity.[8] It takes a radical upheaval in Victor's life for the chance encounter between the two characters to occur. In a comically rapid succession of events, the film introduces us to a frazzled Victor waking up to an empty bed: his wife has left him. He then packs his children off to a skiing resort, where they will stay with their grandmother until the end of the film, and rushes off to the office to find out that he has inexplicably been laid off. He spends the whole film desperately trying to get someone, anyone, to listen to his pathetic tale of what he sees as a double betrayal. Anyone would do except, of course, Michou, who *has* been listening intently all along, even if he claims to be following Victor only to get him to buy him a drink or a meal here and now. Unfortunately, the film thus implies, it takes the sudden disappearance of his job, his partner, and his family for Victor to finally have enough space in his life to acknowledge the presence of people like Michou, the ultimate Other and alter ego.

For in spite of Victor's paternalistic assumptions, the film insists primarily on the similarity, not the differences, between the two characters. Although Victor never becomes aware of it, Michou is exactly like him in that he is without a job (although chronically, it seems), without a partner, and without a family. And it will remain Victor's blind spot that he needs Michou more than Michou needs him. While Victor's loneliness is due to his exasperated wife's departure, Michou's solitude is an act of love. When he left the tiny apartment he shared with his brother in a housing project, he lied to Djamila, pretending that he had found a room elsewhere. But since Victor never listens to his companion and because Michou refuses the role of the pitiful homeless, we only find out about Michou's tragedy little by little, through snippets of apparently irrelevant conversations. Throughout the film, the two characters appear together on the screen, often in close-ups, like a man and his shadow, or like a man seeing himself in a mirror, Victor failing to realize that he is constantly provided with a version of himself. Only at the end of the film does he finally come to terms with the fact that his own crisis simply cannot be distinguished from what the French called "la crise" in general—a persistent feeling of economic social and political malaise that includes a complete failure to deal with new multicultural realities and exclusion. Victor's professional and emotional problems cannot be solved independently from Michou's and will not find any solution until he listens to the question that the film keeps asking, relentlessly, patiently: How is it possible to live with other people's otherness when classic recipes supposed to bring about Republican equality and harmony have long ceased to work, even if the slogans survive as stereotypes? How does one represent other people's different history, different ethnic origins, different social classes, and different desires without stereotyping them?

In the film, upper-middle-class characters tend to refuse confrontation with otherness and to hide conflicts under hypocritical stereotypes about tolerance and France's ideal of "*terre d'accueil*" (land of asylum). The film keeps asking what it means to confront irreconcilable parameters of difference without using stereotypes to perpetuate the status quo and mask conflicts. Is some amount of stereotyping a form of homeopathy? One of the subplots in *La crise* is a debate about the respective merits of homeopathy and allopathy. Homeopathy is a form of medicine that is metaphorically related to the principle of the *pharmakon:* both a poison and a cure, the pharmakon sabotages the illusion that perfect hygiene and perfect health would result from the administration of medicine. In *La crise*, a homeopathic dose of racism seems to be the possible cure to the proliferation of unrecognized forms of racism. It is as if we could not choose to eradicate racism but had to accept living with a carefully chosen set of expressions of certain forms of racism. The plot also makes the point that homeopathy and allopathy are economic issues, with allopathy being on the side of capitalist logic. When one of the heroines, a doctor's wife, barges into her husband's waiting room and proceeds to expel the patients who are seeking homeopathic treatment, she angrily explains that their family is going bankrupt and can no longer afford expensive cars and houses and second houses and trips abroad, all because of homeopathy.When her husband was practicing allopathy, she remembers, he used to see sixty patients a day, send them home with a big, fat prescription, and things were fine. Now, he spends hours with each of his patients, chatting instead of working. How does he expect her to balance the books? Allopathy is the medicine of commercial profit, whereas homeopathy, which cannot accommodate the demands of upper-middle-class consumerism, is also seen as the idealistic response to a profit-oriented medicine that has ceased to honor its own principles.

At the same time, the film is quite clear what type of stereotyping is intolerable and unacceptable. For example, cozy, comfortable stereotypes appear more scandalously racist than Michou's predictable litany about what foreigners do to us. When Victor and his sister Isabelle have dinner with the socialist deputy and his wife, Serreau shows that the host and hostess are two remarkable experts in "*langue de bois*" (politicalese) and two perfect representatives of the hypocrisy of the so-called *gauche caviar* (literally, caviar-eating socialists). The whole scene revolves around the fact that all four characters share the same definition of what is racist and nonracist. The characters also share exactly the same definition of what constitutes acceptable social practices. This scene is about a perfect consensus, and the film suggests that such a level of harmony should already be a warning sign, that it is treacherous, deceptive, and full of hidden violence. The presence of stereotypes creates a cozy feeling of comfortable agreement among the members of a group. This perfect harmony and agreement are the symptom of stereotypical dysfunctionality, of a grotesquely hypocritical benevolence that Serreau intends to ridicule and indict. To this effect, she builds the scene as the juxtaposition of two complementary and simultaneous dialogues. While the two men discuss politics in the living room, the two women carry on an exactly symmetrical conversation in the kitchen.

In the first scene, Victor listens to the socialist politician who expresses stereotyped views about racism in general (in typical left-wing langue de bois), then expresses his own stereotyped views about a supposedly tolerant and nonracist French people.

—Le député: "Il y a un problème de racisme, comment enrayer ce fléau?"
—Victor: "Non moi j'ai confiance en le peuple français, au fond il est tolérant, généreux . . . "
—Le député: "Oui enfin 15 percent votent pour l'extrême droite, beaucoup plus même par endroit, c'est tout de même, c'est tout de même . . ."
—Victor: "Je sais c'est terrible . . ."
—Le député: "Non c'est même une honte, c'est une véritable honte."

[—The Representative: "There is a "problem of racism! How do we stop this plague?
—Victor: "I wouldn't worry, I trust the French people. It is basically a tolerant and generous people . . ."
—The Representative: "Well, I am not sure about that, 15 percent vote for the extreme right, more in places, that's quite . . ."
—Victor: "I know, it's horrible . . ."
—The Representative: "It's more than that. It is a shame, truly, it is a disgrace."]

The camera interrupts the politician on this word "*honte* (shame) and cuts to a shot of Isabelle and the hostess in the kitchen. Thanks to the irony of editing techniques, the comment now functions as the introduction to the next scene, where Isa allows and even implicitly encourages the politician's wife to indulge in a long string of violently racist generalizations about the women she hires for short periods of time and treats like domestic appliances. We thus learn all about the respective merits and shortcomings of "les Portugaises, les Maghrébines, les Asiatiques, les noires etc." (Portuguese, Arab, Asian, black women). The monologue of the politician's wife is worth quoting as an example of perfectly stereotypical syntax. Her tirade also announces Michou's long speech, preceding it only by a few seconds. I have deliberately reversed the film's chronological order to highlight Serreau's techniques. It is crucial for the structure of the film that Michou's tirade occurs right after a perfectly symmetrical speech by the politician's wife: when I isolate Michou's series of "ils . . . ils . . . ils . . ." what is lost is the echo with an earlier series of "elles . . . elles . . . elles . . ." that the film foregrounds without any mercy for the self-righteous upper-middle-class characters. Before Michou's arrival, the hostess and her guest had been having exactly the same type of conversation, not about "foreigners" in general but about Portuguese, Asian, and Moroccan women and their supposedly natural characteristics. As viewers, we will soon perceive this speech as the origin of an echo, the series of equally perfectly formed racial stereotypes uttered by a racist Michou eventually sounding blatantly similar to what the rich and refined and supposedly antiracist character has to say. What we have here is the most minimalist formulation of ethnic stereotypes, the formula I have isolated as a possible definition of the genre. What is produced here is a series of "*idéologèmes*": [9]

—Isabelle: "Vous avez toujours votre Marocaine-là?"
—La femme du député: "Non, ça fait longtemps. Non, maintentant j'ai une petite Philippine."
—Isabelle: "Elle est bien?"
—La femme du député: "Oh formidable, oh les Asiatiques, c'est vraiment ce qu'il y a de mieux. Sérieuse, propre, discrète, travailleuse. Non parce que les Portugaises, elles sont très propres, mais voleuses. Les maghrébines elles sont très bien avec les enfants mais alors le ménage, c'est une véritable catastrophe. Quant aux noires, elles sont toujours fatiguées. Oh non vraiment, les Asiatiques, elles sont comme ça!"

[—Isabelle: "You still have that Moroccan girl of yours?"
—The politician's wife: "Oh no, she's been gone a long time. Now, I have a little Philippine."
—Isabelle: "Is she any good?"
—The politician's wife: "She's great. Asians are the best. Serious, clean, discreet, hard working. You know, Portuguese women are neat, but they steal.

> Arabs are great with kids but don't ask them to clean house. As for black women, they are always tired. No, seriously, Asians, thumbs up!"]

Such dialogues might explain critics' tendency to remember the film as formulaic. The woman's opinions are so recognizable as ethnic stereotypes that hardly any interpretive skill is required to identify them. Isabelle's opening sentence is hardly more subtle with its objectionable use of the verb "*avoir*" (to have) and of the possessive pronoun followed by the adjective of nationality ("votre marocaine" [your Moroccan girl]). But her hostess sounds like a parrot repeating bits of congealed stereotypical syntax. An ironic interruption of the politician's moment of self-righteous indignation, the passage allows the film to give a concrete example of its theoretical hypothesis: the difference that matters is not between positive and negative stereotyping. The rest of the film will show why Michou's racist tirade may be preferable to this type of stereotyping, but in the meantime it makes it clear why the politician's wife is guilty of the same type of racist language structures. Besides, "les Asiatiques, elles sont comme ça!" is just as racist a statement as "Les noires sont toujours fatiguées," even if we are more tempted to oppose the second than the first. The absolute symmetry of the two statements here demonstrates the futility of establishing a hierarchical distinction between the two statements; the first one is not compliment, only another formulation of the same stereotype. I am not sure I always remember that rule when there is no time to think.

The film makes this argument several times, but the heroes never seem to learn the lesson. Toward the end of the story, Victor is all alone, Michou having given him up as a bad job. Finally becoming aware of the extent of his self-centeredness, Victor decides to pay Michou a visit. He eventually crosses the invisible border that separates his world from Michou's suburb. Only then does he discover that his racist companion's surrogate mother is of Arab origin. The scene is in many ways a mirror image of the dinner party and a reinterpretation of what Michou meant when he calmly claimed that of course he is a racist.

On arrival, Victor's surprised and shocked disbelief makes him incapable of uttering anything but the most blatantly racist benevolent banalities. Michou having stepped out for a minute (to buy champagne to celebrate his brother's obtaining the "RMI"),[10] Victor is greeted by Michou's brother, who seems to know all about him, although they have never met. When Djamila calls out from the bedroom, asking who has just arrived, Michou's brother explains:

—Le frère de Michou: "C'est ma femme, elle est malade, elle peut pas se lever."
—Victor: "Comment elle s'appelle?"
—Le frère de Michou: "Djamila."
—Victor: "Ah elle est Arabe?"
—Le frère de Michou: "Vous aimez pas les Arabes?

—Victor: "Si si si, bien sûr bien sûr que j'aime les Arabes, je les adore même. Non non c'est pas ça c'est parce que Michou m'avait dit, enfin il avait l'air, non j'aime beaucoup les Arabes moi."
—Le frère de Michou: "Vous voulez boire quoi?"

[—Michou's brother: "It's my wife, she's sick, she can't get up."
—Victor: "What's her name?"
—Michou's brother: "Djamila."
—Victor: "She's an Arab?"
—Michou's brother: "Don't you like Arabs?
—Victor: "Of course I do, of course I do, of course I like Arabs, I *love* Arabs. It's just that . . . Well, . . . It's Michou, he said . . . No, no, I love Arabs, I do."
—Michou's brother: "What'll it be?"]

What is striking about this scene is the way in which the image contradicts what Victor says. Michou's brother has not said anything about his wife's nationality or ethnic background, and she remains invisible at first. But, previously alerted by a little girl who gave him directions, Victor already suspects that the person's name is Djamila. He is the one who insists on bringing ethnicity to the fore by asking something he already knows and by formulating the real question behind what could have been a polite inquiry. This question is not only put to a perfect stranger but asked about a woman about whom Victor has just been told that she can't get up. Under the circumstances, it could be deemed curious that Victor is apparently more obsessed by the woman's ethnic origin than concerned about her health. Michou's brother dispenses with the unpacking I have just gone through. He does not take the trouble to point out to his guest that his wife's ethnic identity is less relevant than her illness, for example. From that point of view, it is quite logical of him to pick up on the irrelevance of the question with a comment that highlights the implicit fusion between Djamila and all Arabs.

What is particularly violent in Victor's automatic and stereotypical reaction is that, as usual, he has not really understood the question. He immediately decides that "Vous n'aimez pas les Arabes?" means exactly the same thing as "Vous n'aimez pas Djamila?" (Don't you like Djamila?) or "Vous n'aimez pas ma femme?" (Don't you like my wife?) because he never for a second imagines that the question could be something else (and something more) than an implicit and stereotypical accusation of racism. When Michou's brother asks him: "Vous n'aimez pas les Arabes?" Victor's gut reaction is an emphatic denial that is meant to protect him from any suspicion of racism when in fact it displays his paternalistic habit of stereotyping all Arabs as the beloved exotic. "Je les adore même" is a ridiculous statement, first because it smacks of overcompensation (why would anyone adore *all* Arabs anyway?) and because the sentence is built on the very model that the film has taken

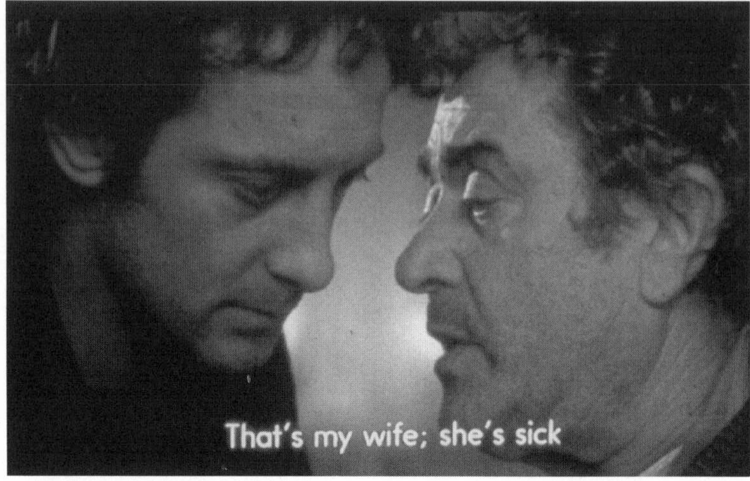

Figure 3. Bernard Cazassus (Michou's brother) and Vincent Lindon (Victor) in Coline Serreau's *La crise.* Reproduced by permission of the actors, Coline Serreau, and Canal+. Photo: BFI Stills, Posters and Designs.

great trouble to discredit as a racist stereotype. What Victor does not know yet is that Michou's brother himself certainly does not like, let alone adore, all Arabs. In fact, he loudly proclaims that he hates "tous les Arabes racistes" (all racist Arabs) for disowning his wife when she married a Frenchman. It is therefore extremely ironic that Victor should desperately try to defend himself against what he mistakes for an accusation simply because his own stereotypes interpret the situation.

The irony of this misunderstanding is reinforced by the way in which Serreau uses close-ups. During the first part of the exchange, the screen is entirely occupied by the two men's faces, Victor on the left, his host on the right. There are very close to each other, Michou's brother leaning over at one point to whisper in Victor's ear to make sure that Djamila will not overhear. At that point, the scene is very intimate. There is a sense of exchanged confidences, of trust between the two characters. Although Victor does not know this man, it is obvious that Michou, who cares a lot more about Victor than Victor cares about him or than Victor realizes, has talked about their meeting, about Victor's problems, about their odd friendship. A lonely Victor is immediately welcome and accepted as part of an extended family. The camera reinforces the physical proximity between the two men and symbolizes the presence of a strong yet invisible link between them by an extreme close-up. Surprisingly perhaps (but this is precisely something that should alert viewers), when the brother asks "Vous n'aimez pas les Arabes?" his position in the scene does not

Figure 4. Vincent Lindon (Victor) in Coline Serreau's *La crise.* Reproduced by permission of Vincent Lindon, Coline Serreau, and Canal+. Photo: BFI Stills, Posters and Designs.

change. His tone is not different (not more aggressive, just curious), and he remains very close to Victor's face, the frame still focusing on the faces of two men talking to each other (fig. 3). But Victor does not notice that nothing has changed, that the question is not an attack, and that he is still part of a magic circle of affection. His first reaction is to move away, hands up in front of him as if to protect himself from an impending blow. As Victor protests, "I do, I do, I love Arabs," he backs up, away from the brother as if he suddenly represented a threat. The camera follows him, not altering its angle, and as a result, it cannot focus on Victor's face without losing sight of his interlocutor (fig. 4). A sudden void appears where the brother used to be. Victor is left alone, disconnected, estranged, repeating like a parrot: "I *love* them." It is up to Michou's brother to interrupt his hysterical speech by asking him what he wants to drink. The camera then reunites the two men on the screen, but the angle is slightly wider, as if we had to see them from further away to get them both into the picture, as if a distance had been introduced, a tear in the fabric of human relationships that cannot be patched up right away (fig. 5).

Naturally, this scene also presents us with the same recurring problem as all the other cultural representations of stereotypes. Like Pieterse's *White on Black* (1992), Serreau's film presents the viewer with a list of stereotypes that critics may deem dangerously infectious. What in this film allows us to distinguish between the presence of actively racist stereotypes and the satirical and supposedly harmless representation of stereotypes? Can Michou's and the

Figure 5. Bernard Cazassus (Michou's brother) and Vincent Lindon (Victor) in Coline Serreau's *La crise*. Reproduced by permission of the actors, Coline Serreau, and Canal+. Photo: BFI Stills, Posters and Designs.

politician wife's tirades function like an effective critique of racial stereotypes or will stereotypes permeate the film itself and finally dominate the stage that is supposed to exclude them? Is this scene a moment of pyrrhic victory, a failed ideological intervention where, as viewers, we are put in the same position as the guest and recruited as accomplices of the politician's wife for more or less excusable reasons of powerless politeness? Or does it tell us something valuable about racial stereotypes, does it encourage a form of recuperative activity that we may be encouraged to use in the presence of equivalent forms of ethnic stereotyping? After seeing the film, do we know more about what can be done or replied when someone says: "Les Asiatiques, elles sont comme ça!"? Unlike Smaïn and *Le thé au harem d'Archimède*, *La crise* does not steal stereotypes. Unlike Marie Féraud's story, it does not give them away as a present, and it does not try to avoid them. What specific activity, then, does this cinematographic text deploy in the face of stereotypes?

Serreau's film seems to know that it is facile and not very productive to denounce the hypocrisy, condescension, and contradictions of upper-middle-class antiracist politics. This 1992 comedy has obviously learned the discouraging lessons of the 1980s. The "Touche pas à mon pote" (Hands off my buddy) ideal has not won out, and even liberal journalists prefer to concentrate on the spectacle of rioting *banlieues*, predicting social apocalypse.[11] *La crise* thus adds its own doubts and questions to the work done by sociologists and historians who wonder how to go beyond the tricky opposition between racism and antiracism that now has the flavor of another political cliché.

Here the repetition of stereotypes suffers from what could be dubbed a Flaubertian symptom: the illusion that by writing *Bouvard et Pécuchet*, the author would completely, radically, and permanently shame his contemporaries and cure them of their stupid beliefs and preconceived ideas.[12] The intertextual echo would be to Flaubert's *Sottisier*. Serreau is writing an imaginary entry in *Le dictionnaire des idées reçues* or in Begag and Chaouite's "Dictionary of fixed ideas about people who move about" (Begag and Chaouite 1990). The entry would be something like, Racisme: "être contre dans les dîners en ville" (Racism: be against it at dinner parties).[13] In this case, the decision to represent stereotypes in order to denounce them is almost useless. No one would ever want to identify with the politician's wife, for example. The stereotype is seen as the language of the stupid Other, it has nothing to do with what "we" (whoever "we" are) do or think.

This scene does teach us something about stereotypes, something that can be used precisely whether the stereotype emanates from the right or the left, from the deputy's supposedly benevolent antiracism or from Michou's openly racist hatred of the foreigners with whom he lives. The scene forces attention on what is apparently the less important and harmful aspect of stereotypes: their formal construction. Serreau proposes not to ignore the ideological violence but resists the temptation to oppose the stereotype with another stereotype. She shows that such dialogues are already stereotypical themselves and that by ignoring the obvious bait, an analysis of the formal qualities of the stereotypical statement can be just as political and certainly more efficient than a knee-jerk reaction.

If we follow that lead, Serreau's criticism proves quite finely tuned to current political realities and a much more meaningful than it seems at first. One useful intervention made by the film is to criticize the theoretical stereotype that stereotypes are essentially a right-wing discourse. The film has learned that as seductive as Barthes's theories about stereotypical discourses were in the 1970s, they are clearly less relevant during the last two decades of the century. It is clearly not possible anymore to entertain the illusion that left-wing intellectuals will save us from stereotypes. Serreau's attacks are not restricted to a denounciation of hypocrisy: even when the socialist representative and Victor are at their most sincere, their language is discredited by the diseased syntax of stereotypes: "il y a un problème de racisme" (There is a problem of racism), or "Non moi j'ai confiance en le peuple français, au fond il est tolérant, généreux" (I wouldn't worry, I trust the French people. It is basically a tolerant and generous people) are what Pierre Barbéris would call "juicy" stereotypes (Barbéris 1994, 10). These are formulas whose formulaic qualities are obvious to everyone except to the author of the statement. "*Juteux*" (juicy) is said of scandals, of (often sexual) gossip, it not only evokes an excess of illicit jouissance but it also aptly conveys the tragic *and* comic impression of a high-voltage current caused by the discrepancy between the glaring stereotypical quality and the intensity of the speaker's political stance.[14] According to Barbéris, this is a crucial aspect of stereotypes. In the preface of the published proceedings of a Cerisy colloquium on *Le séréotype*, he writes:

> Point capital: le stéréo est-il parole de droite dénoncée par une conscience de gauche? Mais j'essaierai de le montrer: les meilleurs stéréos et les plus juteux sont des stéréos de gauche qui ont cessé de dire le réel. (10)
>
> [Crucial point: are stereotypes a right-wing discourse denounced by a left-wing consciousness? As I will try to demonstrate, the best, the juiciest stereos are left-wing stereos that have lost touch with reality.]

Serreau's film as a whole echoes Barbéris's suggestion that we pay more attention to the history of the reception of stereotypes. In the 1990s, the image of the bourgeois as most likely producer of racist stereotypes is obsolete. What needs to be considered is the nightmarish entanglement of left-wing and right-wing racisms that sometimes find uncannily similar stereotypical expression. Once the historicity of ethnic stereotypes is established, the film also proposes at least three interesting alternative tactics to the impossible refutation of stereotypes.

The first of those tactics is a form of interruption that functions like an alarm signal and is well adapted to filmic practices. The film does not directly attack the content of the politician's stereotypes, but the whole moment is denounced as a stereotyped simplification based on a violent gesture of exclusion. Victor's universe can only remain benevolently antiracist as long as his definition of racism and his definition of good neighborly conduct is kept separate from Michou's universe. Whenever the two worlds meet, Michou and Victor act like distorted mirror images. They defamiliarize each other's definitions and each provides, for the other, the possibility of interruption and friction, which exposes the fallacy of consensus.

We already have an inkling that the dialogue between two upper-middle-class men is kept artificially simple by the physical exclusion of the proverbial third: the homeless, working-class, and overtly racist character who is defined as "otherness." What makes the dialogue between the middle-class heroes stereotypical is not that the characters agree with each other (they do not) but that they agree to the terms of the debate. In fact, they reinforce each other's vision of the world even when they seem to disagree. Their definition of what racism and otherness are depends on a gesture of exclusion and separation between social classes, between rich and poor, between the city and its suburbs. Victor is inside, Michou is outside, waiting, alone.

Only his absence from the predinner conversation allows us to enjoy an uninterrupted, perfectly stereotyped dialogue. But while the four characters who are having dinner inside have temporarily managed to exclude him, the film as a whole does not forget his existence. While the others are inside, Michou's image intrudes both as a digression and as a political statement: a rather long silent and almost static shot is inserted in the middle of the animated conversation. Deserting the living room, the camera suddenly focuses Michou, who is standing outside by the gate. Now, in the background, we distinguish the massive old house where the other characters are having dinner. His lonely silhouette interrupts the flow of stereotypes and the silent shot changes our point of view for five or six long seconds. The film uses Michou as a potential interruptor, as a parasitical presence, a level of difference that highlights the reductive quality of stereotypes.

At that moment, the film underlines Michou's role as the element of cultural noise in the system. Interestingly enough, Michou is standing by an open gate that I read as the symbol of the failed desire to keep him outside. The gate exists, ready to be shut at any time, but there is also a pretense of free circulation between the homeless, unemployed suburbian and the offensively affluent socialist manor (fig. 6). The film capitalizes on the rare moments of encounter between the characters and uses editing to thematically emphasize separation and to create moments that the viewer experiences as disruptive and uncomfortable interruptions. We have no choice but to follow the camera back and forth between Michou and Victor. As long as Michou remains outside, stereotypes go unchallenged, which turns the dialogue into a completely meaningless exchange.

Ironically, the characters are unaware that their comfort depends on the sharing of stereotypes about racism and antiracism. What is important in that scene is the emphasis both on the physical absence of a possible contradictor and on his proximity. Michou's visible presence is a reminder that something remains unsaid. The film constantly warns us that the possibility of interruption is the price to pay for internal contradiction. Because the upper-middle-class characters are keen to preserve the appearances of benevolence—indeed, because they think of themselves as good, moral, benevolent people—they cannot claim exclusion as a practice. As a result, they are implicitly opening themselves up to interruption. The possibility of interrupting any coherent flow of discourse in the film is preserved by the fact that the violence inside one system does not see itself as violence. Because the socialist family of politicians and their affluent guests are incapable of seeing through their own racism, because they do not think that there is anything contradictory worth hiding, they finally invite Michou to share their meals and his views. In a sense, benevolent racism does have an advantage: It contains its own desire or contradictory need for interruption. From an homeopathic perspective, we could say that the

Figure 6. Patrick Timsit (Michou) in Coline Serreau's *La crise.* Reproduced by permission of Patrick Timsit, Coline Serreau, and Canal+. Photo: BFI Stills, Posters and Designs.

stereotypical consensual drone is paradoxically begging to be interrupted by some country rat.[15] Needless to say, Michou's presence shatters the fragile and artificial harmony, and his language functions like a magic mirror where his hosts' words are suddenly exposed as brutal stereotypes.

The second of the tactics used in the film plays on what I have called the high level of iterativity of stereotypes. *La crise* capitalizes on the fact that stereotypes are formally similar to both citations and proverbs. They can have an author, an origin, but they operate primarily as though they were anonymous and supposedly timeless pieces of wisdom. Stereotypes can be mistaken for benevolent banalities or ignorant generalizations only as long as they are not identified as stereotypes by the speaker or the listener. If comments about a racial group are received as stereotypes, they require a different type of intervention from those that circulate as supposedly self-evident truths. Before being denounced as stereotypes, such statements keep being repeated as moments of cultural wisdom and collective cultural knowledge. Like mathematical theorems, they do not depend on the authority of an author. When the hostess says, "Les Portugaises sont très propres" no one would ever ask, "Oh, where did you read that? Who said it? Cite your sources." The stereotype is a simulacrum in the Baudrillardian sense of the word: the repetition of an original declaration that really never exists.

La crise proposes an interesting antidote to the authoritative anonymity of stereotypes. In the scene where the politician's wife shares her wisdom about Asian, Arab, and Portuguese women, the logic of anonymity is reversed. A whole number of perfectly recognizable stereotypical statements are given a very recognizable origin and author: a spoiled upper-middle-class woman. In other words, there is repetition, but with a difference. As Daniel Castillo Durante puts it,

> N'empêche que réapproprier, c'est avant tout re-prendre, donc répéter. Cette réappropriation du corpus à la lettre équivaut parallèlement à l'insertion d'une sorte de ventriloquie. Le lieu d'une théâtralité polyphonique. (Castillo Durante 1994, 64)

> [And anyway, to reappropriate is to repossess and to repeat ("reprendre" has both meanings). Reappropriating the letter of the corpus goes together with the insertion of a type of ventriloquy. The place of a polyphonic theatricality.]

Like Castillo Durante, I take literally the concept of "property" present in "reappropriate." The film attributes the statement in the same way as a given quotation is attributed to an author who gets both the credit and the responsibility of what has been said. For all the viewers of *La crise*, one very real fictional character can now be said to be the author of the statement (in the same way as "Tartuffe" or "Monsieur Jourdain, le Bourgeois Gentilhomme" may be quoted). After seeing the film, whenever I hear someone say "Asians, thumbs up!" I can add, mentally or out loud, "as the politician's wife says."[16] In this scene, it is not simply a question of alluding to implicit stereotypical images ("The Wandering Jew," "veiled women in the orientalist harem"). By giving a manifest content to the stereotypical matrix, the character produces a quotable sentence rather than an anonymous stereotype. This "théâtralité polyphonique" circumscribes the stereotype and puts it on the spot, highlighting its comic potential and discrediting it as anonymous truth, especially if, as is the case in *La crise*, the film takes the precaution of denouncing such perfectly formalized stereotypes.

Finally, the third and perhaps most controversial and dangerous of all the film's tactics is an attempt at displacing the negative energy present in stereotypes as if someone was using a weapon to shoot a symbolic target rather than a human being. This highly dangerous use of stereotypes is not always possible and, in the film, it depends on the extremely manifest character of the stereotypes. For the politician's wife to become the plausible author of a recognizable citation, the quotability factor must be even higher than usual. Quotable sentiments are remembered because they are memorable—because they are sound bites or slogans. Here, the film is precisely capitalizing on (rather than worrying about) the memorable simplicity of stereotypical statements that have been stripped of all complex nuance. The more formally perfect a stereotype, the easier it is to remember its exact wording, and as a quote the more eminently reappropriable it becomes. I think this is the reason why the politician's wife is forced to regurgitate absolutely basic forms of racial stereotypes: the woman's discourse sounds like a fill-in-the-blanks quiz, or like a mass-mailing computer file. All her sentences follow the same pattern: The data file under "adjectives" would read: "sérieuses, propres, discrètes, travailleuses, très propres, voleuses, très bien avec les enfants, toujours fatiguées" (serious, clean, discreet, hard working, very neat thieves, good with kids, always tired).

Not only has she become the author of stereotypes, but the formally perfect stereotype turns the sentence into a mechanized utterance. After depriving the stereotype of its autonomy and anonymity by linking it to one speaking subject in particular, the passage robs the speaking subject in question of its humanity by exposing the mechanical construction of her statements. The film turns the author of stereotypes into Henri Bergson's laughable puppet.[17]

The use of almost outrageously perfect stereotypes is also crucial when laughing at stereotypes entails the risk of laughing at the stereotyped. The cultural wars waged in the presence of something called positive and negative images are about whether one has the right to be amused by the repetition of stereotypes, or more crucially, whether it is possible to manipulate stereotypes without harming someone. In the first chapter, I suggested that racial stereotypes (including the critical representation of them) should perhaps be identified and labeled like bottles of bleach that are best kept out of the reach of children. Do I mean, then, that a film like *La crise* necessitates training or education? Is the manipulation of stereotypes a hazardous activity? In the same manner as a film like Gillo Pontecorvo's *La bataille d'Alger* would be automatically censored as "violent," the passages I analyzed are violently racist if by "racist" we mean including scenes that feature racist statements.[18]

Serreau's cynical though tender proposal is that we resign ourselves to accept the comic potential of stereotypes and clichés that have achieved a sort of formal perfection. I suggest that the representation of formally perfect stereotypes is akin to the transformation of war into a violent sport, or perhaps to the sublimation of real and unacceptable violence into some sort of symbolically violent art that spares its victims. Didier Alexandre quotes Victor Hugo on the relationship between the use of clichés and the will to seduce a sexual partner (Alexandre 1993). Before Freud wrote about the potentials of sublimation, Hugo wrote this:

> Un poëte est un être indifférent, divers . . .
> Et qui, tout en criant: c'est Vénus dans sa conque!
> C'est Léda sur son cygne! Hébé! Turlututu
> Ne veut pas plus charmer cette femme, vois-tu
> Qu'un archer dans un tri ne veut tuer la cible.[19]
>
> [A poet is a being indifferent, contrarious . . .
> Who, while he cries out: Here's Venus in her conch,

> Here is Leda on her swan! Hey hey hey, ha ha ha,
> Has no more intention to charm the lady
> Than an archer, at practice, would want to kill the target.]

In the same manner, it may be that *La crise* plays with stereotypes like the archer plays with his bow and arrows, knowing full well that they are lethal instruments, that they are never safe, that people can use them to kill, knowingly or by accident. A first reaction to the image could be that we should always beware of people who choose a bow and arrows as a form of entertainment. Should we worry about individuals or works of art that mark a predilection for the recognition and satirical repetition of stereotypes? Concerned educators about to show the film to a class of students may wonder, for example, if *La crise* hoards metaphorical arrows that may be used by less playfully minded archers. The film apparently has taken sides in this debate and asserts sadly that if arrows are always potentially dangerous, even more dangerous are people whose violence is constantly repressed, denied, and whose hobbies are not efficient cultural safety valves ("C'est même une honte, c'est une véritable honte" [It is a shame, truly, it is a disgrace]).

The film suggests that each viewer is responsible for striking a very delicate and precarious balance by establishing distinctions, not between racism and antiracism, but between different forms of racism: those that require immediate reaction and opposition, and those that are better left unchallenged. The position is pessimistic because it renounces the ideal of a zero-tolerance threshold. But it is also a demanding attitude in that it requests that we rethink which forms of racism we consider obvious or not. For example, the scene between the two very civilized socialist women strongly recommends that we refuse to condone apparently harmless banalities. It is crucial that we learn which stereotypes are still lethal weapons in our context, that we decide when it is the right moment to condemn apparently idle chitchat. In the film, Serreau interrupts the scene with the cruel picture of Michou left alone outside like a dog at the entrance of a supermarket.

On a more delicate issue still, the film suggests that we should know when to refrain from intervening. Sometimes, the intervention would only result in a moment of self-righteous pleasure that would only be protecting a symbolic target from some sort of cultural archer. When Victor finally interacts with Michou, his family, and his friends, he discovers the complete uselessness of challenging a form of racism that he simply does not understand. The whole scene leads up to that moment of role reversal, Victor finally admitting his utter confusion—"Je n'y comprends rien" (I don't get it)—while Michou the sponger pours him a glass of champagne.

Victor is speaking with Michou's brother about Djamila when the door opens and Michou walks in, announcing:

—Michou: "J'ai dit à Mohammed et Farid de venir et aussi à Lucien. Ah vous êtes là Monsieur Victor?"
—Victor: "Salut Michou"
—Michou: "Ben ça tombe bien mon frère fait une fête pour son MI là, j'ai acheté du champagne. Alors, vous avez trouvé facilement?"
—Victor: "Mais dis-donc je croyais que tu étais raciste."
—Michou: "Ah oui pourquoi bien sûr que je suis raciste."
—Victor: "Mais Djamila?"
—Michou: "Ah oui mais Djamila c'est pas pareil, Djamila c'est la femme de mon frère puis d'abord elle m'a élevé c'est comme ma mère alors c'est pas pareil."
—Victor: "Et alors qu'est-ce que tu racontes que tu peux pas blairer les Arabes?"
—Michou: "Ah mais c'est vrai que je peux pas les blairer, mais sauf Djamila parce que Djamila, c'est pas un Arabe, c'est une femme."
—Victor: "T'as invité Mohammed et Farid c'est pas des femmes ça?"
—Michou: "Oui mais eux c'est des copains depuis l'école c'est pas pareil eux."
—Victor: "Michou, j'y comprends rien."
—Michou: "Mais y a rien à comprendre Monsieur Victor, un verre de champagne? Pour une fois que c'est moi qui vous offre à boire . . . "
—Victor: "Oui oui . . . "

[—Michou: "I invited Mohammed et Farid and Lucien, too (long pause, Michou is obviously moved to discover that Victor has come. Very softly:) So you're here, Mister Victor?"
—Victor: "Hi, Michou."
—Michou: "Well, good timing. My brother is having a party to celebrate his RMI. I bought some Champagne. Did you find easily?" (His brother leaves the room).
—Victor: "But hang on, I thought you were a racist."
—Michou: "Sure I'm a racist, why?"
—Victor: "But what about Djamila?"
—Michou: "Oh, yes, Djamila, ah, but that's different, Djamila is my brother's wife, and anyway she raised me. She's like my mother so it's not the same."
—Victor: "So why do you go around saying that you can't stand Arabs?"
—Michou: "But that's true! Can't stand them, except Djamila because she's not an Arab, she's a woman."
—Victor: "You invited Mohammed and Farid, they're not women are they?"
—Michou: "Yes, but we went to school together, they are my buddies, so it's not the same."
—Victor: "Michou, I don't get it."
—Michou: "But there's nothing to understand, Mister Victor. Will you have a glass of Champagne? My treat for a change . . ."
—Victor: "Sure . . ."]

While Victor's overall racist perceptions of race relationships leads him to imply that in order to even accept Djamila whom he does not know, he must first love *all* Arabs, Michou's own brand of racism forces him to introduce a rather preposterous theory of the exception to justify the fact that the violence of his stereotypes is not addressed to the people he cares for but directed against an abstract symbolic target.

The pessimism of Serreau's film is that it implies that we always have to choose between two forms of racism: one that claims not to exist but in effect is a classist form of racism, or one that exists and refuses to even criticize itself but results in practices of cohabitation. The cohabitation is conflictual, volatile, and full of sadness, tragedies, and rancor, but it exists nonetheless. From that perspective, the party scene at Michou's apartment is remarkable: in the same manner as Victor had invited himself to the socialist politician's dinner, he also crashes the informal party thrown by Michou's brother when he finally receives governmental financial help. An apparently innocent question about whether Michou will inform his wife's brother of her imminent death reveals unsuspected layers of tragedy in this family's life. Michou's brother, it turns out, hates Arabs, and the reason is that his wife was never allowed to see her family again after marrying him. Her mother died without having seen her. Their own son, who died when he was twenty-five, had never known his relatives. This sudden outburst is an answer to Farid's gentle request: "Fais-moi plaisir, arrête de dire du mal des Arabes" (Do me a favor, stop going on about Arabs). As an Arab himself, the friend in question is precisely in the position of the potential target of racist stereotypes, and he may find himself hurt to the quick by the brother's unfair generalization. But it is noticeable that he makes a conscious decision not to intervene. He asks for a change of protocol as if the subject was completely innocent. It would be a personal favor ("fais-moi plaisir" [for my sake]), and he gives up as soon as he realizes that his request has awakened tragic memories. If he authorizes the stereotype, it is not because he is cowering in fear or powerless, but because he interprets the scene as a case of the archer playing with a bow. He is not at risk, nor, paradoxically, are other Arabs.

Here, stereotypes are what allows Michou's brother to turn his own powerless anger into a spectacular show of contradictory and verbal anger that his friends can actually live with without losing their own dignity. They do not accept the brother's conclusions. They do not like his vituperations against "les Arabes." They are not indifferent to the power of the brother's tirade. They are affected by the use of the stereotype. They register its presence and object to it. But clearly, here, stopping the circulation of anti-Arab grand declarations is not identified as a top priority. As in Marie Féraud's story when Si Bachir keeps quiet, a conscious moment of nonintervention is the opposite of indifference. They do try to object to the blanket statement, but they soon give up, as if Michou's brother was definitely not a worthy interlocutor that needs convincing at all cost.

Here though, Michou the racist finds a perfect way out of stereotyping. He raises his glass and offers a toast "A la santé des copains Arabes" (To our Arab friends). I see this sentence as the compromise the film (and Victor as the helplessly lost character) has been looking for since the beginning of the story. This is the only toast that Michou and Farid and Mohammed and the racist brother agree to drink to. Here is a sentence that is repeated out loud by all the participants. It is the definition of a new border, or rather, this is the end of a search for a border between "real" Arabs, stereotyped Arabs, the Arabs I know, and those I imagine. Rather than a frontier, it is a protocol of cohabitation. "A la santé des copains Arabes" is not completely idealistic in the sense that it accepts to be exclusionary: "Arabs" are still disinvited as a whole abstract people against whom the brother is implicitly allowed to fulminate. At the same time, the film has successfully demonstrated by now that such sentences could be just as racist as "A bas les Arabes" (Down with Arabs). Benevolent racist declarations such as "Les Arabes je les adore" have been discredited as the ultimate hypocritical statement and authorized by people like the politician's wife. "A la Santé des Arabes" (To Arabs), by now, would be too similar to "Les Asiatiques chapeau" and "Moi, je les adore les Arabes" not to elicit a justified feeling of suspicion.[20]

"A la santé des copains Arabes" is also inclusionary but tautologically so: By definition, people invited to Michou's parties are his friends. The fact that they all agree to limit their toast to "les copains Arabes" is a compromise for the "copains Arabes" who allow themselves to be contaminated and become participating witnesses in their buddy's use of racist stereotypes, but it is also an obvious compromise for Michou's brother, who ends up renouncing a worldview where no Arab can be a friend of his. The loophole of the exception theory, in principle an untenable position, does not redeem the brother's racism. At the same time, his form of racism is here treated as tolerable, or rather not worthy of a confrontation because it is the only way to cohabit and drink with him. What the film suggests, however, is that the brother is perfectly happy with his own self-contradictions and, even more important, that homeopathic treatments of social fracture involve tolerating his outbursts.

The type of reappropriation advocated here is risky. The strategies adopted, more or less successfully, by the economy of the film suggest two possibilities. First, it may be possible to treat the use of stereotypes as a sport or a form of art (make a cliché of the cliché, frame the stereotype as if we were about to put it in a museum for people to see). And concurrently, it may be that we have to accept the presence of stereotypes in small doses, as a healing practice. Such highly questionable activities of reappropriation do not restore any kind of political innocence. Rather, they make the highly pessimistic point that a certain level of stereotyping, a certain form of stereotypical, racism, may be the lesser of two evils. Paradoxically, a degree of extreme optimism is also entailed in the belief that the group is capable of dealing successfully with a certain level of racial stereotyping and the film sets an example. By taking the risk to use dangerous stereotypes as theatrical props, or as the bow used by the archer, it suggests that there is a possibility of conscious formalization of stereotyping that we should not necessarily be afraid of or try to censor.

Chapter 6

Cheating on Stereotypes

Emile Ajar, Calixthe Beyala, and Didier Van Cauwelaert

Stereotypes are impossible to eradicate.[1] Stereotypes evolve but never disappear, and when we think we have identified them, they are already at work in our own innermost thoughts and narratives of ourselves and of others. The most pessimistic definitions equate language itself with stereotyping, as if our sentences could be understood only once they have been put together as idioms, familiar combination of words whose meaning requires reference to intertextual echoes rather than unique and context-specific acts of interpreting. Some conceive of every single sign as the potential carrier of solidification, sameness, and repetition—that is, of death (Touratier 1979; Castillo Durante 1994). Yet even the broadest conceptions of stereotypical constructions imagine a way out, a little niche carved within language where the speaker or the writer finds relief from diseased images, from stale clichés, from solidified formulations. In *Leçon*, Barthes visualizes the opposite of stereotyping as a mixed metaphor of flight and cheating. Because stereotypes are a type of language, Barthes maintains that stereotypes can be outfoxed through a subversive and nonconformist use of language. To avoid petrifaction, solidification, and thoughtlessness,

> il ne reste, si je puis dire qu'à tricher avec la langue, qu'à tricher la langue. Cette tricherie salutaire, cette esquive, ce leurre magnifique, qui permet d'entendre la langue hors-pouvoir, dans la splendeur d'une révolution permanente du langage, je l'appelle pour ma part, littérature. (Barthes 1978, 16)
>
> [the only thing left, is, if I may say so, to cheat with language, to cheat language. This healthy cheating, this evasion, this magnificent deception, which lets you hear a lan-

guage beyond power, the gorgeous spectacle of a permanent revolution of language, I call it literature.]

Assuming that literature is, in and by itself, the answer to stereotypes is wishful thinking, or rather a forceful, performative confining of literature to curious limits that seem to contradict Barthes's obvious desire for liberation from the straitjackets of conformity. As it is, literature is too often harnessed to institutionalized canons to be safe from the stereotyping effects of monumentalization. Some scenes from Pierre Corneille's *Le Cid* have been stereotyped into French children's minds by virtue of their conventional teachability. They thus have virtually no value as antidotes against stereotypical thought unless we find a way as grown-ups to hear them freshly or differently. Even Barthes, a great believer in rereading, may have found it difficult to think of Corneille's tragedies as "cheating language."[2] But perhaps it is unfair to argue with his formulation. At least, let us embrace his ideas of "cheating" and of acting directly on the level of language since the two tactics seem so close to elaborating the politics of grammar we have been seeking. The addition of an *s* to the word literature may be all that is needed to move from formalism to a form of reading and writing capable of declining stereotypes both at the ideological and at the poetic level. If literature can no longer be thought of as an independent paradise, free from the influence of institutionalized power and from the intrusion of stereotypical thought, at least there might be answers in *some* literatures, in some literary texts whose conscious goal is to decline stereotypes.

Some texts or, to be more accurate, some styles, or some ways of writing choose to practice the art of what Barthes calls "*esquive*" (dodging, eluding). Recommending esquive is a way of recognizing that the subject is engaged in a type of fight or duel. Language is like a drawn sword, and we are advised to acknowledge the element of violence. But esquive also favors a nonviolent response that requests swift and adroit movements rather than confrontation. What Barthes calls literature and cheating does not resuscitate the tradition of dialogue as a duel where two partners use wit like a weapon. Instead, cheating language involves not responding to violence with violence. Stereotypes are not dismissed as mere linguistic events; they are taken seriously, as potentially harmful swords. But no heroic counterassault is to be expected. Esquive is another of the forms of nonintervention that I have explored above as possible methods of defusing stereotypes. In this chapter, I analyze a slightly different tactic that combines direct and spectacular cheating of language with an apparent indifference to the scathing political indictment that accompanies linguistic and poetic manipulations.

I look at three novels that refuse to deal with stereotypes as an enemy that must be fought on its own turf. As readers, we are not constructed as bloodthirsty spectators expecting a battle between gladiators, between the forces of evil and the saintly text. Instead, the authors invite us to participate in a "splendid" cultural feast where the spectacle is a revolution arising from the unresolved clash between the rigidity of stereotypes and the freedom of poetry. The result is something like an impossible hybrid, an improbable stereopoetic language that has inherited both memorability and originality. The three authors do not distinguish between the *idéologème*, and its manifestation. Their narrators invent their own phrases and expressions, defacing language, adding or subtracting from set phrases like someone spraying or carving graffiti over public images, like someone grafting a mustache under Jean-Marie Le Pen's nose on a campaign poster.

Emile Ajar's *La vie devant soi* (The life before us), Calixthe Beyala's *Le petit prince de Belleville* (The "little prince" of Belleville) and Didier van Cauwelaert's *Un aller simple* (A one-way ticket) display extremely high levels of irony and extremely low levels of didacticism, although the novels confront some of the most distressing aspects of racism, xenophobia, and anti-Semitism. *Un aller simple*, for example, focuses on recent controversial French immigration policies regarding the treatment of so-called *clandestins* or illegal aliens.[3]

Twenty years separate the first book from the last two, which were published within the space of two years. The social and political context has obviously changed radically between 1975, when Ajar received the Prix Goncourt for *La vie devant soi*, and 1994, when the same prize was awarded to Van Cauwelaert for *Un aller simple*.[4] (When the 1975 Prix Goncourt was awarded to an obscure Ajar, no one suspected that he was none other than Romain Gary, who had already had the pleasure of turning down another Prix Goncourt in 1956.) For Beyala, *Le petit prince de Belleville* inaugurated a new cycle, since it is the first of her "Parisian" novels, after a series of texts set in Africa.[5]

The three texts cannot be unproblematically classified and celebrated as "Francophone" novels whose writing and structure reflect a growing interest and fascination with phenomena of cultural métissage, *créolité*, and *créolisation*.[6] In Ajar's case, the label is almost anachronistic, and in the two other novels there is no attempt to reclaim an identity that the narrators were taught to despise (Cliff 1985). If Ajar, Beyala, and Van Cauwelaert belong to something called postcolonial studies, it is, at best, obliquely and without claiming the position as a privilege or a redress. No specific ethnic identity is claimed or even explored. Unlike Leïla Sebbar's Sherazade and other characters, Aziz, Momo, and Loukoum (Beyala's protagonist) are not interested in how Odalisques are portrayed in Western culture (Sebbar 1982, 1984, 1985).

If we compare the three texts with Aimé Césaire's poetry or with Patrick Chamoiseau's *Texaco*, another recent Goncourt Prize winner, other differences appear. Where Césaire's and Chamoiseau's works may present serious linguistic obstacles even for educated French readers, Ajar, Beyala, and Van Cauwelaert's deceptively colloquial styles are not intimidating; they give readers a false impression of simplicity.[7] Their language moves constantly between the familiar and the strange, the (stereo)typical and the unexpected. Often, lulled by a perfectly classic structure, the reader finds his or her attention suddenly awakened by an incongruous noun, a bizarre adjective in the wrong place at the wrong time. No attempt is made to represent Francophone communities whose language has been silenced by centralizing attempts, whether linked to colonialism or not.[8] We are not invited to discover non-Parisian Francophone languages, nor do we find a sustained reproduction of a certain jargon, of regional cultures or of a given social class.[9] Yet the texts often leave us frustrated and confused by the absence of a predictable word or, on the contrary, by the addition of an astonishing supplement to a set phrase. Generally speaking, the cheating consists of a constant shuttling between the banal and the extraordinary, the completely known and the completely unknown.[10]

The feeling of alienation and distance from the norm is vague and unsettling. It is necessary to examine the text very closely to actually identify what difference is introduced, what subtle displacement provokes such strong moments of foreignness, such radical changes of mood. I call this type of discourse "stereopoetic" because the difference between Ajar's prose and our implicit (and probably inarticulable) definition of "normal" prose is the same elusive gap that separates prose from poetry; it is a question of definition and a not very useful case-by-case argument. A better analogy is that of poems and songs: reading the lyrics of a song can in no way give credit to a performance that combines the written word and the melody. The same sort of difference is created when Ajar, Beyala, and Van Cauwelaert challenge our knowledge of "modèles littéraires" (literary models) (Barbéris 1994, 10), or genres, or assumptions about what it means to be a native speaker.[11]

Let us examine the conditions of enunciation that allow the characters and narrators to reinvent language and decline stereotypical invitations. In the three novels, the narrator is a child or an adolescent: a young Jewish child in Ajar's *La vie devant soi* and a young Malian in *Le petit prince de Belleville*. In *Un aller simple*, the situation is complicated by the fact that the narrator is "un enfant trouvé par erreur" (a case of mistaken foundling) (5) whose race, origin, and identity are never specified; the novel makes a point of not knowing whether its own hero is white or not, though his self-constructed identity definitely—almost essentially—turns him into an Arab:

> Je me trouvais donc à Marseille, en qualité de Marocain provisoire, avec permis de séjour payable à chaque renouvellement. Tant qu'à faire un faux, on aurait pu carrément me donner la nationalité française, il me semblait, mais c'est vrai aussi que je n'avais pas voulu mettre le prix. (8)

[So I was in Marseilles as a temporary Moroccan with a cash-on-renewal permit. It seemed to me that if they were going to forge it anyway, they might as well have given me a French passport but it is also true that I had been cheap about it.]

In all three novels, the voice emanates from the multicultural and poor suburbs of a big city: Belleville for the first two, the northern suburbs of Marseilles for *Un aller simple*.[12] In the same way as Mathieu Kassovitz's *La haine*, Malik Chibane's *Hexagone* and *Douce France*, Karim Dridi's *Bye-bye*, and Bernard Blier's *Un deux trois, soleil* (also filmed in Marseilles) can be brought together under the umbrella of their banlieues-films in spite of their obvious and profound differences, literary historians may eventually decide to classify the three books as banlieues-novels. The voices emanating from Belleville or northern Marseilles invoke and displace the stereotypical images attached to neighborhoods where the percentage of immigrants is thought to be particularly high. As is so often the case, this reference to immigration is both the key to phantasmic interpretive grids and a completely useless concept, since none of the heroes can hope to benefit from Césaire's exhortation to return to the native land.[13]

The authors' critiques of racism and anti-Semitism are filtered through children whose political consciousness is supposed to be practically nonexistent. The young narrators succeed, notwithstanding, to destroy the stability of commonplaces they apparently believe in by preserving a complete (and perhaps ignorant) independence from the rules of grammar and semantic coherence. Their humor seems almost involuntary, as its source is primarily a series of apparently haphazard errors of vocabulary, approximative uses of idioms, and faulty syntax.

To a certain extent, the young narrators renew the tradition of the eighteenth-century "Candide" or "Ingénu," although it is quite clear that they do not stand for the stereotype of the idyllically controllable good savage, of the innocent child. Besides, they are candid insiders and not wise outsiders. As Jean-Marie Volet puts it, "at no time does the reader get the impression that the author has fallen victim to her own game and slipped into the gentle mood of Utopian innocence" (Volet 1993, 311). Beyala's reference to Antoine de Saint-Exupéry's "little prince," a blond, blue-eyed, angelic little alien, only generates cruel bases for comparison between the literary hero of the fairy tale and the little prince of Belleville. The two *petits princes* are caught in an ironic double act. They seem to be trapped inside mirror images of each other, as if they were the embodiments of the two heroes of Baudelaire's 1862 poem "Le joujou du pauvre" (The poor boy's toy) (Baudelaire 1962, 92–94): each on one side of the gate, separated by symbolic barriers that condemn one to the tragic thrills of playing with dead rats . . . or stolen car radios (Aziz "se débrouille," i.e. makes a living stealing car radios).

We could even interpret Beyala's title as a deceptive attempt to make us concentrate on Loukoum as a *petit prince*, for in the novel a second character exists who could well play the role of the rich boy in Baudelaire's "Le joujou du pauvre." The boy who plays with expensive toys on the other side of the gate of respectability, perhaps the "little prince" of Belleville, is not Loukoum but rather Pierre Pelletier, the wonderful white classmate who helps Loukoum with his homework and teaches him how to read. When Loukoum describes him, he says: "Il a un visage de petit Français de l'époque des princes, avec de cheveux tout bouclés" (1992, 51) (His face is that of little French boy in the time of kings and princes, with his hair all curly) (1995, 31). The resemblance to Saint-Exupéry's illustrations of his own book is almost too good to be a coincidence.

The ethnic identity of the young heroes is always problematic and always clearly foregrounded, even if the racial construction is denounced as an effect of delusion and self-fulfilling prophecies. For all intents and purposes, Momo, Aziz, and Loukoum are treated as if they were, respectively, Arabs or black. There is no attempt to erase ethnic categories in the hope that a universalizing principle of integration will make ethnicity irrelevant. But the way in which the novels cope with ethnic identity is quite remarkable; it is never a principle of inclusion or exclusion in and by itself. Because of their identities, Momo, Loukoum, and Aziz are sometimes inside and sometimes outside, and they never imagine that integration would allow them to simply move from an exterior to a supposedly homogeneous interior.

Raised and educated in their multiethnic French neighborhoods, the young heroes move between perfect adaptation and complete alienation. At one level, they are perfectly at home in the larger entity called France. They are all perfectly at ease with the language, and Momo and Loukoum are at home in French urban and even Parisian culture. They do not correspond to the postcolonial image of the diasporic traveler. The only environment they have ever learned to decipher is their *banlieues*. At nineteen, Aziz says, "je n'ai jamais encore quitté les Bouches-du-Rhône" (9) (I have never left the department of Bouches-du-Rhône). At another level, they are completely rejected, marginalized, even excluded from this very same society that treats them as foreigners. Their language is the only adequate representation of this constant motion between being inside and being outside, between being a native and being a foreigner. The three heroes are fluent in code switching rather than in one specific language. And code switching is particularly well adapted to the principle of constant evasion, elusive and adroit dodging.[14]

Code switching (in and out of stereotypes) becomes the language of a constant oscillation between inclusion and exclusion capable of incorporating both racist and antiracist comments, playing with echoes of political clichés. Sometimes, an expression whose meaning depends on its invariability is slightly altered by the narrator, the transgression producing an amusing moment of uncertainty: “Madame Rosa avait un système de plus en plus nerveux” (Ajar, 68) (Madame Rosa had an increasingly nervous system). In Beyala’s text, we learn that Madame Abdou particularly appreciates one of her visitors who systematically asks about her “fibrome” or lump whenever she sees her. But just as the reader starts wondering what is wrong with Madame Abdou and whether the lump or tumor in question is a life-threatening disease, the narrator reveals that she does not have a tumor in a breast or in her uterus for example, but . . . in a jar: she had kept it there after having it surgically removed. The text acts as if there were no difference between “to have a car” and “to have a disease.” Madame Abdou “a un fibrome . . . dans un bocal” (1992, 10) (“has a lump . . . in a jar”) (1995, 5). On the one hand, the children modify apparently solidified units of language, demonstrating a complete independence from linguistic norms, but then suddenly, like puppets, they start parroting racist stereotypes that we have heard a thousand times and whose violence contrasts with the apparently childish tone of previous passages. Without warning, we are treated to a whole string of racial slurs about Jews and blacks. “Décidément, on ne peut pas faire confiance à un nègre” (1992, 40) (Really, you can’t trust a nigger) (1995, 23), exclaims Loukoum. He also informs us that “les nègres sont pas intelligents” (1992, 32) (Niggers aren’t smart) (1995, 52). As for Momo, he explains that “les juifs ont toujours le disque triste” (Ajar 1975, 230) (Jews are always out of sorts).

At times, what is fixed and immobile is manipulated in an apparently apolitical moment of humorous transgression; at other times, the most basic level of originality is abandoned and replaced by sentences that even the most conventional author would probably refuse to take credit for. Throughout the texts, stereotypes stand out as though framed and displayed in a gallery, but they are never discussed, criticized, or denied. No attempt is ever made to substitute a racial slur with a (still racial) compliment. No book could be further from the reappropriative choices of some proponents of Negritude, for example. Whether the stereotype is flattering or insulting, the texts treat it in a similar manner.

Often, a direct intervention against the supposedly impeccable truth of stereotypes occurs at the level of logical articulations. As stereotypes tend to assume a direct link between being Jewish or black and having other characteristics as a result, the formulation of a cause-and-effect sequence is a delicate juncture that the novels often transform in victorious moments of adroit declining. Thus, when Loukoum says:

> D’ailleurs, je suis le plus grand de la classe, le plus fort aussi. Normal, puisque les Noirs sont plus forts que n’importe qui. C’est comme ça. (Beyala 1992, 8)
>
> [Besides, I am the tallest in my class, the strongest as well. Quite normal, since black people are stronger than anyone. (1995, 2)]

the text has already given us the means of seeing through the apparent clarity of its "besides" and reference to normality. If I had included what comes before the quotation (the frame that surrounds the pinned-up stereotype), it would be obvious that this is a moment of exuberant declining where the text indulges in the pleasures of internal contradictions for the sake of showing that the stereotype is a *desire* for truth rather than the truth. "Besides" is a logical mistake, as I demonstrate below.

Similarly, Ajar launches an attack on "because," inviting us, in the future, to do the same to people who seriously explain that "les Portugaises sont très propres parce que . . ." (Portuguese women are very neat because . . .). Momo says: "J'allais sur mes dix ans, j'avais même des troubles de précocité parce que les Arabes bandent toujours les premiers" (Ajar, 22) (I was almost ten, and I had precocious problems, because Arabs always have hard-ons before anyone else). The two examples use the same strategy: The text feeds us apparently undeniable facts. Apparently, the black child is taller and stronger than his peers, and the young Arab has reached puberty at ten. Because the facts are curious, they seem to beg for an explanation, even if only stereotypes come to mind.

The narration pretends to go along with the racial clichés that supposedly account for the curious "facts," but it soon becomes obvious that this tolerant indifference is in reality a clever form of self-defense against stereotypes. Momo's and Loukoum's apparently indulgent acceptance is quite different from what Si Bachir decided to do when confronted with the racist old lady. *Le petit prince* displays a certain amount of laissez-faire, the better to confound the stereotypical logic. When a stereotypical "fact" is bandied about ("black people are stronger"), the text refrains from an ideological knee-jerk reaction. Faced with similar statements, we might, for example, invoke the exception to the rule. We may want to mention another black person who does not fit the stereotypical equation, or we may be tempted to scrutinize the black individual in question and find perfectly acceptable reasons for his physical development other than his race.

The novels adopt quite a different strategy, suggesting that we should beware of how we read statements presented as "facts" when they occur in a racialized or ethnicized environment. What we may be used to identifying as a fact is a juncture at which the narration wants us to avert our eyes from a simple problem (the "fact" in question is not a fact) and to squander our energy trying to theorize a situation that was never there to being with. (As we will see, the question of *why* Loukoum is strong for his age really need not be answered.) What we interpret as a fact is shown to be a form of discursive and ideological temptation. In the context of ethnic stereotyping, the grammar of facts and figures, with its accompanying level of articulations, is fetishized; it is an open invitation to plunge into our own list of preconceptions. In order to rationalize and control what we believe to be an unexplainable difference, we enlist the power of stereotypes. We fill in the blanks without realizing that the predicate is problematic because it erases all doubts about the construction of that reality. The search for causes would be very different indeed if, instead of accepting the sentence as it is written (Loukoum is stronger than his friends because . . ."), we mentally supplied a slightly modified proposal: "If it is true that Loukoum is stronger than his friends, then. . . ." The novels show how we could adopt precisely such a reading tactic by deceiving us deliberately: the narrators are lying, providing us with prefabricated truths.

The facts that made it necessary for the narrators to provide some kind of racialized explanation are simply inaccurate. Loukoum and Momo are not stronger than their peers, they are simply compared with younger children. Both Loukoum and Momo are several years older than their official age. Ironically, that discrepancy between the children's real and social age is the result of their disenfranchisement as ethnic subjects. In other words, those "facts" are the *results* of stereotypes rather than the reality of a cultural difference that can be studied, theorized, or explained through the logic of stereotypes. Loukoum admits, "J'ai sept ans pour l'officiel, et dix saisons pour l'Afrique. C'était juste pour ne pas prendre de retard à l'école" (Beyala 1992, 8) (I am seven years old for the record and ten seasons old for Africa. That was just so I wouldn't be put back in school [1995, 1; trans. modified]). As for Momo, when he asks Madame Rosa: "Pourquoi m'avez-vous dit que j'avais dix ans alors que j'en avais quatorze?" (Ajar 1975, 229) ("Why did you tell me I was ten years old when I was fourteen years old?"), he receives the following answer: "J'avais peur que tu me quittes, Momo, alors je t'ai un peu diminué" ("I was afraid you'd leave me, Momo, so I shrank you a little bit.") In other words, stereotypes are used to explain situations that would hardly be remarkable if the children's real ages were known. And the text cheats by inserting fake articulations between so-called facts and their stereotypical explanations: the series of *d'ailleurs* (besides) and *parce que* (because) are less than subtle traps.

When ethnic stereotypes are not discredited by the exposure of inaccurate facts, they are sabotaged by a different tactic of reappropriation. The texts capitalize on one specific aspect of the stereotypes' memorability. If stereotypes are easy to remember, it is because they are endlessly repeated. As a result, as a well-established axiom in information theory has long demonstrated, they do not carry a high level of new information. Their circulation is precisely facilitated by their lack of new and challenging knowledge. Beyala's and Ajar's novels thrive on this double characteristic, using the predictable refrain of stereotypes as a way of highlighting the completely unexpected end of the sentence where they have inserted the stereotype in question. Both narrators constantly begin sentences with familiar clichés, with pompous, self-righteous, and banal statements that make them sound like little parrots. And suddenly, when readers' expectations are at their lowest, a completely unexpected twist appears, a genuine surprise that challenges preconceptions. Here, the memorability of repetitions is in competition with the effect of surprise. The ostentatious stereotypes are apparently allowed to go unchallenged, but their power is immediately undermined by the refreshing originality of the children's reformulation. Stereotypes that are normally remembered because they function like endlessly repeated commercials are made to function like secondary frames to a most unexpected and therefore extremely striking statement that may well take precedence in the reader's memory.

Momo constantly says things like, "Les juifs sont très accrocheurs surtout quand ils ont été exterminés" (Ajar 1975, 59) (Jews are very stubborn, especially when they have been exterminated). This hybrid statement is the typical product of a tactic regularly used in the three novels. The narrator starts a sentence with a worn-out formula, an old hackneyed statement that makes him sound as though he is imitating grown-ups. We may have the impression that the young child does not own his words, that he acts as a channel for a language that speaks him in the same way as we used to say "*ça parle*" (it speaks) when Lacanian psychoanalytical parlance was hegemonic in literary criticism.

Stereotypes impose their language on Aziz, Momo, and Loukoum, who act like ventriloquist's puppets, traversed by an anonymous and collective dominant voice. Or so we think. Until we reach the end of the sentence, the children can be interpreted as rather typical colonized, alienated subjects who have no choice but to perpetuate negative myths about their own communities, forced as they are to share the racist, xenophobic, and anti-Semitic premises of the language they have learned to speak. Yet the end of the sentence usually shatters the image of the puppet. Suddenly the child speaks for himself and adds his own unexpected commentary. Under the pretense of adding a last detail to the stereotype ("*surtout quand*" [especially when]), they completely modify the overall meaning.

Like the unexpected bit of new information, readers are likely to be framed, trapped by their expectations and smug confidence in their own intelligence. At first, as grown-ups, educated readers, we may fall straight into the trap: We feel superior to the childish narrator. We know he should not indulge in sentences starting with "Jews are . . ." as 99 percent of all such sentences will end up being useless if not dangerous. But it soon becomes obvious that Momo's tactics are far more complex. We are correct to supply quotes around the children's words and to assume that they are taking their cues from adults or repeating what gets repeated around them. But far from having internalized ethnic stereotypes, the children are capable of using precisely them in a way that exposes and ultimately betrays their stereotypical logic. If the beginnings of such sentences deprive the narrator of any personal voice, the final twist functions like his signature: Here is an individual, personal, signed statement. Inside such sentences, two conflicting logics are allowed to coexist: an anonymous and collective stereotypical thinking (thought by no one in particular about certain ethnic communities in general) and a specific individual statement for which the narrator must take full responsibility. This straight-faced yet highly amusing shuttling between obvious stereotypes and surprisingly personal statements is what gives the novels their peculiar flavor. The narrators are both trapped by language and capable of using congealed structures as a sort of trampoline, bouncing up and down between original flights of their imagination and the gravity of predictable formulas.

The authors have adopted a similar defusing tactic. Stereotypes rely on the possibility of drawing boundaries around territories and individuals. The children believe or pretend to believe in the existence of origins, of the distinction between "we" and "they" and then become "poachers" (De Certeau 1984). But it is clear that they treat the notions of territory, of origin, even of nationalities as metaphors that children must go along with because they are grown-ups' stories. And they treat language as the symptom of this discrepancy between their own narrow margin of freedom and what is always already said, articulated by some anonymous collective and inherited culture. The narrators are not victims; they are not believers. They pretend, they go along, skeptically.

The peculiar use of nouns and proper names is emblematic of this sort of *esquive*. Like their language, the heroes assume several identities defined by reference to either ethnic groups or individuals. The three novels question and blur the distinction between a common noun and a proper name, especially between words used to describe an individual as a member of a community ("black, Jew, Arab") and as unique subjects whose name is arbitrary and not determined by racial or ethnic qualities. The issue is all the more important as minority subjects usually find themselves reduced to the element in their identity that others consider sufficient to define them. Most of the time, the difference between a name and all the other words that can be used to describe a subject is linguistically quite clear and simple to maintain. Here, on the contrary, the names of people, of things, and of communities are used as if they had become interchangeable. In the end, the line that separates the name of a person from the name of a community reveals itself as easy to cross.

This issue of the name is of the utmost importance in a context where authenticity and origin justify all kind of violence and excesses. When the novels use proper names as if they were the names of things or the names of groups, and when they use the name used to refer to whole communities in order to talk about one specific individual, the whole concept of identity is called into question. When Ajar writes, "On l'appelait le Nègre pour des raisons peu connues, peut-être pour le distinguer des autres noirs du quartier, car il en faut toujours un qui paie pour les autres" (1975, 204) (We called him the nigger for obscure reasons, perhaps to tell him apart from the other blacks of the neighborhood. Let's face it, someone has to pay for the others), he plays with some people's tendency to equate skin color and identity. "Le Nègre" is only understandable (by which I do not mean acceptable) in a context where everyone is white except one individual whose name is then erased and replaced by the physical marker of his or her community. But in the example given by Momo, amid a whole community of black people, the reference to "the" black man makes little sense. What happens, then, is slightly different from the simple repetition of something overheard by the child. The narrator recognizes that the phenomenon is rather strange and would normally demand an explanation that he cannot really give. Consequently, "le Nègre" starts functioning like a real person's name, as only one member of the black community bears that name. Strangely enough, by singling out one black man among others and calling him "le Nègre," the other inhabitants of the neighborhood, regardless of their own skin color, are both using a potentially racist linguistic structure and depriving that very same structure of its raison d'être if not of its power. In *La vie devant soi*, the black community is not absent at all and "le Nègre" cannot function as the stereotypical substitution of a whole community by one of its members. But usually, what is unacceptably reductive and highly paradoxical about people calling someone "le Nègre" (or the Jew) is that they are, at the same time, forcing one individual to become the representative of an abstractly imagined community and acknowledging the fact that this very community is completely absent from their environment. This authorizing absence of a group is all the more problematic as the individual singled out as the typical member is supposed to exhibit all the stereotypical features of those other individuals with whom he or she is compared and for whom he or she stands. Both Sander Gilman and Frank Felsenstein have studied the remarkable moment of rejection when a nonexistent community is reinvented for the purpose of excluding it. Either presence or absence can be invoked as the verification of delusional narratives about the scapegoated community. If "they" are in my neighborhood, I can show you what they do and how unacceptable the situation is; if they are away, I can warn you about what would happen if they were allowed to return. Felsenstein shows that even after two hundred years of exclusion, the Jewish community was still stereotyped by the British and that a new wave of anti-Semitism followed an attempt to readmit the community into the country.

In this example from *La vie devant soi*, the politics of grammar oscillates between an optimistic and a pessimistic take on the issue of categorizing. The beginning of the sentence is optimistic, implying that it is possible to find a context that neutralizes the repeated stereotype. And yet, the narrator's attempts to explain the unusual formulation implicitly warns us that it would be premature to rejoice. In a sense, what is introduced here and immediately canceled out is a qualitative difference between a stereotype and a racial slur.

Most of the time, calling someone "le Nègre" is an extremely violent racialization, a doubly racist condemnation of the individual and of the race itself. Because it makes no sense to call someone "le Nègre" among other black people, the narrator is capable of disentangling the words from the slur. And yet, his assumptions about why this black man is singled out immediately reintroduces the spectrum of the scapegoat and the idea of responsibility. (Somebody must pay for something, but what?) In other words, although the ludicrous name is at first dissociated from a purely racial slur, the apparently nonideological use of the stereotype is not innocent. Those who use the expression are not exonerated, and the text suggests that their use of this pseudo–last name is an exclusionary tactic.

In *Le bouc émissaire* (*The scapegoat*, 1982) René Girard suggests that the scapegoat is never essentially different from the other members of the group, and that the creation of difference is a by-product of the identification of the scapegoat. While commonplace definitions of scapegoating assume that whoever is different from the group will be noticed and then accused of all evils, Girard suggests that the choice of an emissary victim comes first. Once the scapegoat is chosen, his or her own identity is constructed as different. Girard's insight provides an interesting explanation of Momo's formulation and, read through this grid, the sentence is a quite relevant commentary on current analyses of Maghrebi immigration in France. Conveniently forgetting that those so-called immigrants were born and educated in France and are as permanently settled as any French citizen can ever hope to be, some commentators continue to try and explain any disturbing social phenomenon as the effect of specific migratory behavior. In contemporary France, it is often suggested that Arabs function and will continue to function differently from previous generations of immigrants.[15] Their difference is different from other forms of differences. They cannot be assimilated, their integration is jeopardized by their religion, their non-European culture. Even liberal discourses that recognize that Arabs are being scapegoated usually blame their plight on current economic circumstances, rationalizing that the French are looking for a scapegoat because of their deep-seated anxieties. I would suggest, however, that the scapegoating does not occur as a result of a supposedly greater discrepancy between a unified French culture and the (again, supposedly unified) immigrants' culture. If Girard is correct, Arabs are rationalized as different because they are stereotypically scapegoated and not the other way around. This means that no matter how much the difference between "l'Arabe" and the hegemonic Other decreases, someone will continue to have to pay. That is, someone will be called "l'Arabe" almost by default, Ajar suggests. By suggesting that someone must pay no matter what, by suggesting that it is not even worth mentioning what it is that one must pay for, Ajar's novel insists that scapegoating would continue to blaze a trail of difference through any community and in the absence of any identifiable danger. Stereotypes are always there, ready to supply the necessary elements for any scapegoating enterprise. Stereotypes will manufacture difference in the middle of sameness. "Le Nègre" does not disappear even when the phrase has become nonsensical and comic. Even if it becomes a proper name, the adjective used to refer to a whole community does not completely lose its potentially devastating effect. The word "Nègre" is still used to force one individual to bear the burden of representativity of otherness defined as an undesirable characteristic.

Ajar's reformulation suggests that the principle of the stereotype plays on the fundamental ambiguity in the distinction between proper names and common nouns. In the context of Belleville, if someone is called "le Nègre," the phrase functions both as a nickname—a name that is proper, owned by one unique individual even if it is not an official identity—or as a common noun. Stereotyping reflexes turn the names of ethnic groups into undecidable units that share some of the characteristics of both proper names and common nouns. When a proper name is narrowly associated with someone's race, religion, or ethnicity, its functions are blurred and adulterated. The proper name loses its power of differentiation and is no longer capable of endowing one individual with a uniqueness irreducible to any form of regrouping. The mystery of otherness is lost and replaced by the dull but also pacifying comfort of generalizations. What Levinas calls "*Autrui*" (that irreducible otherness in others) disappears from our mental map (Levinas 1969).

Instead of meeting a unique subject, instead of creating for ourselves a new and specific narrative that will gradually be equated with the always incomplete impression of "knowing" another person, we will replace the as-yet-unwritten tale of knowledge with a spurious process of recognition. The unknown other is paradoxically recognized as always already known, his or her identity being imagined as a list of stereotypes.

In the end, a sort of generic body-name is created. "Mohammed" becomes synonymous with "Arab" and with all Arabs. This is a direct consequence of an ambiguous mental category that seems so harmless in the abstract that a concerted effort at resisting it would be perceived as intolerant: that of the "Jewish name," for example. Like the so-called Jewish nose, the Jewish name is always trapped by layers of historical stereotypes. The idea that someone's name "sounds" Jewish results from the fact that we do not always insist on distinguishing between a Jew's name and a Jewish name. Language, in this instance, is a bit sloppy, and the cultural use of the blurred boundary is fraught with potentially dangerous (or comic) misunderstandings. In French, layers upon layers of cultural assumptions are implicitly revealed by a slight asymmetry between what would be called "*un nom arabe*" (an Arab name) and "*un nom bien français*" (an all-French name). Perhaps words are like guns: they don't kill unless someone uses them to that effect. Yet I wonder what determination is needed to insist on opposing the type of ideological grammar that creates false parallels between "*un nom juif*" (a Jewish name) and "*un nom bien de chez nous*" (a good old French name).

To expose the consequences of such stereotypical formulas, it is always possible to adopt reversal tactics. If our name is more or less implicitly branded as undesirably foreign, it is possible to cherish that name, to wear it with ostentatious pride. But the novels and films studied here adopt quite a different principle of resistance. Like recent fictional autobiographies or semi-autobiographical novels written by Caribbean, Beurs, or Maghrebi authors, they are both culturally informed by their postcolonial predecessors and apparently convinced that no linear progress or ideological development allows them to wear their mark of nominal difference with unmitigated pride. Perhaps the fact that many Beur narrators are children explains that no transcendent triumph over self-deprecation is to be taken for granted. Historically, people such as Césaire and Fanon may have paved the way, but each individual must relearn the lesson of stereotypes. Azouz Begag often plays with names. We have seen how, in *Béni ou le paradis privé*, his main character would rather be called "Béni" (which sounds like "blessed" in French) rather than Ben Abdallah. Van Cauwelaert goes even further by reversing the principle. Even though the novel does not give us one single clue about the child's race or ethnicity (all we know is that he was pulled out of the wreckage of his parents' car after an accident), his arrest and subsequent deportation demonstrate that his foster mother was absolutely right when she tried to explain that it is the name that creates the race, that the name is the source of one's ethnic identity, regardless of what someone actually looks like. Call someone Aziz, and he will be an Arab. Here is the story of the narrator's identity/name/ethnic identity:

> La voiture était une Ami 6 de race Citroën, alors on m'a appelé Ami 6 en souvenir. Ce sont mes origines, quoi. Avec le temps, c'est devenu Aziz. Mamita, qui est née Rom en Roumanie où elle a été stérilisée par les nazis, dit toujours que c'était une mauvaise idée de m'abréger comme ça, parce que, petit, j'avais le type français—d'après elle, les noms qu'on donne, ça déteint.

> [The car was a Citroën Ami 6. So they called me Ami 6 in memory. Those are my origins if you will. Eventually, Ami 6 became Aziz. Mamita, born a Rom in Romania where she was sterilized by the Nazis, always says that it was a bad idea to shorten me like that because, when I was little, I looked like a French boy—she reckons, you give someone a name, and the name rubs off.]

I suppose it is both tempting and reductive to assume that if a narrator tries to dissociate him- or herself from the name that will be received as an ethnic marker, that attempt is always a symptom of a painful alienation, the signature of an oppressed postcolonized subject. But Van Cauwelaert's text shows that we should not generalize. *Un aller simple* suggests that the apparently contingent connection between name and race is more systematic and predictable that the apparently natural connection between race and skin color or "type." What we see is not what we get. What we call people, is, however, exactly what they get in the end.

The narrators never explain, never theorize, and yet their strategic adoption of a fluctuating and apparently incoherent definition of what a name is could be described as the activist tip of the theoretical iceberg. I cannot say that a solid theoretical foundation informs their reappropriation of the proper or ethnic name, as such metaphor precisely glorifies a type of origin that is undermined by the narrators' humorous and apparently casual treatment of their own names. Without ever sacralizing either definition, without formulating their assumptions, the narrators constantly move from one definition of the name to another, sometimes claiming their individual identities, sometimes their statuses as members of groups, dreaming up new connections and new definitions.[16]

"Je n'étais qu'un môme, comme son nom l'indique" (Beyala 1992, 153) (I was only a kid, as the title indicates), says Loukoum. But this narrator has precisely no title to claim. The fact that he is a kid does not to justify the extreme powerlessness he has inherited. The beginning of this short sentence, is unremarkable, but, as usual, the end of the statement functions like a punch line, destabilizing a whole series of preconceptions. For the reader of *Le petit prince*, this "comme son nom l'indique" may sound both very familiar and still difficult to interpret. The elusive quality of the apparent simplicity is immediately revealed by attempts at translating it literally into English, for example. Should we understand the sentence to mean "as *his* name indicates" (did he mean *my* name?), or do we have to settle for "as the word "*môme*" indicates"? Or should we adopt a prescriptive attitude and simply declare that the use of "comme son nom l'indique" in this context is a grammatical mistake, an error. The pronoun is certainly up in the air. But then we would be policing some ideological frontier not unlike the border between nation-states. The slight distortion, emphasized by the inadequate translation, reveals that within the French language the boundary between name and word is porous, exposing stereotypical categories as severely damaged constructions. The child's name, precisely, does not appear. Yet the strangeness of the formula is a signature. In this case, authorship is a mark of chosen grammatical otherness. Children are vulnerable and innocent, or so the cliché tells us. Loukoum, on the other hand, criticizes the careless equation between his own lack of power and his young age. The stereotype of vulnerable childhood can easily mask the specific reasons for Loukoum's powerlessness. Loukoum is not just any child, and his situation is not reducible to his age. While the quoted cliché ("je n'étais qu'un môme") tends to accredit the comforting theory according to which it is only normal for a child to be so powerless and vulnerable, the reappropriation of the stereotype suddenly throws into stark relief the specific reasons why Loukoum's childhood is exceptionally tragic and confusing.

Saying "comme son nom l'indique" is meant as a shortcut. Usually, the phrase allows us to dispense with some form of explanation, of development. We rely on the fact that the audience will recognize an obvious reference and agree to tap a source of shared knowledge. In Beyala's novel, the phrase works precisely the other way around. It rereads the mental activity that consists of trusting someone's implicit claim to a layer of shared references. As a result, not only is the expression highlighted in this passage but subsequently it will continue to sound intriguingly and amusingly defamiliarized in other contexts. In the same way that the politician's wife unwillingly creates memorizable counterstereotypes in *La crise*, Loukoum effectively disarms a potentially dangerous series of equivalencies between a name and what is in it. Beyala disrupts a sensation of familiarity, shatters the impression of a shared cultural patrimony. The connection between all the minds dwelling on the same side of the border is suddenly exposed as a mosaic of discontinuities. Sentences such as "comme son nom l'indique" could now function as a signal, a revealing symptom of the presence of stereotypes that estrange rather than bring together members of the same linguistic community. When Momo meets the children of his upper-middle-class friend, he again uses a technically incorrect or at least incomplete formula: "Ils étaient vraiment sans aucun rapport" (222) (they didn't translate), he says.

At other times, the name does not disappear but proliferates and multiplies. For example, both Loukoum and Momo have names and what are normally thought of as nicknames, used only in private, among families and friends. Yet far from functioning like some kind of trivial detail, the nickname functions like a ghost, redoubling the heroes' identity, revealing and playing with arbitrary conventions. The first sentence of *Le petit prince de Belleville* reads: "Je m'appelle Mamadou Traoré pour la gynécologie, Loukoum pour la civilisation" (Beyala 1992, 8). Once again, necessarily imperfect efforts of translation highlight the areas of linguistic transgression. As the published translation correctly interprets, the sentence means: "My name is Mamadou Traoré according to my birth certificate; in everyday use it is Loukoum" (Beyala 1995, 1). Or, more literally, "My gynecological name is Mamadou Traoré. My civilized name is Loukoum."

Surprisingly, the child seems to equate the name he prefers with "civilization," perhaps to the surprise of readers who will note the orientalist connotations of "Loukoum." But what matters is that the child formulates the potentially schizophrenic split between several models and therefore refuses to internalize the contradiction. The postcolonial subject, expected to shift gears depending on the context, prefers to accumulate all the levels of experience in one strange sentence. Mamadou/Loukoum rewrites in his own way the difference between Béni and Ben Abdallah, the "écart" or split between what Fanon called Black Skin and White Masks (1967). Stereotypes and prejudices increase the painful separation between the two inseparable aspects of the child's identity but he finds original ways of negotiating the relationship to his own name.

In the first sentences of *Le petit prince de Belleville*, the negotiation directly resists the binary opposition between "we" and "you" (to which the reader implicitly belongs). If we wonder about the specific function of the "pour" that follows the two different names, we are forced to recognize that a whole theory of identity is presupposed. Usually, when a name is followed by "pour," the reader expects a clarification of the type "pour les intimes" or "pour les amis" (my friends call me . . .). It would be perfectly unremarkable for Loukoum to write: "Je m'appelle Mamadou Traoré, Loukoum, pour les intimes" (My name is Mamadou Traoré, my friends call me Loukoum). The intended audience would thus be separated into two categories: the narrator's friends and the others. In a sense, we are being asked to choose our side. Or at least we have to admit that the double name reflects a double identity (as well as the possibility of moving back and forth between several identities), and also that the difference between the two points depends entirely on an opposition between "les intimes" and others. But as we anticipate something like "pour les intimes" to function as the frontier between the two names, our expectations are frustrated and the distinction is framed by an incongruous opposition between gynecology and civilization, a binary pair that is apparently totally incomprehensible.

The separation between "we" and "you" is not abolished, but it starts functioning differently, displacing other comfortable pairs of concepts, asking insidious questions. Could the difference between "pour les intimes" and "for the rest of you" function like, or be the equivalent of, the opposition between "la gynécologie" and "la civilisation"? Gynecology is supposed to be a science or a medical practice, not an official filing system. As Beyala's translator quite aptly suggests, shouldn't the child's "real" name be a matter of the birth certificate rather than of gynecology? Is the text actually going as far as to say that there are links between gynecology and the collecting of information performed by state officials? Is the child actually reformulating Foucault's vision (1975, 1977) of a carceral society where hospitals become an extension of the prison? [17]

The narrators are thus capable of explicitly refusing the principle of association between their names and the stereotypes attached to them. They distance themselves not from their origin and from a certain ethnic group but from the value (or lack thereof) attached to certain origins and ethnic groups. Momo and Loukoum can both claim that they are proud of being "Arabe" and "Nègre" and still reject their official names, preferring "Loukoum" and "Momo," which they find more in keeping with their dignity, even if other characters may be stereotypically inclined to show respect by avoiding the familiar nickname. For example, as Momo is having a conversation with his grown-up friends, Ramon and Madame Nadine, they are suddenly interrupted by the arrival of the couple's two children. The mother introduces the narrator:

—Venez, je vous présente notre ami Mohammed, dit la mère.

Elle aurait pas dû dire Mohammed, ça fait cul d'Arabe en France, et moi quand on me dit ça, je me fâche. J'ai pas honte d'être arabe au contraire mais Mohammed en France, ça fait balayeur ou main-d'oeuvre. (222)

[—Come on in, let me introduce our friend Mohammed, the mother says.

She shouldn't have said Mohammed, it sounds like any old Arab asshole in France, and when people call me that, I get angry. I am not ashamed of being an Arab, in fact, I am proud of it, but Mohammed, in France, you see a garbage collector or a construction worker.]

Here, we have the opposite of the common name transformed into a proper name. Instead, the proper name can no longer to distinguish between "les intimes" and the rest. The phrase "notre ami Mohammed" is suddenly denounced as an ironic oxymoron since Mohammed means "garbage collector," "worker," or even "asshole."

The exact same principle is deployed in one of Beyala's scenes: Like Madame Nadine in *La vie devant soi*, Lolita, one of Loukoum's classmates, is portrayed as a generous character devoid of xenophobia and racial prejudice. But her intentions are betrayed by her way of using names. Lolita and Loukoum are apparently in love with each other, their "affair" continuing in *Mamant a un amant*, the sequel to *Le petit prince de Belleville*. The text makes it clear, however, that the presence of an interracial couple, or even their friendship, should not be equated with a simple solution. In fact, it is always difficult to ascertain whether Beyala's novels celebrate such possibilities or mock those who imagine that here is an adequate response to institutionalized racism.

Lolita always uses her friend's gynecological name, Mamadou, a choice the narrator obviously finds tasteless, even if the alternative sounds just as unappealingly exotic. Is the text warning us against such assumptions? At least, we are invited not to confuse the respect owed to an individual and the respect we systematically show for "l'officiel" (the record) or gynecology, which pairs a body and a name without criticizing the principle of cultural inheritance and origin.

When Loukoum arrives, Lolita introduces her friend:

Je vous présente mon ami Mamadou, elle a fait.

Loukoum, j'ai rectifié.

Je n'ai pas honte d'être nègre. Mais Mamadou, ça fait tirailleur sénégalais. Je n'allais tout de même pas entretenir la colonisation. (Beyala 1992, 163)

[Please meet my friend Mamadou, she said.

It's Loukoum, I corrected.

I am not ashamed of being black. But Mamadou sounds like Banania, you see a Senegalese rifleman. I was not about to support colonization after all.]

Even more explicitly than Momo does, Loukoum suggests that there is a link between neocolonialist mentalities and the names used by white characters. The children's intervention forces us to listen again to old banal formulas such as "my friend Mohammed," "my friend Mamadou" and to check whether the accusation is not at least partially justified.

As for Van Cauwelaert, he uses the opposite strategy to expose the contingency of racial and national identities. Because Aziz had to buy his passport, his "race" depends on the arbitrary choice of a last name adopted when his first set of fake IDs was manufactured. "J'ai aussi un nom de famille: Kemal. Je ne sais pas d'où ça vient. C'était peut–être l'année de K" (6) (I also have a last name: Kemal. I don't know where it comes from. Perhaps it was a K year). The reference to pedigrees accuses the system to treating him like a dog, but Aziz seems to accept the hypothesis quite calmly. On the other hand, his "pride" consists in refusing to adopt an identity that must be based on official papers:

Et puis si les gens ont besoin d'un faux papier pour se rendre compte que je suis français, je préfère rester arabe. J'ai ma fierté. (9)

[And if people need a fake ID to realize that I am French, I'd rather remain an Arab. I have my pride.]

The absence of official and legitimate lineage functions like an ironic counterstereotype. Momo says: "Au début je ne savais pas que je n'avais pas de mère et je ne savais même pas qu'il en fallait une" (Ajar 1975, 13) (At first, I was not aware I did not have a mother and I did not even know it was mandatory). Playing on the multiple meanings of "il faut" (one needs or one must), Momo challenges the confusion between prescription, need, and necessity. As for Loukoum, he quickly discovers that he "was immigrated just for family welfare payments" (Beyala 1995, 19, trans. slightly modified) ["j'avais été immigré juste pour les allocations familiales" (Beyala 1992, 34)]. Once again, the reappropriation of stereotypes operates at the level of grammatical and semantic distortions. If the dictionary is to be believed, immigrate is an intransitive verb, which makes the passive voice "to be immigrated" definitely incorrect. It also sounds strange, which is not necessarily the same. When writers want to reproduce the typical way of speaking of certain ethnic groups, they may choose to adopt constructions that would be considered substandard by grammarians but will, on the other hand, sound perfectly authentic to native speakers. Dropping the "ne" of negative verbal syntagmas is a completely innocuous way of signaling a colloquial dialogue. In other contexts, a glossary may be provided to allow the author or director to continue to use words that the reader is expected not to know (the director of *Hexagone* is apparently perfectly aware that his public may not be fluent in verlan). But in the three novels examined here, the type of agrammaticity seeks visibility.

Like a ghostly echo, "to be immigrated" keeps the trace of other sinister passive voices, such as "to be deported," as in Aziz's case. While the meaning of the sentence seems to accept the worst stereotypes about the reasons why Malians immigrate (all they want is to abuse the system), a barely noticeable use of the passive voice suddenly deprives the statement of its commonsensical thrust.

Similarly, Momo knows that his community cannot pretend to believe in the sanctity of origin and authenticity. He is well aware that he lives in a universe of fake IDs, of fake identities. Madame Rosa has her own forger as other people have their lawyer and "elle pouvait même prouver qu'elle n'avait pas été juive pendant plusieurs générations" (Ajar 1975, 35) (she was able to prove that she had not been Jewish for generations). In a most disturbing reversal of a supposedly aristocratic ritual (counting the generations of one's noble lineage), Madame Rosa invents a ritual of nonbelonging, of anti-identity. Not only are biological filiations uncertain, but their value is systematically denied by foster parents who invent an extremely strict set of ethics to replace stereotypical assumptions with new unofficial rules of generosity and solidarity.

It is very clear, for example, that a whole theory of contingency and rights is at work when Madame Rosa explains that the parent who deserves the child is not the biological father or mother, especially if the filiation in question manifested itself through the abandonment of the baby as the result of a more or less lucrative transaction. No Solomon is necessary here: when the "real" parents show up to claim their little princes, they are quickly kicked out, with the children's complicity. When Loukoum's biological mother starts yelling that she has got "documents" that prove that she has the right to claim her son, "M'an" retorts,

> Ça existe pas de droit, M'amzelle, j'le jure, au nom d'Allah. Y a que des devoirs et on peut pas dire que vous accomplissez les vôtres. . . . Moi les documents qui prouvent les choses ne m'intéressent pas. (Beyala 1992, 129)
>
> [Right has nothing to do with it, Mademoiselle, I swear in the name of Allah. There are only duties and I can't say you fulfill yours. . . . I am not interested in documents that prove things.]

This disregard for documents will certainly not facilitate the task of those who swear only by registers and official names. Similarly, when Momo's father, freed from the psychiatric institution in which he was confined after murdering his wife, barges into Madame Rosa's house to pick up his son, she suddenly pretends that Momo was raised as a Jew by mistake and that she has unfortunately made what she calls an "identical error" ("une erreur identique"): "L'identité, vous savez, ça peut se tromper également, ce n'est pas à l'épreuve" (Ajar 1975, 198) (You know, identity can get it wrong too, it is not foolproof). Far from gratuitous puns and amusing semantic approximations, the mothers' responses practice the art of avoiding the institutionalized violence of official identification processes. They propose a countermodel of filiation where people can choose a narratively constructed identity rather than inherit their rights and privileges thanks to the contingent accident of their place of birth.

Momo often chooses his parents among friends and neighbors: "Je pensais souvent en le regardant que si j'avais choisi un père, ce serait le docteur Katz que j'aurais choisi" (Ajar 1975, 31) (Watching him, I often thought that if I had chosen a father, I would have picked Dr. Katz). And it also seems possible to refuse a racial, cultural, or literary heritage that would be synonymous with alienation and madness. After literally neutralizing Momo's biological father—his heart stops when he understands that his son has become Jewish—Madame Rosa coldly and rather illogically concludes: "Et puis, un père qui a été psychiatrique, c'est pas du tout ce qu'il te faut parce que des fois c'est héréditaire" (203) (Besides, a psychiatric father, that's the last thing you need, in case it's hereditary).

The message of this implausible tale of reverse causality is, however, quite clear. The transmission of an origin, of a religion, of a language, of formative narratives is an activity that requires responsible interventions, and it is much too important to leave to chance. In our unreasonable world, it would be an unreasonable decision. Because history pretends to make you the inheritor of an alienated or racist father does not mean that you should be exonerated from the responsibility of rewriting your cultural heritage. The idea is to avoid reproduction or inheritance as the reproduction of intolerable structures.

Conclusion

Stereotypes and History from Astérix to Assia Djebar

The memorable quality that saturates most stereotypes has a directly distressing consequence for academics: Stereotypes are easy to teach.[1] Of course, we also know by now that iterativity goes both ways. Most teachers have at some point decided that it was worth stereotyping their thought to make some statement more memorable, in order to transmit it to an audience. It does not take much imagination to realize that the tactic is double-edged, but at the same time it is hopelessly optimistic to expect socialized human beings to spend their lives without ever being exposed to stereotypical constructions. All academic disciplines probably indulge in a love-hate relationship with the human faculty we loosely think of as memory. We tend to despise forms of memory that supposedly bypass conscious thinking processes, and we would like to think that mechanical rote memorization is a thing of the past as a pedagogical strategy. However, we celebrate memory as a valuable and indispensable part of our cultural environment. The assumption is that each type of memory involves very different mental skills. Sometimes, I wonder if we would not be better off exploiting the gray areas of overlap between the two types of memory rather than risking the development of a collective discourse that relies heavily on memorable, stereotypical, repeatable statements. The stereotype thieves—Isa and her host in *La crise*, Aziz, Momo, and Loukoum—all rely on memory for certain of their effects, but they are not actively involved in a conscious attempt to create memorable statements. If it happens, it is a by-product of their success.

When memory meets history and nations and state education, the result is quite different and sometimes spectacularly problematic. We have seen that it is possible to deploy imaginative tactics to counteract ethnic stereotypes, but what would happen if our identity itself was built like a stereotype by the history lessons that we learn as children, lessons that tell us who we are as a people, as a nation? Nothing is more dangerously unstable than the "we" in the previous paragraph, since the stereotype I will scrutinize here has everything to do with the construction of a community that different subjects may find violently exclusionary in spite of its benevolent rhetoric.

As Pierre Barbéris has remarked,

> tout stéréo dépend toujours étroitement:
> —d'un appris et donc d'un apprendre: école sauvage et buissonnière de la "sagesse des nations," école institutionnelle avec ses musts mémorisés et propagandes sous toutes ses formes hétéro-, intoxication et autre intoxication, culture, propagande;
> —de médias de diffusion, étroitement liées aux modes d'inculcation: oralité conforme, livres de classe, modèles littéraires, presse, radio, télévision, tout ce qui véhicule sur le mode de la répétition et d'un certain par coeur. L'apprendre, on le sait, n'est jamais neutre ni innocent. Mais son efficace dépend largement des moyens de sa diffusion. (Barbéris 1994, 10)
>
> [each stereotype depends on:
> —what is learned and therefore on the process of learning: on the haphazard teachings of "the wisdom of nations," on institutionalized schools with their memorized canonical musts, and on all kind of heterodisinformation, heteromanipulations and other manipulations, culture, propaganda;
> —on media of dissemination closely related to methods of teaching: conformist orality, textbooks, literary models, the press, radio, television, and on everything that circulates as repetition and through memorization. The teaching and learning apparatus, as we all know, is neither neutral nor innocent. But its effectiveness depends mostly on means of circulation.]

In these last pages, I explore the possibilities of both taking into account and resisting the almost unavoidable quality of effective teaching, especially when what is taught is the same as what is doing the teaching. That is, the truths of institutionalized education are collectively invented by the same "wisdom of nations," or perhaps by their "imagination," as Benedict Anderson might say (Anderson 1991). I will concentrate not only on what is stereotypical in what is learned but also on the stereotypical image of the learning subject constituted by what is learned and memorized.[2] By unsimplifying what is learned, it may be possible to imagine a nonstereotypical learner not satisfied by stereotypical visions of otherness because his or her own identity would not fit within the stereotypical distinction between "I" and "the Other."

But let me start from what can be the beginning of history lessons, from the most recognizable stereotypes in French or, for that matter, international historical discourse: a little phrase that, when quoted ironically, is all that one needs to satirize both a certain history of France and the entire colonial project: "our ancestors the Gauls." This little phrase, particularly its reference to "*my* ancestors," functions exclusively as a memorable stereotype. Here ancestors are both a stereotype and an invitation to transform myself, the reader, into a stereotypical learner that will resemble the object of study. The phrase functions like the beginning of a formula; it is the equivalent of other types of stereotypes. It takes, perhaps, a leap of bad faith to equate the "my ancestors" in "nos ancêtres les Gaulois" with the role assigned "les Portugaises" in *La crise*. But to follow the hypothesis to its logical extreme: What if "my ancestors" were not only a discursive but also a derivative construction, the by-product of acts of monumentalized stereotypification? What if my ancestors were *created* as stereotypes, rather than remembered?

Judging from the most recent reinvention of Clovis—one of "our" problematic ancestors whose identity can be claimed as easily by the Christians (as the first king to have been baptized) as by the secular Republicans who remember him as part of a "French" history—our ancestors seem to be the effect, rather than the cause of those national days that have been called "guided memory tours."[3] As Barbéris points out, they are closely dependent on the power of the media, and they structure events into memorable units, repeatable at will. Pierre Nora notes that a "*lieu de mémoire*" (place of commemoration) can easily become a "*lieu common*" ("common place") of memory (1992, 13), and commonplaces are easily structured as stereotypes.

Of course, when I stop worrying about the element of bad faith involved in equating "mes ancêtres les Gaulois" and "les Portugaises sont très propres," I also wonder about another pitfall: Should I bother flogging a dead horse? Does anyone believe any more that "our" ancestors looked like some serious version of Astérix-le-Gaulois? It may indeed be the case that this stereotype is not active anymore, that it has lost its currency precisely because we identify its stereotypical character. After all, it is now more or less unanimously accepted that it was inept to teach young colonized Africans that their ancestors were blond, blue-eyed warriors. But once again, the repeatability of the stereotype protects its poisonous core by making it look innocuous. Besides, it is obvious that in this case irony definitely does not shield us from the effects of the formula. I find the sardonic invocation of the formula "our ancestors the Gauls"—the very same formula once used by those who believed in it—a worrisome rhetorical gesture. By assuming that this is a dead stereotype, that everyone knows that it is idiotic, I do not then think about what exactly in this formulation fascinated and pleased. I suddenly fear that it is really a bit facile to poke fun at all those who used the formula during the colonial period in Africa or Asia or the Americas, now that the obviousness of its stupidity has become a hegemonic opinion, another cliché. As Charles-Robert Ageron notes in an article devoted to the Colonial Exposition of 1901,

> il devient difficile d'imaginer ce temps, proche encore, où triomphait avec bonne conscience, l'impérialisme colonial. Qui veut célébrer la République se garde de se

rappeler qu'elle s'est enorgueillie, quasi unanimement, de son oeuvre coloniale. (1984, 561)

[it becomes difficult to imagine that time, still quite near, where colonial imperialism triumphed in good conscience. He who wishes to celebrate the Republic would do well to remember that it took great, virtually universal pride in its colonial creation.]

Under the Third Republic, for example, what critical act, what intuition pushed some teachers to recognize that the history of this France was not universally valid? And what about classes today? Might I be teaching grandiose nonsense on the order of "our ancestors the Gauls" without realizing it? Is it not dangerous to assume that some sort of average level of education and political consciousness protects anyone from stereotypical knowledge memorized so long ago that its origin cannot be remembered?

As usual, we can hope that there is some point to defamiliarizing those mythical Gauls. Putting the expression itself into the frame of a historical narrative might defuse its stereotypical power, as Eugen Weber shows in *My France* (1991). The author points to something that should be obvious, and about which we think so little: "our ancestors the Gauls" themselves have a history, not as Gauls, but as a sentence, as a national symbol, and it was not always fashionable to claim that lineage. "Like camembert and vandalism, nos ancêtres les Gaulois are part of the legacy of the Revolution" (21). Weber's first chapter examines the evolution of symbolic power and the pertinence of the word "Gaul" as a political and electoral weapon: "Assertion of Gaulish descent stressed emancipation from servitude or the need and moral duty to bring this about" (33). He shows, for example, that the Revolution assimilated the Franks to the nobles, and the Third Estate was thus supposed to descend from the Gauls. However, the Revolution seems to have preferred Athens and Sparta to Alésia (23). The Franks, not the Gauls, were often constructed as our ancestors. As for Napoleon, when he felt the need to invoke a hero from the past, he usually preferred Charlemagne, not Vercingetorix or Clovis. Weber elegantly shows that the "Gauls" are certainly not natural ancestors and that they have a history as a national "commonplace of memory."

In other words, we now know that fighting stereotypes with stereotypes is never such a great idea and that resisting stereotypes with complex and sophisticated processes of defamiliarization may also miss the mark. It is not enough to show that the Gauls are not our "real" ancestors to deprive the stereotype of its power. In order to oppose, in the present, the immense affective power of the commemorative stereotypes that are likely to become idiotic in the near future, we need a warning sign, something that alerts us. And in the case of "our ancestors the Gauls," the grammatical element that should function as a red light is not the specific reference to the Gauls themselves but the conjunction of the adjective "our" and the word "ancestors." That is a telltale clue to the prefabricated aspect of the formula. The first-person adjective elicits reflexes of origins, legitimacy, authority, and lineage, and it is an invitation that claims unconditional loyalty. When the two words are brought together, "the moment of my ancestors" emerges, a rhetorical moment that is a dangerous symptom of propaganda at work. This stereotypical moment is avoidable if we refuse to accept the invitation to correspond to the identity thus invented.

Rather than attempting to analyze official ceremonies of commemoration, I will therefore survey the failures of the system of stereotypical historicization. I will look closely at all those moments when propaganda is declined and fails to turn into a memorized iterative stereotype, because either irony prevails, or the internal contradictions of a certain discourse are stronger than the solidifying forces of repetition, or a new learning subject emerges, ready to embrace new objects of study. Often, the creation of that new subject is a violent event because it sabotages the old stereotypical order. At the least, a discontinuity occurs that leaves a trace in our textbooks or literary narratives.

Sometimes, sabotage takes the form of profanation. A monument is destroyed, graffiti are carved on a commemorative plaque. Obviously, profanation is not an acceptable cultural practice. And calling a gesture a "profanation" forecloses discussions about the meaning of the act in question. Yet it is worth recognizing that such moments as "the moment of my ancestors" tend to refuse political or cultural criticism. Unless I actually admit that there may be some theoretical validity to the identification of "the moment of my ancestors"—that is, until I am willing to consider such a moment as a great purveyor of stereotypical formulas—"our ancestors the Gauls" does not permit irony.

For example, I blaspheme when I suggest that we could teach something new (construct new learning subjects) by systematically replacing "our ancestors the Gauls" with "our ancestors the Fellaghas," or "our ancestors the Moudjahiddin." The new formula would be just as problematic, just as idiotic, even though I now cringe before the judgmental adjectives. Imagine teaching, quite seriously, without a hint of irony "our ancestors the Fellaghas" instead of "our ancestors the Gauls" in the primary schools of the richest suburbs of Paris, precisely those suburbs where the number of "second-generation immigrants" would be statistically negligible, and not in the Goutte d'or neighborhood, for example, where people imagine that there is an imagined large population of children of Algerian origin. The issue of the replacement is precisely not to produce more "authentic" ancestors but to underline the frictions produced by the grouping of "our" with "ancestors." I am sure that the project would encounter a maximum amount of resistance, not only from those who believe in "our ancestors the Gauls" but also from those who would wish to make the Moudjahiddin true ancestors and national heroes.

In this specific historical case, no substitution is innocent, and this one even less than others. Even if I take into account the obvious attempt at structural reversal, my critical parody of the "moment of my ancestors" is obviously blasphemous because the present does not allow me to criticize the grammar of that statement.[4] Clearly, in France, the Algerian war does not tolerate flippant commemorations. It is bad enough that history books written for a wide public are still a recent phenomenon. And yet, I suggest that the provocation implicit in the ironic "moment of the Fellaghas" would be a way of renouncing that "moment of my ancestors" in favor of more ambivalent narratives that would defuse the stereotypical weapon of textbook history. But such forms of discourse and spectacle would be deemed unacceptably provocative because they would, for example, refuse to celebrate only victories, refuse to praise heroes, and refuse to believe that history does not make irredeemable mistakes.[5]

The Algerian historian-autobiographer-novelist Assia Djebar manages to walk this literal and political tightrope. Her work best theorizes and therefore disarms historical stereotypes. Internationally known and acclaimed for her uncompromising feminist stance, for the beauty of her lyrical and visionary prose as well as for the epic dimension of her rewriting of Algerian pasts and presents, Djebar also succeeds in inventing a literary genre that constitutes a radical intervention for the teaching of history. Her work as a whole, and two novels in particular, could be taught in parallel with conventional history books as a way of providing a framework of interpretation that would reveal both the inevitability of stereotypical constructions and the absolute necessity of recognizing their presence.

Both *L'amour la fantasia* (Fantasia: An Algerian Cavalcade) and *Le blanc de l'Algérie* (The white of Algeria) are autobiographical novels that seek to write and rewrite the immensely complex history of Algeria, to imagine and remember at the same time. *L'amour la fantasia* (1985) creates narrative and visionary links between the colonial conquest and the war of national liberation of 1954–1962, resuscitating or rather exhuming stories that some official accounts had carefully buried. *Le blanc de l'Algérie*, written in 1995, is a bold and defiant literary monument, a moving and extraordinarily unconventional *tombeau* to dead Algerian authors, who are lovingly placed within a history that many consider blasphemous because the author's immensely generous way of paying her respects amounts to a categorical refusal to enshrine and mummify her literary predecessors and longtime companions.

Djebar is fascinated by language, and her autobiographies are indistinguishable from a constant and meticulous attention to stories and idioms. Her ceaseless scrutiny of the effects of language, her meticulous analysis of words as well as her interest in historical reconstructions, allows her to find intriguing solutions to the problem of stereotyping. For example, I argue that one of the invaluable discoveries of her novels, autobiographies, and historical narratives can be described as the apparently minimalist yet strongly meaningful shift from "my" ancestors to "the" ancestors ("*les* Ancêtres"). This tiny difference, which often gets lost in the English translation, is a gift to the reader who discovers the possibility of preserving the notion of cultural heritage while rejecting the necessarily stereotypical reductions of nationalist commemorations.[6]

In *L'amour la fantasia*, Djebar reveals, unearths, or brings to light (the choice of metaphor is crucial and mimetic in relationship to the text) one of the most odious episodes of the war of conquest that made Algeria a French colony: General Pélissier's 1845 massacre of a tribe of five thousand Berbers. None of the Berbers lived to tell the tale. Men, women, and children had hidden in caves where they thought they would be safe, but they all died when the French army smoked them out. If Djebar's only merit was to draw attention to the gruesome ruthlessness of the colonial conquest, her novel would already be worth recommending to French history students. It is an invitation to compare the often totalizing logic of textbooks (Who won the battle, who lost? Who was the conqueror, who was the conquered?) to this careful recording of minute human details and the explicit mixture of imagined and remembered or rewritten stories, a position that questions the very definition of historical facts.[7]

But *L'amour la fantasia* goes further than redefining the framework of interpretation; it confronts the sometimes contradictory imperatives of language, narrative, nationalism, and ethics. The narrator of the novel is fascinated by Pélissier's reaction to the mass murder for which he is responsible. After the deed, the officer ordered the bodies brought out into the open. Then, he wrote his report to the parliament. In *L'amour la fantasia*, Djebar explains:

> Les corps exposés au soleil; les voici devenus mots. Les mots voyagent. Mots, entre autres, du rapport trop long de Pélissier; parvenus à Paris et lus en séance parlementaire, ils déclenchent la polémique: insultes de l'opposition, gêne du gouvernement, rage des belliscistes, honte éparpillée dans Paris où germent les prodromes de la révolution de 48.
>
> Canrobert, lieutenant-colonel en garnison dans ce même Dahra, livrera son jugement plus tard: "Pélissier n'eut qu'un tort: comme il écrivait trop bien et qu'il le savait, il fit dans son rapport une description éloquente et réaliste, beaucoup trop réaliste, des souffrances des Arabes." (1992, 93)[8]

> [The bodies exposed to the sun; here they have become words. Words travel. Words, among others, in Pélissier's overlong report; when they arrive in Paris and are read at a parliamentary session, they unleash a polemic: insults from the opposition, embarrassment from the government, rage from the warmongers, shame scattered in Paris where the premonitory symptoms of the '48 revolution germinate.
>
> Canrobert, lieutenant colonel at the garrison of the same Dahra, will deliver his judgment later: Pélissier made only one mistake: he wrote too well and he knew it. In

his report he wrote an eloquent and realistic description—much too realistic—of the Arabs' suffering.]

What Djebar discovers is that Pélissier's flagrant error was to get his public interested in the story of somebody else's ancestors. That is, apparently, heresy. It happened by chance, by mistake, not because he was trying to commemorate an event but because his grammar, or the style of his commemorative discourse, provoked an almost mimetic reaction. Pélissier could not leave the dead corpses alone; he had to take them out in the open. Mesmerized by his account, we become like him. We can no longer bury the case. If Canrobert is to be believed, Pélissier committed the sin of writerly pride. Today, we may be outraged by Pélissier's decision to kill the Berber tribe and mentally catalogue him as a war criminal, but the concept is anachronistic, and the story does not owe its power of revelation to hindsight. It is the *contemporary* reaction to Pélissier's report that Djebar is interested in, and the shattering of a stereotypical consensus occurred as the result of specific characteristics of the text rather than as a "normal" human reaction to what we can now unanimously describe as atrocities. Pélissier provoked an outcry among the parliamentarians not because he was a monster, but because he was too successful as an artist, as a writer. His "lieu de mémoire," his commemorative monument, is, literarily speaking, particularly successful. Obviously, that coincidence chafes. He was not criticized for having established commemoration where there was none (he was not criticized for having told the truth), but he was blamed for creating a space of memory that one cannot easily summarize nor describe except in terms of literary criticism: "an eloquent and realistic description—much too realistic." Implicitly, we are told that certain commemorations would be more acceptable if they were expressed in nonpoetic language, in bad writing. The memory of the massacre thus becomes the site of an intolerable coincidence: The truth is told because of Pélissier's literary ambitions. The commemorative text is diverted in the name of literary fame rather than in the name of human values. Confronted by that gesture, Djebar's originality is to preserve a double and contradictory reaction of gratitude and denunciation that finally complicates the idea that the French and the Algerians are forever condemned to respect two distinct and hostile set of ancestors.[9]

In her *Transfigurations of the Maghreb*, Winnifred Woodhull notes that there is a sort of counterpoint between Pélissier's gesture (he exhumes the bodies rather than letting them lie buried in the cave-tombs as other officers did) and that of Djebar, who brings the massacre to light (Woodhull 1993, 84). What interests me here is precisely that the ceremonial consists in *exhuming*, not in giving a burial place or in constructing a monument. Yet at the same time, the novel itself is a monument, though its very shape is hollowed by Djebar's refusal to celebrate "her" ancestors in a simplistic manner. Normally, or rather mythically (as with Antigone), the scandal is to deprive the body of proper burial. To bring into the open the story of these rapidly decaying bodies is to suggest that here, commemoration is not on the side of marble but on the side of what is normally considered a profanation: exhumation, decomposition. Every act of commemoration that refuses the "moment of my ancestors" always contains an element of profanation because it produces a cultural text that is not a monument nor a funeral ceremony but rather a destruction of the very idea of tombstones and burial. Naturally, such complicated nonmonuments will be both feared and attacked by those who tell simpler narratives of who the ancestors are, of what historical truth is. And Djebar takes great risks.

Here, the commemorative site is synonymous not with a funeral ceremony but with a form of exhumation that recalls both the act of vandals and the autopsy. The taboo question this text raises is whether it might be appropriate to commemorate an ignoble act by means of an another ignoble commemoration. Pélissier's report is so remarkably split and ironic that it does not correspond to any of the stereotypical motives for memorializing (the "never again" or an act of mourning that touches "us" in so far as "we" belong to the same family, facing the enemy that must be kept separate in our memories). Pélissier, who had just murdered five thousand people, obviously had no ancestors among the dead rotting in the sun. And that absence of direct ancestral relationship distinguishes him from Assia Djebar, who could easily claim all the dead as her ancestors. She does anchor her commemoration in an "us" bound up by a certain idea of legitimate lineage, so in a sense it appears that her text is in great danger of being immediately reappropriated by those who search for stereotypical narratives about "our" ancestors. At first, Djebar's commemorative gesture seems perhaps less subversive than that of the damnable officer because her text appears to follow a logic of the national, or at least a principle of identification with "my" people.

Au sortir de cette promiscuité avec les enfumés en haillons de cendre, Pélissier rédige son rapport qu'il aurait voulu confidentiel. Mais il ne peut pas, il est devenu à jamais le sinistre, l'émouvant arpenteur de ces médinas souterraines, l'embaumeur quasi fraternel de cette tribu définitivement insoumise . . . Pélissier . . . me tend son rapport et je reçois ce palimpseste pour y inscrire à mon tour la passion calcinée *des* ancêtres. (97, my emphasis)

[Emerging from this promiscuity with the corpses dressed in scorched rags, Pélissier writes his report, which he would have liked to keep confidential. But he cannot. He became forever the sinister, the moving surveyor of those subterranean medinas, the almost fraternal embalmer of that definitively unsubjugated tribe . . . Pélissier . . . passes me his report and I receive that palimpsest to inscribe upon it in turn the charred passion of *the* ancestors.]

On the one hand, the presence of "ancestors" modifies completely the space from which memory (or memorability) emanates by introducing a lineage, a historical "us" that links the narrator to the burnt Berber tribes and that excludes all non-Berber readers who do not have any ancestors there. It is clear that *L'amour la fantasia* is not written from the point of view of French colonizers, even if the text is addressed to a French-speaking audience that includes them. But note that Djebar does not write "my" ancestors. With this gaping absence of a possessive pronoun (and "possession" here takes on its strongest possible sense), Djebar changes the whole matrix of stereotypical historical narratives. History remains a palimpsest and is not treated like a repossessed object. Djebar allows layers of writings to accumulate rather than proposing an alternative genealogy that would be constructed on the same model as the one she wishes to contest.

The novel thus manages to both exhume and create a commemoration that does not look like an erected monument. Pélissier unearthed his dead victims in an admission of guilt or at least of responsibility, while Djebar recognizes that "no ceremony lasting an hour or a day [would] take place, they [would] not be bathed nor enshrouded" (92) and her own text is itself a linguistic nonceremony, a nonevent, a structuring absence that speaks louder than words. It is in the absence of a culturally codified ceremony that the nonstereotypical commemorative power of the act resides, and it is the originality and the merit of Djebar's text to mirror and echo the historical profanation without diminishing its ambivalence. Her novel becomes a new story that refuses to give Caesar his laurels. Pélissier is "the *almost* fraternal embalmer of that definitively unsubjugated tribe" (my emphasis). And because the fraternal solidarity that Pélissier embodies evokes the fraternity of the French constitution as well as the duel between Cain and Abel, I prefer it to a "we" that would appeal to the real, authentic ancestors and would unavoidably veer toward the stereotype of common mourning. Djebar's criticized attachment to the French language may be a symbol of the decision by a postcolonial author to refuse the simple reclaiming of a different heritage that one could glorify in exactly the same way as the "Gauls" of the stereotype. Djebar's text is attentive to those moments of blasphemous encounters between commemoration and exhumation because they best articulate the contradictions that official texts tend to erase. Pélissier's report does not try to eliminate his complicity; he does not try to clear himself nor to forget. But because he is complicitous in the massacre to a literal degree, his text becomes the incongruous model of the guilty commemorator who does not position himself as the hero beyond reproach. And because he is responsible for the act of barbarism that his report keeps in the public record, he may become a model to every historical subject who can neither completely disengage him or herself from a national past nor renounce the right to judge it intolerable.

For example, if I had said, at the beginning of this text, that I wanted to dedicate my thoughts to the memory of Félix Germon, whose body was unearthed during the profanation of the Jewish cemetery in Carpentras on May 10, 1990, I would not have known how to formulate my dedication without falling into the stereotypical language that saturated the media at the time. The story was turned into a symbolic battle between the National Front and human decency. Personally, I thought it was a bit of a shame for Mr. Germon and his relatives. But what to do? In order for my act to be as effective as Pélissier's, will it be necessary for me to write a "too realistic" story that will inevitably cause violent reactions among the public? And if I refrain from realism in the name of good taste, am I refusing to intervene, to accept that my positioning cannot be that of the neutral observer? Naturally, should I choose to write a Pélissier-like report, I immediately offer my text up to charges of voyeurism and unhealthy sensationalism. Almost three years to the day after the exhumation, Alain Peloux wrote:

> Le 10 mai 1990, deux soeurs venues se recueillir sur la tombe d'un proche enterré dans le cimetière israélite découvraient avec horreur le corps d'un défunt exhumé et placé sur une tombe dans un simulacre d'empalement. Sur la dépouille profanée de Félix Germon est déposée une étoile de David tandis qu'une énigmatique inscription funéraire est placée entre ses jambes: "Souvenir des voisins." (Peloux 1993, 11)

> [May 10, 1990, two sisters who had come to pay their respect to a close relative buried in the Jewish cemetery discovered, to their horror, a corpse dug up and placed on a tombstone in simulation of an impalement. A Star of David had been placed on the profaned remains of Félix Germon while an enigmatic funeral inscription was found between his legs: "a souvenir from the neighbors."]

Three years after the event, why take up all the macabre details published by the newspapers in 1990, including the much-discussed "simulation of an impalement"? It was certainly not the only possible discourse. In 1990 and later, certain voices had opted to hide either the details or even refused to mention the event itself (for reasons, I hasten to say, which were not necessarily of the order of denial or indifference). One year after the profanatory exhumation, for example, an article in *Le Monde* was entitled "The Silences of Carpentras" (Bernard 1991). It must be noted that the "silences" in question were certainly not passive; *Le Monde* was talking about a deliberate decision of non-commemoration. One of the paper's journalists had interviewed a member of the Jewish community, and he had expressed surprise that no ceremony had marked the anniversary of the profanation. To his question, he got the following answer from Joseph Amar, vice president of the Jewish cultural association: "Why would you have us commemorate that act of barbarism?" Here, the absence of commemoration is justified by the fear of seeing the memorializing gesture confused with the act that it commemorates, as if barbarism might contaminate the ceremony or the discourse itself. Similarly, one year after the profanation, the 1991 issue of *Universalia* (the yearly supplement to the *Encyclopaedia universalis*) reports the event but makes sure not to make the same mistake as Pélissier: no "too realistic description," no controversial details. The article is entitled, "France: Indignation after the Profanation of the Jewish Cemetery of Carpentras" (46): "Dans la nuit du 9 au 10, trente-quatre sépultures du cimetière Juif de Carpentras, un des plus importants et des plus anciens de France, sont profanées" ("During the night of May 9–10, thirty-four tombs in the Jewish cemetery of Carpentras, one of the oldest and largest in France, were desecrated"). And the article insists on a wave of so-called unanimous indignation that swept France after the news was reported:

L'indignation des milieux politiques est unanime: tandis que François Mitterrand appelle les Français à "se ressaisir," Michel Rocard exprime son "horreur," et tous les dirigeants de l'opposition font part de leur soutien à la communauté juive. Seul Jean-Marie Le Pen, qui dénonce "les professionnels de l'anti-racisme" s'élève contre une "provocation." L'enquête policière s'oriente sans résultat vers les milieux des skinheads et de l'extrême droite méridionale. Le 14, alors que de nouvelles profanations de cimetières juifs, mais aussi catholiques ont eu lieu les jours précédents et qu'une cérémonie religieuse a réuni la veille à Carpentras des personnalités de tous les horizons, ainsi que des milliers de personnes, le Conseil représentatif des institutions juives de France (CRIF) auquel se joignent tous les partis politiques sauf le Front National, appellent "tous les hommes et les femmes qui refusent la haine, l'intolérance et l'exclusion" à participer, à Paris, à une manifestation "pour la justice, la liberté et la démocratie." Environ deux cent mille personnes piétinent, plus qu'elles ne défilent, entre la place de la République et celle de la Bastille. Fait sans précédent, le président de la République se joint pour la première fois à une manifestation non officielle, suivi par un grand nombre d'hommes politiques, de la majorité comme de l'opposition. (Lorsignil et al. 1991, 46)

[The political world is uninamously outraged. While François Mitterrand calls upon the French to "pull themselves together" Michel Rocard expresses his "horror," and all the leaders of the opposition reiterate their support for the Jewish community. Only Jean-Marie Le Pen, who denounces the "professional antiracists," speaks out against a "provocation." The police investigation targets the skinhead community and the extreme right of southern France, but no arrests are made. The 14th, while new profanations of Jewish but also of Catholic cemeteries occurred during the previous days and while, the night before, a religious ceremony brought leaders from all political parties to Carpentras, as well as thousands of demonstrators, the Representative Council of Jewish Institutions in France (RCIF), joined by all the political parties except the National Front, call "all men and women who refuse hatred, intolerance and exclusion" to participate in a demonstration in Paris "for justice, liberty and democracy." About two hundred thousand people crowd, more than march, between the Place de la République and the Place de la Bastille. In an unprecedented act, the President of the Republic joins an unofficial demonstration and is followed by a large number of other political leaders from the majority as well as the opposition.][10]

The tone is measured, no detail of the profanation is cited; only the consequences of the profanation, the demonstrations, the public manifestations of solidarity seem to be worth citing. In other words, we remember a series of public and collective actions that "we" can be proud of, in which we could fully participate.[11] History invites us to side with an antiracist France governed by a president whose exceptional gesture is celebrated by the press. We are also invited to believe that the profanation was condemned by a unanimous political spectrum. One forgets that the reaction was not unanimous. One wishful adjective is not enough to eliminate the presence of the National Front from French politics. We are expected to believe, in spite of past history, that "we" would all be enraged by any profanation of a Jewish cemetery.

What had happened to all this commemorative energy on January 1 and 2, 1993, when two Jewish cemeteries were profaned in Strasbourg? Which Pélissier was missing from this other act of barbarism committed far from an audience capable of reacting indignantly to a "too realistic" description? If the French can pride themselves on the fact that France was "unanimous" (or rather visible in the media) in condemning the exhumation of Félix Germon, was that rage not a function of a story that itself was profanatory, that like Pélissier's account refused to bury the details, dragging the body into the light at the risk of abjection? I am not trying to absolve the journalists whose motives were perhaps sordid—that case has been tried very often. But I suggest that the macabre stories have the same consequences as Pélissier's report. They unearth what, in the act itself, remains unacceptable, unforgettable. If on the contrary, for example, a newspaper editor had refused the story because it made the commemoration uncannily similar to the profanation itself, it might have nipped in the bud the desirable outbreak of demonstrations and the eminently necessary political consequences that correspond to the polemic that Pélissier's report unleashed in the parliament.[12] Naturally, there is no guarantee that I better serve the memory of Félix Germon by keeping alive the memory of the insult that was inflicted upon his body, with which my act of commemoration is now complicitous. Even supposing that I could be, like Pélissier "a good writer," capable of "realistic and eloquent description" (and what happens if I'm not?), my act of commemoration does not put him to rest and does not erase the outrage. But perhaps I am putting the problem incorrectly. Perhaps I must seek out, rather than regret, those moments of commemoration where coincidences proliferate (a "good story" is coupled with an "ignoble event"), where disturbing resemblances abound (the insult resembles the commemorative act), or, on the contrary, where disturbing symbolical reversals beg to be interpreted ("to unearth" comes to mean the same thing as "to bury with dignity"). The parasitical noise that interferes with the ambivalent commemorative ceremony (that polemic which occurs after Pélissier's report, or my confusion about the dedication that I could have offered the old man) prevents memory from congealing and becoming a ready-made cliché, a stereotypical "moment of my ancestors." More important, it prevents the act of commemoration from being coopted by an ideology, by politics, by those parties that express their indignation and refuse to recognize their share of responsibility in the event that now elicits indignation and horror. As Césaire says,

> On s'étonne, on s'indigne. On dit "Comme c'est curieux! Mais bah! C'est le nazisme, ça passera!" Et on attend, et on espère; et on se tait à soi-même la vérité, que c'est une barbarie, mais la barbarie suprême, celle qui résume la quotidienneté des barbaries. (1989, 12)
>
> [People are surprised, people are indignant. They say, "How curious! But never mind! It's Nazism, it will pass!" And they wait, and they hope; and they never admit the truth, that it is barbarism, yes, but only the supreme barbarism that sums up everyday barbarism.]

In recalling my own ancestors, I tend to forget that I choose and that I invent a collective family tree. I thus risk falling into a naturalizing definition of history that suggests that I am personally answerable for everything that history books define more or less arbitrarily as the past that belongs to me as a historical subject. I suggested earlier that it was probably blasphemous to joke about "our ancestors the Fellaghas," and it may well be worth asking what an author can do when blasphemy becomes a crime punishable by death. In *Le blanc de l'Algérie* (The white of Algeria), Assia Djebar courageously answers the question by writing a most unconventional literary monuments to three of her close friends murdered in 1993, the first two in Algiers and the third one in Oran[13]:

> Mahfoud Boucebci: psychiatre et auteur, mort le 15 juin 1993, à 54 ans, à Birmandreis (Alger) (assassiné).
>
> M'Hamed Boukhobza: sociologue et auteur, mort le 27 juin 1993, à 55 ans, à Alger (assassiné).
>
> Abdelkader Alloula: auteur dramatique, atteint le 11 mars 1993, à Oran, mort à Paris le 15 mars, à 55 ans (assassiné). (1995b, 278)
>
> [Mahfoud Boucebci: psychiatrist and writer, died June 15, 1993, at fifty-four years of age, at Birmandreis (Algiers) (murdered).
>
> M'Hamed Boukhobza: sociologist and writer, died June 17, 1993, at fifty-five years of age, in Algiers (murdered).
>
> Abdelkader Alloula: playwright, shot March 11, 1993, in Oran, died in Paris on March 15, fifty-five years old (murdered).]

Once again, Djebar's text grapples with death, with history, and with the desire to invent ceremonies and rituals that will not betray the friendly ghosts who continue to haunt her. Throughout the book, the narrator speaks to her lost friends and they answer: "ces chers disparus; ils me parlent maintenant; ils me parlent. Tous les trois; chacun des trois" (15) (My dear lost ones; they talk to me now, they talk to me. All three of them, each of the three). While the media usually respond to an intellectual's death with a prepackaged collection of images and reductive formulas, *Le blanc de l'Algérie* suggests that a dialogue still takes place and that the form of the commemoration is negotiated between the living and the dead, the living refusing to abuse the privilege of the monologue. Each of the dead she evokes is resuscitated through a narrative that explores not only the context of his or her death but the possible model offered by people's reaction to this disappearance.

Often, Djebar's unconventional reports breaks the mold of stereotypical commemorations by refusing to abide by certain implicit narrative laws. For example, when she remembers a colloquium held in Brussels in 1988 to celebrate Kateb Yacine's work in the presence of the author, her memory resuscitates the novelist and essayist through a most unexpected detail. She does not remember a particularly meaningful speech (Yacine had announced that he would not comment on the Algerian situation) or a particularly striking and flattering delivery or remark; she remembers his feet. "De la salle où je me trouvais, je fus assez vite fascinée par les pieds de Kateb. . . . il allongeait ses jambes et soudain, ses pieds dans des baskets assez volumineux prirent pour moi toute la place sur l'avant scène" (182) (From the room where I was, I rapidly became fascinated by Kateb's feet. . . . he stretched his legs and suddenly, his feet in his rather bulky sneakers took up all the room for me). Djebar's text refuses to sing the conventional and official song of praises, and yet a strange and unforgettable vision manages to express, or perhaps to demonumentalize, the obvious admiration she has for Yacine's work. Statues and sneakers are incompatible. The rather grotesque close-up on inelegant sneakers and the narrator's affectionate respect are not. Yet, disturbed by the conventional setting, she is suddenly capable of formulating her distaste for the very principle of commemoration:

> Un malaise me prit. Je sortis discrètement. Debout en bas, devant une tasse de café, je fus rejointe par Nabile Farès. J'ai essayé d'expliciter devant celui-ci ma gêne: comme un noeud en moi contre ce genre de commémoration, peut-être aussi contre toutes les commémorations. (183)
>
> [Suddenly, I did not feel well. I left discreetly. Downstairs, as I was standing in front of a cup of coffee, Nabile Farès joined me. I tried to formulate my uneasiness: like a knot in me against that type of commemoration, perhaps against any type of commemoration.]

The most unconventional aspect of Djebar's literary monument is her desire to unite apparently incommensurable deaths on the same narrative tombstone. Her refusal to heed the call for legitimate ancestors takes the form of a list printed at the end of the book, where each individual is celebrated regardless of which side he or she was on. In Djebar's memorial, the very principle of the list is deconstructed by her deliberate refusal to constitute sets of people according to stereotypical formulas (nationality, ethnicity, or even gender). In this self-critical list, the reader finds not only the expected heroes killed during the war of independence, but also intellectuals murdered by anonymous Algerian hands in 1993, and perhaps most remarkably, people who committed suicide, or who died in an accident, or were claimed by illness. Djebar's list of her dead is the opposite of a nationalistic cemetery overshadowed by a national flag. The list thus pays the same respectful homage to Mouloud Feraoun, a victim of the war of liberation ("romancier, mort le 14 mars 1962, à 49 ans, à Alger [assassiné par l'O.A.S]") (277) (novelist, died March 14, 1962, forty-nine years old, in Algiers [murdered by the O.A.S]), to Josie Fanon, who killed herself ("journaliste morte le 13 juillet 1989, à 60 ans, à El Bier [Alger] [suicide]") (journalist, died July 13, 1989, at sixty years of age, at El-Biar [Algiers] [suicide]), and to her husband Frantz Fanon, who died at thirty-six of leukemia ("essayiste, psychiatre, mort le 6 décembre 1961, à 36 ans, près de New York [leucémie]"). The very first name on this list also represents a deliberate will to refuse certain apparently obvious partitionings between (literary) ancestors: "Albert Camus: romancier, auteur dramatique, mort le 4 janvier 1957, sur la route de Villeblevin, Yvonne (accident de voiture)" (Albert Camus: novelist, playwright, died January 4, 1957, on Villeblevin Road, Yvonne [car accident]). Camus's presence alongside the Fanons is bound to be perceived as an intolerable gesture of provocation by some and as a remarkable poetic and political statement by others.

Finally, the most daring intervention of Djebar's monument is to create parallels between groups of individuals that history represents as two completely waterproof communities. *Le blanc de l'Algérie* refuses to separate the past and the present, Europeans and Arabs. The author does not only speak up against torture as a thing of the past, she specifically denounces what she sees as a sort of perverse heritage that cuts across generations, nations, across the colonizer/colonizer divide: "Maintes fois, je me suis demandé comment s'est faite la passation dans cette capitale du soleil, la passation entre tortionnaires?" (216) (I often asked myself how this transfer between torturers had occurred in this sunny capital). The book even demystifies the sacred opposition between the liberators and the oppressors during the war of national liberation, suggesting that some Algerian rebels were killed by other Algerian rebels who then turned their victims into official war heroes. The narrator tells several versions of how Abane Ramdane was killed by his own and regrets that his *tombeau* or literary monument remains to be written. In the meantime, Abane Ramdane is portrayed as a wandering ghost whose relationship to other dead authors remains a matter of chance encounter (151).

Traditional ceremonies, the invocation of "our" ancestors, on the other hand, often presuppose a homogeneity of our present about to become the substance of our past, an abstract entity stereotypically imagined as unifiable. Yet just as there are ideas and acts that we wish to oppose in the present, there is no reason to accept or refuse the past as a unit, even if we cut it into positive or negative periods, defeats and victories, moments of resistance and moments of collaboration. "My ancestors" are, unfortunately, the Vichy regime as well as De Gaulle's call to resist. And the consequences of the choices we make today are not less weighty.

If I recoil from the stridency of profanatory acts of commemoration as the only antidote to stereotypes, other ambivalent narratives are possible that would just as effectively put into question commonplaces of memory. Opposed to the "moment of my ancestors" are not only profanatory exhumations but also literal and metaphorical disfigured monuments that inscribe memory as a hodgepodge palimpsest, eternally written over with more or less legitimate inscriptions. Like the rewritten stereotypes of Ajar and Beyala's novels, disfigured monuments both benefit from and sabotage stereotypical iterativity. The disfigured monument can effectively take the form of a tombstone marred by graffiti, of a stele upon which vandals have left their mark. But the disfigured monument can also take a less tragic and certainly much more official shape. By "disfigured monument" I mean a historical scribbling that changes its mind about earlier stories without really erasing the former version, even if it has become quite unorthodox. Take, for example, the statue of Joséphine de Beauharnais that stood in the Parc de la Savanne in Fort de France until it was decapitated in the summer of 1991. The anonymous executioner left behind an ambiguous monument, a reflection of the ambivalence of the statue of the empress. This form of unclaimed disfigurement is not structurally different from the will to dememorialize that ends in the destruction of other statues, changes in the names of cities (Leningrad reverting to Saint Petersburg), and changes in protocol, however desirable they may be (such as François Mitterrand's refusal to visit Maréchal Pétain's tomb after 1993). Rather than interpreting these modifications as instances of repentance, or even as positive changes, one could perceive them as the ironic principle of the disfigurement of monuments. As soon as a commemorative plaque is installed, as soon as a date and a name are canonized, an undermining process begins, opposing voices are heard, rewritings appear, that forever threaten the official and consensual meaning of the commemorative act. If that undermining process had been at work in the 1940s, then Vichy would perhaps not have the same significance today.

Several conflicting narratives may coexist in official history, and memories subsist, linked like the two faces of an ironic Janus. A memory never replaces another memory; the first one is not erased but disfigured or rewritten. It survives like a disordered and contradictory text, both in individual memories and in official texts. It would, for example, be very amusing and very instructive to study the administrative disorder that occurs when the names of cities or streets are modified. How much confusion and how many comic or tragic misunderstandings are doubtlessly caused by the impossibility of erasing layers of individual memory, even if the eraser is official, governmental? To replace Leningrad with Saint Petersburg is an act of commemoration undermined by its own logic. It makes apparent that Saint Petersburg is a name just as charged with ideology and history as the one that temporarily replaced it. Moreover, the new name does not forget Lenin, but only superimposes itself on him. It only symbolizes the lack of consensus that surrounded Lenin's memory and the instability of all attempts at commemoration. The change of name makes me doubt that it is reasonable to name eternal cities after heroes. In spite of what Baudelaire says, the heart of mortals apparently changes more rapidly than the form of cities.

That ambiguous moment of disfiguring, however, may be a most interesting moment when two memories overlap, and it bears witness to the ambiguity of human memory. As sociologists Christian Bachmann and Luc Basier write: "La temporalité propre aux imageries fait qu'elles ne se s'annulent pas brusquement mais qu'elles se raturent et se désintègrent" (1989, 40) ("The temporality specific to images results not in a sudden canceling out but in a crossing out and disintegration").[14] To want to forget at any cost is never a guarantee of forgetting, just as a desperate will to remember is not a guarantee of memory. And it may be desirable not to suppress, to in fact encourage contradictory overlaps of memories, those superimpositions that prevent an ideology from triumphing too easily, from imposing its privileged story. Because if some can congratulate themselves on seeing Lenin's statue lying in pieces, others might consider that those pieces are a healthy warning to those who believe that statues of liberty are inalterable. We may prefer the ceremonies that confirm the fundamentally double and ambivalent quality of those official memories that constitute the history of a nation. We may want to refuse the principle according to which one only commemorates victories and not defeats, the principle according to which governments invite only the former victors to commemorative ceremonies. The mirror effect or *mise en abyme* of Pélissier's text by Djebar's is another form of superimposition, of Derridean "*rature*" (simultaneous erasure and palimpsest), of an accumulation of memory that resists the burial or the anniversary ceremony. On the other hand, other formulas are possible. In a 1992 article, for example, Patrick Jarreau evokes the case of that burdensome date March 19, 1962, that saw an end to the Algerian war after the signing of the Evian treaty. The controversies around that date denounce the often transparent principles that govern commemoration. No one reexamines the fact that this date itself became an event. Simply, if one takes as a point of departure the principle that official history is bent on making the national heritage a series of glorious stories, a heroic saga, it is clear that March 19, 1962, does not necessarily fit the bill.

Les mairies communistes de la Seine-Saint-Denis avaient donné ce nom à des rues ou à des places, se souvient M. Eric Raoult, député (RPR) de ce département. Elles répondaient ainsi à une revendication de la FNAC, la fédération nationale des anciens combattants, qui souhaite la commémoration régulière de la fin de la guerre d'Algérie. L'Union nationale (UNCAFN) est opposée, elle, à cette célébration: fête-t-on Waterloo ou Azincourt? . . . Le 19 mars, dit M. Raoult, c'est la fin du conflit, mais ce n'est pas le 11 novembre 1918 ou le 8 mai 1945. Ce n'est pas une date de concorde nationale. On y a laissé un peu de l'honneur de notre pays. (17)

[Mr. Eric Raoult, (RPR) deputy of Seine-Saint-Denis, remembers that the communist mayors of that department had given this name to some streets or squares. They were responding to a request made by the FNAC, the National Federation of War Veterans, which wanted a regular commemoration of the end of the Algerian war. The National Union (UNCAFN) was opposed to that celebration: Is Waterloo or Agincourt celebrated? March 19, said Mr. Raoult, is the end of the conflict, but it isn't November 11, 1918, or May 8, 1945. It is not a date of national harmony. Some of our country's honor was lost there.]

In other words, commemoration is in bad faith and accepts its status as stereotypical discourse. This is what Uderzo and Gosciny, authors of the famous *Astérix* series, have remarkably illustrated by inventing characters who start yelling hysterically when asked where Alésia is (Uderzo and Gosciny 1968, 12, 19). In French history books and in some national imaginary and mythic narrative, Alésia is as powerful a symbol as "our ancestors the Gauls." Every one knows that Alésia is the place where Vercingetorix surrendered to Julius Caesar. Alésia stands for a symbolic defeat. It means the end of that imaginary nation reinvented as the Gauls. In Uderzo and Gosciny's *bande dessinée* (comic strip), no one wants to remember this defeat. According to the village authority (Abraracourcix, the leader), Alésia simply does not exist. But Uderzo and Gosciny's heroes demonstrate the impossibility of forgetting. The question "Where is Alésia?" refuses to go away, and every time it is asked, the characters who are expected to know the answer refuse to give any information and throw a spectacular tantrum instead. They repeat that they do not know where Alésia is (figs. 7–8).

As a result, the word "Alésia" is repeated over and over again, forcing readers to remember it like the proverbial pink elephant about which we should not

Figure 7.
—He is right, you guys, go the Arverne region, Check out the wonderful scenery. . . .
—Visit Gervovie, the place of our great immortal victory. . . .
—What about Alesia?
—Alesia? I don't know of any Alesia! I don't know where Alesia is! No one knows where Alesia is!
Source: Uderzo and Gosciny's *Le bouclier Arvene*, p. 12. Reproduced by permission of Éditions Albert René.

think. Like Djebar's text, for different reasons, *Le bouclier Arverne* writes history by forcing us to remember Alésia when the characters are trying to bury it in forgetfulness. By exhuming the victims of the massacre, Pélissier gave them a historic and decent tomb; by trying to forget Alésia in order to privilege Gergovie (where Caesar was defeated), the *Astérix* characters only highlight the impossibility of voluntary forgetfulness as well as the unavoidable accumulation of historical layers that stereotypical ceremonies of commemoration want to mask. March 19, 1962, is not a date of victory for France, nor would I wish to see it celebrated out of principle simply because it was a victory for Algeria. On the contrary, it seems interesting that the polemic was not reduced to an attempt to debaptize those streets once called "Rues du 19 mars 1962":

Cependant, lorsque le RPR avait conquis ou reconquis plusieurs de ces mairies, en 1983, il n'avait pas débaptisé les "rues du 19–mars-1962," mais ajouté, à la suite de cette date, la mention: "et de tous les combattants d'Algérie." (Jarreau 1992, 17)

[Nevertheless, when the RPR had gained or regained several of these city halls, in 1963, it had not unbaptized the "Rues du 19 mars 1962", but added, following that date, the appendix: "and of all the veterans of Algeria."]

One epitaph was added to another and, in the process, the commemorative monument became a place of questioning rather than a place that dictates a certain memory. Presumably, all veterans were remembered, regardless of which side they were on. Here, adding to the inscription and crossing it out are

Figure 8
—What about Alesia?
—Alechia?
—What ish Alechia? Hmm? What about Aleshia? We don't know where Aleshia ish!
(As a result of this attitude, which has lasted for centuries, the location of the Gauls' defeat remains rather mysterious to this day. Regrettable nationalism!)
Source: Uderzo and Gosciny's *Le bouclier Arvene,* p. 19. Reproduced by permission of Éditions Albert René.

one and the same action. No one tries to erase a previous narrative, but the grammar of the statement is modified. The "and" replaces the "or" (Alésia or Gergovie is celebrated according to which side one happens to be on) and the "all" refuses to take sides.

I will end this reflection with a text that seems to have understood that commemoration can occur through the refusal to define an event in terms of defeat and victory. That text proposes, at least temporarily, to separate the narrative of history from the narrative of memory. It is another novel by Mehdi Charef, *Le Harki de Meriem* (1989a), whose hero is a Harki (an Algerian who fought on the side of the French during the war).[15] A character excluded from commemorations, the Harki could well be the archetype of official nonmemory, the symbol of ceremonies that cannot resort to stereotypes because no traditional commemoration can claim him. I imagine the Harki as a doubly tragic figure, as the dark side of the unknown soldier to whom one will always bring flowers no matter which government is in place, because he incarnates patriotism in general, virtue, and so-called universal sacrifice. While the tomb of the unknown soldier incessantly forgets that it is inserted into a national discourse, the Harki reminds us unceasingly that commemorations manage the imagination of a nation-state like an old, inexhaustible cliché. The Harki is the very type of the problematic historical character because he falls into the chasm of nonsense, silence, and nonrepresentation that opens between two national histories. Twice vanquished, as a Frenchman who "lost Algeria" and as an Algerian rejected by the new state, the Harki discovers that he never had any ancestors, neither ancient Gauls nor Moudjahiddin. And yet, the curse is inherited via those national myths that the Harki puts into question. In Charef's book, Selim, the son of the Harki, is assassinated by three punks who blame him not for being an Algerian or an immigrant (he is neither as he was born in France of a French father), but for having a French identity card yet looking like an Arab, "a face painted in blue, white, and red stripes" says his assassin (Charef 1989a, 28). It is this "and" that they cannot bear. More than a racist crime, we are faced here with a crime against the very idea of hybridity. The hero's hybridity is what questions national memory and the "moment of the ancestors." Symbolically, the three assassins eliminate this ambiguous son of two histories, killing that which represents an intolerable interrogation of the opposition between enemy and ally, between "us" and "foreigners," between our victory and their defeat, between what must be commemorated and what one has the right and the duty to forget. The fate of this Harki's son would not be different from that of all the children of immigrants if, again, as if by magic, the question of the tomb had not returned to present itself in terms that no commemoration had foreseen. If Selim is, in France, a victim of anti-Arab racism, he is not by virtue of that fact recognized by Algeria as a legitimate victim who had fallen on the field of honor like those killed by Pélissier. Algeria does not claim him fraternally. On the contrary, a hysterical immigration officer refuses his sister entry into the country because she is the daughter of a Harki. The lifeless body of the Harki's son, which the father did not want to bury in France and which Algeria refuses to accept, floats in a sort of commemorative nonplace, stuck between borders like a historical aberration. This body cannot be brought out into the light, it cannot be accommodated; it is a mute and nevertheless loquacious accusation, a criticism of all those who expect of individuals a stereotypical alliance to a certain definition of the national past.

All war veterans have a little bit of the Harki in them whether they know it or not, and there is some Harki in each individual who suddenly decides to refuse or at least contest the "moment of my ancestors." There is some Harki in anyone who has the sudden intuition of the principle of stereotypical commemorations. Because the Harki cannot invoke either his or her ancestors the Gauls nor his ancestors the Moudjahaddin without eliciting a crisis of interpretation, they are the tragic alter egos of the *Astérix* characters. They present us with the human consequences of those theories that cartoons make fun of. The son of a Harki who died in France and whose "country" denies burial is paradoxically united with the young soldiers sent by the French government to die in Algeria in the name of "*Algérie française.*" No mention of the war of Algeria appears in the cemeteries, as if no discourse could to take responsibility for their deaths. Could the figure of the Harki be the antidote to the temptation of the stereotype?

Notes

Introduction (pp. 1–20)

1. Who we are—that is, the position we occupy within the spectrum of recognized and thus predictable racial, ethnic, or gender identities—does not protect us either from being stereotyped or from the assumption that we agree with stereotypes about other ethnic groups; the experience of being exposed to racist, sexist, or, more often, racist *and* sexist stereotypes depends only partially on our own identity. I am not suggesting that we are all equally victimized by some sort of anonymous stereotyping cosmic force. It may be the case that every culture displays a similarly disturbing ability to stereotype others, but some stereotypes are decidedly more cruel than others, and members of traditionally stereotyped groups are much more likely to suffer from them. Most theories treat stereotypes as an inherent (if undesirable) part of any discourse of representation. Sander Gilman concludes, for example, that trying to "stop the production of images of the Others . . . would be the task of Sisyphus" (Gilman 1985, 240). Yet the fact that stereotyping can be analyzed as an anonymous and abstract activity does not free us from a recognition of who is stereotyping and who is suffering at a given moment in history. As Elisabeth Young-Bruehl notices, "there is no generalized 'prejudiced person' who projects one desire or even one set of desires on any victim who happens to be there, any 'scapegoat.' Similarly, there are no groups where all prejudices are exercised by all members" (Young-Bruehl 1996, 69). See also Barbara Christian's story about how her daughter was excluded from a mock trial team in her high school because she spoke too well—i.e., because she did not fit the profile of the "stereotypical black girl, in other words, a gum-cracking, slurred-speaking sassy girl—an image, unfortunately, even teachers often have of who black girls are supposed to be" (Christian 1996, 120).
2. "Vacances à Marrakech," by Guy Bedos and Sophie Daumier. Public Recording, Paris, Bobino, September 16, 1970 (Barclay).
3. Such stereotypes are all the more devastatingly dangerous as new immigration policies packaged with the Pasqua laws of 1993 have introduced the notion of "comparable" housing standards as a prerequisite for the granting of documents to recently immigrated foreigners.
4. Directed by an Italian filmmaker at a time when discussion of the war in Algeria was still a complete taboo, *La bataille d'Alger* is a landmark in the evolution of images. Pontecorvo accepted the daunting challenge of confronting the similarities between the ideals and the methods of both camps. Without ever condoning or justifying terrorism or violence, the film addresses the representation of the Arab as terrorist. The stereotype is qualified (Pontecorvo reveals that Algerian civils were killed by European bombs, too) and its cultural implications (of essentialist deviousness and cowardice, for example) carefully contextualized when the leaders of the FLN are given a chance to explain their point of view.

5. "Beurs" or "Rebeus" are approximative inversions of "Arabe" used in the slang of the *banlieues.*
6. For an analysis of the variations between the different versions of *Tintin au Congo*, see Marie-Rose Maurin Abomo's "Tintin au Congo ou la Nègrerie en clichés" and Jean-Marie Apostolidès's pleasantly sarcastic comments in the passage entitled, "Impressions d'Afrique" (Apostolidès 1984, 21 ff.; Maurin Abomo 1993).
7. For a comparison between the concepts of hybridity and *métissage*, and for a definition of *métissage* as both an identity and a practice, see Lionnet's introduction to *Autobiographical Voices* (1989, 1–29).
8. See Annie LeBrun's *Statue cou coupé*, where she suggests that *Texaco* should not have been awarded the prize. Her criticism is part of a polemic intervention in the internecine cultural wars between pro-*créolistes* and pro-Césaire Caribbean factions. LeBrun violently criticized the authors of the manifesto, *Eloge de la créolité* (Raphaël Confiant, Patrick Chamoiseau, and Jean Bernabé) for constructing "creoleness" as a celebration of hybridity, multiculturalism, bilingualism, and also as an increasingly violent rejection of Césaire's Negritude. She suggests that their literary production leaves a lot to be desired when compared to the universal and timeless appeal of Césaire's masterpieces.
9. See McClintock 1995 for an analysis of why the adjective "postcolonial" may be ironically displaced by the construction of new, economically driven federations. What she calls "Fortress Europe" may "signal the emergence of a new empire" (13). At the same time, even those European desires for hegemonic unity are split by internal contradictions and haunted by their own ironic shadows. It is not only that there is Africa in Europe, the reverse is also true. At the heart of Europe is a "we" that can describe itself as African. As Appiah puts it in *In My Father's House* (1992), "we" cannot forget Europe: "for us to forget Europe is to suppress the conflicts that have shaped our identities; since it is too late for us to escape each other, we might instead seek to turn to our advantage the mutual dependencies history has thrust upon us" (72).
10. I remain convinced that creolization is a valuable if often painful condition. Curiosity for the history of those people hybridized by colonization may also lead to a crucial discovery of hybridity as a critical stance. A conscious perception of oneself as necessarily hybrid may be the precondition to a full yet critically distanced participation in civil societies of the West. In that sense, it may not be an essentialist mistake to systematically look to formerly colonized communities for adequate answers to stereotypes. Yet hybridity cannot be mistaken for a new and improved universal condition, nor is it an antidote to stereotyping. As Spivak reminds us in her "Diasporas Old and New: Women in the Transnational World" (1996) an extremely large portion of the world population never becomes diasporic, and their experience cannot not be dismissed as archaic or exceptional. Paul Gilroy's request that we move away from "ethnic absolutism" is both urgent and relevant (Gilroy 1993). It is also important to recognize that the very notion of hybridity may be generated by a dominant nostalgia for authenticity and homogeneity. Some people are perceived as participating in different cultures (African "and" French, or Muslim "and" French, for example), although they may feel that their (one and unique) culture is simply (although there is nothing simple about it) a

combination of what others think of as different and sometimes incompatible cultures. In that case, it is a stereotypical vision that defines the citizen whose parents or grandparents lived in a colonized area as a postcolonial hybrid. The hybrid subject in question may well wonder about the stereotyper's inability to understand culture as one complex and internally divergent whole. For two warnings against the temptation of celebrating hybridity as a necessary liberating condition, see Ha 1995 and Kortenaar 1995.

11. For a disturbing and quite entertaining analysis of how proverbs can be subtly rewritten and robbed of their illusory wisdom, see Pierre Barbéris's "Mistrigris, robe lotus et jeunes filles en short: D'un débat dans la vie à l'autre" (1994).

12. See Richard Dyer's careful analysis of Lippmann's book in the third chapter of *The Matter of Images* (1993, 10–18). According to Lippmann, stereotypes are "the fortress of our tradition and behind its defenses we can continue to feel ourselves safe in the position we occupy" (Lippmann 1956, 96; quoted in Dyer, 10).

13. Stereotypes are much more than statements recognizable for their stupidity and delusional attempts at imposing general truth. They can provoke a strong feeling of comfort, of control and safety based on the impression that sound knowledge is being recalled and applied properly to a given situation. It would be useful to consider the links between the pleasures we derive from stereotyping a powerless abstract other and what Slavoj Žižek calls the "enjoyment" of belonging to a national entity. The psychoanalytical reappropriation of the concept of *jouissance* in the construction of nationality could be adapted to a study of stereotypes; according to Žižek, national identities are predicated on the fear of being robbed of the enjoyment of something no one can adequately pinpoint except as what is in danger of being lost. The strange mixture of fear and desire generated by this way of imagining our own community might be reflected in the complex structure of positive and negative stereotypes (Žižek 1993, 200–237).

14. For a good example of the potential violence of a supposedly benevolent and generous invitation, see the beginning of Frantz Fanon's *A Dying Colonialism* (1965), where he describes how the "sadistic and perverse character of [the] relationships" between an Algerian employee and a European employer can be epitomized by an invitation to a social function:

> In connection with a holiday—Christmas or New Year, or simply a social occasion with the firm—the boss will invite *the Algerian employe* [*sic*] *and his wife*. The invitation is not a collective one. Every Algerian is called in to the director's office and invited by name to come with "your little family." "The firm being one big family, it would be unseemly for some to come without their wives, you understand? . . ." Before this formal summons, the Algerian sometimes experiences moments of difficulty. If he comes with his wife, it means admitting defeat, it means "prostituting his wife," exhibiting her, abandoning a mode of resistance. On the other hand, going alone means refusing to give satisfaction to the boss; it means running the risk of being out of a job (40).

My thanks to Dalila Hannouche for pointing out the significance of this passage.

15. In "The Jewish Nose: Are Jews White? Or the History of the Nose Job" (1995), Sander Gilman makes quite an original contribution to the vexing problem of what it means to respond to an implicit invitation. He starts with an analysis of the racial

politics implied in the rhetoric of personal advertisements, those "announcements of individuals 'in search of' mates" (149). In the interest of saving space and therefore money, authors rely on a stereotypical description of their identity that they encode as a series of letters. Destereotyping the portraits in question, Gilman unpacks the codes (SJW for "Single Jewish Woman" or DW(J)F (Divorced White [Jewish] Female)" much to the relief of some of his readers who are already alienated by the unfamiliar tradition—a sure sign that the invitation does not include them—and then untangles the web of changing assumptions about the relationship between whiteness and Jewishness. (See Gilman 1994 and 1996a for studies of the traditional nineteenth-century pairing between Jewishness and blackness.) Gilman points out that the invitations extended to potential correspondents prove that "individuals were interested in choosing their sexual partners from certain designated groups within American society" (149). The ways in which the personal ads are written is a clear indication of which stereotypical categories of identity function at a given time in a given society. It would be interesting to imagine responses that would decline to adopt the same stereotypical frames of identity. If this proposal sounds like a flippant and disrespectful treatment of what are, after all, love letters, I propose that academics often verify that they do not routinely use exactly the same principle of concatenated letters in papers, articles, or job lists (albeit more discreetly and more subtly).

16. An another example is given by Pierre Bourdieu and Hans Haacke in their *Libre échange* (1994). The authors recognize that there is an increasing level of discursive contamination between the representatives of high finance and transnational trade and intellectuals who often find themselves invited to deliver conferences, even though it is quite obvious to both parties that the general consensus is one of mutual distrust and complete ethical incompatibility.
17. Since the beginning of the nineties, stereotypes have attracted much critical attention and at least four important studies were published in France, Belgium, and Quebec. The proceedings of a Cerisy colloquium added to the already impressive collection (Amossy 1991; Plantin 1993; Dufays 1994; Castillo Durante 1994; and Goulet 1994). I am not suggesting that there is a French or Francophone tradition to which all these authors belong and that delineates their field of research by presupposing a certain definition of stereotypes. Such a sweeping generalization would run the risk of creating an absurdly rigid linguistic frontier and would disregard the relative contingency and not so relative limited scope of my own readings.
18. According to Ruth Amossy, for example, the difference between the cliché and the stereotype is that a cliché is a "discursive frozen unity" that "tolerates neither substitution nor transformation. . . . This is not at all the case with the stereotype, which goes beyond discursive unity and imposes itself in the most diverse forms" (1984, 691).
19. See the second volume of René Dumesnil and Albert Thibaudet's edition of Flaubert's work (1952), including *Bouvard et Pécuchet* (711–987), *Le dictionnaire des idées reçues* (999–1023), and the "Sottisier" (1024–1028).
20. Barbéris chooses to raise the question, "How does it work?" "Sachant que «comment ça marche» implique aussi bien le fonctionnement de la chose que le fonctionnement de celui qui nomme la chose et la fait exister" (Barbéris 1994, 9)

(knowing that 'how it works' implies the way in which the thing works as well as the positioning and function of whoever names the thing and makes it exist).

21. I will also deny that there is a sound reason to assume that this second series of books represents an Anglo-Saxon tradition even if all the authors I mention below write in English. It would be too facile to forget that there are many varieties of English, that I have left out books written in languages that I cannot read, as well as books that our bibliographies do not promote.
22. According to Dyer, Lippmann coined the word in 1922 (Dyer 1993, 10), and Felsenstein concurs: "the word *stereotype* was first employed in its present usage by the American journalist Walter Lippman[n] in an extraordinarily perspicacious book entitled *Public Opinion*, first published in 1922" (Felsenstein 1995, 12). Lippmann, however, is not an obvious reference in books written in French. But then, the word "stereotype" certainly existed long before the beginning of the twentieth century, even in the metaphorical sense. Most scholars writing in French go back to the Grand Larousse, one of the most widely respected French dictionaries, which attests "stéréotype" as a synonym of cliché as early as 1869. I don't think that this discrepancy is necessarily a problem; it is interesting, rather, to see that two myths of origin can successfully coexist without in any way hurting the theories that build on different premises.
23. For earlier constructivist theories of the relationship between stereotypes and the real, see Berger and Luckmann 1967.

1. Stereotypes and Iterativity (pp. 21–40)

1. The quotation comes from an article by Anne Frey, "Les Principes théoriques et pratiques de cet art," published in Manuels-Roret 1979, 384.
2. For three critiques of Alloula's project (including an analysis of the problematic gesture that puts the reader in the same position as that of the stereotyping photographer), see Bal 1991, Betts 1995, and Rice-Sayre 1989.
3. Pieterse's illustrations range from representations of saints sculpted in the thirteenth century to recent commercial posters. He uses stills from films, advertising campaigns, paintings, medical drawings, and caricatures.
4. For a very interesting and informative article on the specific contribution of the French to the discourse of advertising and of the unavoidable intersection between those images and stereotypical identities, see Steel 1996. See also Scott 1993.
5. As Barthes puts it, "Nietzsche a fait cette remarque, que la 'vérité' n'était que cette solidification d'anciennes métaphores" [Nietzsche remarked that the "truth" is nothing but the solidification of old metaphors] (Barthes 1973, 68). If this is true, then there is a stereotype at the core of the very definition of stereotypes as texts turned images.
6. For an analysis of race and "minority status" as "a framework of interpretation," see Butler 1996, 75.
7. "It is not stereotypes, as an aspect of human thought and representation, that are wrong, but who controls and defines them, what interests they serve" (Dyer 1993, 12). Lippmann and Dyer share military metaphors, but while Lippmann adopts a

defensive stance (stereotypes are fortresses capable of sustaining a siege), Dyer sees stereotypes as aggressive weapons.

8. This dilemma is, depending upon the circumstances, a matter of life and death or (or also) a theoretical problem. See David Welch's analysis of Nazi propaganda for example (1993, 66).
9. For a convincing example of the grammatical declension of stereotypes of black bodies in American culture, see Spillers 1987 (cited in Roberts, 2). Spillers's "rosa, rosae, rosam" goes like this: "Sapphire, Brown Sugar, Pussy, Buck, Sambo, Bad Nigger, Uncle Tom." See also Leab 1975.
10. Like all cultural products, stereotypes are also dependent on unpredictable fluctuations: some may disappear from our collective memory, but there is no guarantee that they will not resurface decades or centuries later. Felsenstein points out, for example, that even certain virulent anti-Semitic stereotypes reemerged with a vengeance when it was proposed to readmit Jews into England after centuries of official banishment (pp. 27–57). On the other hand, some stereotypical constructions gradually lose relevance and fade (perhaps temporarily) from immediate habits of representation. For example, Dyer remarks that stereotypes about alcoholism and their predictable fictional narrativizations ("a film about an alcoholic" is either "a tale of sordid decline or inspiring redemption") (1993, 15) have all but disappeared from the official list of "key social or personal problem[s]" (17). Similarly, in a review article of Laurence Mordekhai Thomas's *Vessels of Evil*, Gilman analyzes the potentially crucial divergences between stereotypes of Jews and Africans in the United States. Whereas it is always theoretically possible to emphasize similarities or dissimilarities between races and cultures, such choices are never innocent nor haphazardly transformed into cultural norms. As Gilman puts it: "There was one further problem that American Jews escaped in remarking themselves within the model of Judaism that replaced Jewishness. They ceased to be 'Black.' The icon of Jewish physical difference in the diaspora, the so-called 'Jewish nose,' had been understood as a version of the African nose; it was the stereotype of the nose which related the image of the Jew to the image of the Black" (1994, 44).
11. Sieglinde Lemke writes: "An effective stereotype is one that has entered into common consciousness, that has achieved the status of an 'already read text,' as Barbara Johnson succinctly puts it. It assumes its authority not by being original but rather by means of an expression of déjà vu" (Lemke 1993, 151).
12. See Herschberg-Pierrot 1988, 24. The passage quoted by the author is "Incident de langage dans la famille Langelon." First published in 1938, it is now to be found in Paulhan's *Oeuvres complètes*, vol. 2, 187. My thanks to Christian Garaud for his help with this reference.
13. In one of the examples quoted by Felsenstein (1995), the word stereotyped appears to designate not the stereotyper's object of derision and hatred but the person whose voice, language, and text has been ventriloquized, upon whose ideas something else has been branded. This peculiar use of the passive voice is remarkable because it treats stereotyping as an active process. In Felsenstein's text, the speaker who complains of having been stereotyped is the daughter of a clergyman who, in the nineteenth century, confesses to having been so fascinated, almost pos-

sessed, by *The Merchant of Venice* that it distracted her from preoccupation with God. She describes the book's pernicious influence as a form of stereotyping:

> "The character of Shylock burst upon me. . . . I revelled in the terrible excitement that it gave rise to; page after page was stereotyped upon a most retentive memory, without an effort, and during a sleepless night I feasted on the pernicious sweets thus hoarded in my brain." This one "ensnaring book" she hysterically claimed, was responsible for perverting her mind by initiating a taste for works of the imagination and turning it away from its fitter preoccupation with God. Later, after having recognized the error of her ways and returning with missionary zeal to the Protestant fold, she took considerable delight in endorsing the evangelical work of those attempting the conversion of the Jews." (Felsentein 1995, 313n.17).

Felsenstein refers to Richard D. Altick in *The English Common Reader* (Chicago: 1957, 112–13) and to Charlotte Elizabeth Browne Phelan Toona's *Personal Recollections* (1841), 15, 24, 130–31.

14. Gilman states that every single stereotype is "inherently bipolar, generating a pair of antithetical signifiers ('the noble savage' vs. 'the ignoble savage')" (1985, 27). See also his *Smart Jews* (1996c). Similarly, Anthony Appiah (1993) wonders why movies insist on presenting us with portrait of blacks as "Saints," suggesting that a perverse effect of overcompensation is at work.
15. See, for example, recent criticisms leveled at French antiracist discourses of the 1980s. Pierre-André Taguieff, one of the most articulate opponents of what he sees as useless rhetorical practices, claims that antiracists have lost influence by responding to racist stereotypes with positive images that are themselves stereotypes. But isn't the sheer intellectual brilliance and enormous meticulous historical documenting found in Taguieff's work another of the stereotype's ruses? I certainly do not ask for less theory on the grounds that practice is more effective, but I wonder if the energy required to unravel the million knots of the stereotypical tangle is well spent at this point in time.

2. Stealing Stereotypes (pp. 41–64)

1. One part of this chapter appeared in French as "Du bon usage des stéréotypes orientalisants: Vol et recel de préjugés," *L'Esprit créateur* 34 (Summer 1994): 42–57, edited by Ali Behdad. The part devoted to Marie Féraud first appeared in French in *Parallèles: Anthologie de la nouvelle féminine française*, ed. Madeleine Cottenet-Hage and Jean-Philippe Glennon-Imbert, 144–50. (Québec: L'instant-même, 1996). Reprinted with the permission of the publishers.
2. See Parama Roy's analysis (1995) of Richard Francis Burton's attempts to erase his public identity as an Englishman in order to pass as a member of the Islamic nations he wanted to study. Roy refers to Silverman's description of "double mimesis" and reformulates the principle in the following way: through "his proficiency in Eastern languages and vast knowledge of Muslim culture . . . Burton seeks to create . . . a model of native behavior for natives to admire and imitate, hence the acts of representation that will establish him as both actor and creator of native 'identity.'" Thus, while anglicized natives are capable only of imperfect

acts of mimesis that point to their condition of perpetual lack, they themselves are entirely imitable by the colonizer. The colonizer, in fact, can enact the natives better than the natives themselves can: double mimesis allows the natives to be interpellated as "natives," not just as "mimic men" (Roy 1995, 199).

3. And what exactly does constitute the definition of the family? Is an ethnic group a family? Is a nation? And how does one reconcile the different boundaries created by the analogy? Are transnational companies families? Is it the case that no stealing can take place within groups of similar economic or class interests?
4. The phrase is explained as slang for stealing in the glossary distributed to the audience before the beginning of the film; it connotes leaving a supermarket with a cart full of merchandise. As in *Georgette*, what is at stake here is the right to redefine and name practices. "Se faire un caddie" may not be immediately understandable to the average viewer and will certainly not conjure up negative images of wrongdoing and delinquency. The "se faire" is vague and does not belong to any family of words related to buying or stealing or selling or trade and exchange in general. And yet, the glossary's translation is unambiguous. In the context of the film itself, the discrepancy between the glossary's rendition and the colorful "se faire un caddie" reproduces the gap between Georgette's vision and her brother's.
5. See the chapter "Déclin des banlieues rouges et déviances juvéniles" (Decline of red suburbs and juvenile crime) in Dubet and Lapeyronnie (1992).
6. In *Douce France*, Malik Chibane proposes a different denouement: His "thieves" Jean-Luc and Moussa are able to start their own businesses when they reap the benefits of a burglary they did not commit.
7. Charef's films include *Le thé au harem d'Archimède*, *Camomille*, and *Au pays des Juliets.*
8. Madjid's tactic could be said to be the intertextual inheritor of earlier texts such as Joseph Zobel's classic *Rue Cases-Nègres*: like *Le thé au harem*, Zobel's novel explores the stereotypical racist pattern that associates blacks and stealing but without the ironic distance found in Charef's work. When Mlle Andréa exclaims "cette race dont je porte la couleur, je la déteste" (I hate that race whose color I share) after a fight with a customer, the hero Hassam reacts with dignity and a rather didactic tirade in a language that provides a striking contrast with Charef's casual and colorful colloquial French: "Je ne crois pas qu'aucun Blanc, par exemple, ait jamais crié: 'Je hais ma race' quand un Blanc a commis un vol ou un meurtre. Alors pourquoi, pour une péccadille d'un des nôtres, êtes-vous si prompte à vous désolidariser d'avec tous les nègres du monde et vouer au diable notre race entière." ("I do not think that a white man has ever cried: 'I hate my race' when a white man committed a theft or a murder. So, if one of ours is guilty of a minor offense, why are you so eager to dissociate yourself from all the Negroes in the world and to send our whole race to Hell?") (291).
9. That element of the plot may well disappear from the list of useful narrative techniques if or when certain names become completely integrated and lose their exotic flavor. In the meantime, a foreign-sounding first name continues to be the subject of speculations, negotiations, jokes, fear, and invention in most Beur novels. In Begag's *Béni ou le paradis privé*, Ben Abdallah insists on being called Béni, and his girlfriend's highly emblematic name is France. In Belghoul's *Georgette*,

we never know the little girl's real name since she more or less reluctantly adopts the nickname chosen by an old neighbor whom she visits from time to time. Below, we will see what strategies can be used when a novelist decides to directly confront the stereotypical implications of a name.

10. "Une certaine encyclopédie chinoise—citée par Borges—où il est écrit que les animaux se divisent en a) appartenant à l'Empereur, b) embaumés, c) apprivoisés, d) cochons de lait, e) sirènes, f) fabuleux, g) chiens en liberté, h) inclus dans la présente classification, i) qui s'agitent comme des fous, j) innombrables, k) dessinés avec un pinceau très fin en poils de chameau, l) etc, m) qui viennent de casser la cruche, n) qui de loin ressemblent à des mouches" (1). ("A certain Chinese encyclopaedia [cited by Borgès] in which it is written that 'animals are divided into: (a) belonging to the Emperor, (b) embalmed, (c) tame, (d) sucking pigs, (e) sirens, (f) fabulous, (g) stray dogs, (h) included in the present classification, (i) frenzied, (j) innumerable, (k) drawn with a very fine camelhair brush, (l) *et cetera*, (m) having just broken the water pitcher, (n) that from a long way off look like flies'" [1970, xv].)

3. Investing in Stereotypes (pp. 65–82)

1. An earlier version of this chapter appeared as "Third Cinema or Third Degree: The «Rachid System» in Serge Meynard's *L'oeil au beur~~re~~ noir*," in *Cinema, Colonialism, Postcolonialism: Perspectives from the French and Francophone World* edited by Dina Sherzer, Copyright © 1996. Courtesy of the University of Texas Press.
2. The trio also rests on the assumption that the audience will accept or even eagerly embrace the idea that each character, because of his or her ethnic identity, represents a whole community. Each time, the problem of undesirable representativity as tokenism against a just as undesirable invisibility resurfaces. See, for example, Rob Epstein and Jeffrey Friedman's *The Celluloid Closet* (1995) where Harvey Fierstein says that he would much rather see sissies in films than no gays whatsoever because he fears invisibility more than everything else. See also Smaïn's *Ecris-moi* where he remembers the beginning of his career as one of the members of "Le Petit Théâtre de Bouvard," a popular TV series orchestrated by Philippe Bouvard, whose ambition was to help young stand-up comics and encourage the genre of "café-théâtre": "'Le Petit Théâtre de Bouvard,' c'était . . . une petite cour des miracles réunie autour d'un 'despote éclairé.' Il y avait l'homosexuel, l'Arabe, le Chinois, le Black et la naine. C'était la compagnie des exclus" (*Le Petit Théâtre de Bouvard* was . . . a beggars' opera led by an "enlightened despot." There were the gay, the Arab, the Chinese, the black, and the dwarf. It was the troupe of the excluded) (Smaïn 1995, 29). See the introduction to Dina Sherzer's *Cinema, Colonialism, Postcolonialism*, where she refers to the trio as "the three B's" (1996, 10).
3. One of the most striking differences between the word "nègre" and the word "Beur" is that their statuses within the dominant language are practically opposite. "Beur" is a very recent creation, and it was never an insult; it never functioned like the word "nègre." It is not a derogatory word that a community reap-

propriated as a gesture of rebellious affirmation. Even if some individuals are proud to call themselves "Beurs," there is no consensus about the desirability or even necessity to be named. I think it would be a gross simplification to assume that 100 percent of those who object to the word crave assimilation into the dominant French culture.

4. See Lionnet 1995b.
5. Originally "brown sauce" but mostly used figuratively in the expression "l'oeil au beurre noir" to refer to the bruised face of someone who was involved in a fistfight.
6. It may be worth noting that *verlan* is but one of the highly visible features of the language used in the *banlieues.* Words are formed by inverting the syllables of the original French word, or at least this is how people who usually do not speak *verlan* explain words such as "Beur," "meufs," "keufs," and others. Beur is supposed to be an inverted version of "Arabe." Some contortions and a certain degree of arbitrariness are necessary to explain the desired result, which suggests that *verlan* functions like a language rather than like a strict, mathematical secret code. "Meufs" (women) and "keufs" (cops) are respectively derived from "femmes" and "flics." The homonymy between "beurre" and "Beur" is also part and parcel of the connotations attached to the word. For better or for worse, the pun has proved tempting among critics and sociologists. See Begag and Chaouite 1990 or Hargreaves 1991b.
7. *The Defiant Ones* starring Sidney Poitier, about whom more later. My thanks to Dina Sherzer for helping me with this reference.
8. "Departenance" is both the state and the always incomplete process of departure from one's group of origin, one's supposedly natural community. It is a form of nonbelonging. I have argued before that the figure of the infiltrator (spies, translators, but also cleaning ladies and children) provides us with a much-needed model of participation in the social debate that is based on the understanding that nonparticipation can be a form of desirable identification that refuses the comfortable relationship between belonging and power. The infiltrator, however, does not represent a solution to stereotyping as he or she is likely to reinforce their strength by using stereotypes as a cover to protect their strategic attempts at "passing" (Rosello 1996).
9. The three original plays (*Marius*, *Fanny*, and *César* [Pagnol 1931, 1932, 1937]), were turned into films and directed, respectively, by Alexander Korda (1931), Marc Allégret (1932), and Pagnol (1936).
10. The relationship between Virginie, Denis, and Rachid will prove unusually volatile and difficult to fit into traditional models as the film unfolds. The last scene shows the two men having breakfast together in Virginie's kitchen, a very intimate homosocial atmosphere whose ambiguously erotic potential is denied by the men's discussion of the ever-elusive apartment. Their presence in Virginie's kitchen marks the end of their rivalry only because the film has eliminated her from the team; she is in her own room, with a third lover. For a comparison with other male teams and for an analysis of the role of gender in such constructions, see Fiske 1987. Fiske suggests that in "Starsky and Hutch" episodes, "any woman who attracts the hero has to be rejected at the end of the episode. Male bonding, on the other hand, allows an interpersonal dependency that is goal-centered, not

relationship-centered, and thus serves masculine performance instead of threatening it" (295).

11. As Paul Willemen puts it: "The notion of a Third cinema was first advanced as a rallying cry in the late 60s in Latin America and has recently been taken up again in the wake of Teshome Gabriel's book *Third Cinema in the Third World, The Aesthetics of Liberation* (1982)" (Pines and Willemen 1989, 5). The phrase was also used as the title of a 1986 Edinburgh conference that set out to study "a cinema no longer captivated by the mirrors of dominance/independence or commerce/art, but grounded on an understanding of the dialectical relationship between social existence and cultural practice" (ibid., 2). See also Diawara 1992, esp. chapter 5.

4. Stereotypes as Gifts (pp. 83–100)

1. My thanks to Editions Karthala for granting me the rights to translate and reproduce Marie Féraud's "Oh, le pauvre malheureux!" (from *Histoires Maghrébines* [Paris: Karthala, 1985], 21–23); to Colin Davis, who did the translation for me; and to Russell King, who read a first draft of this chapter and made thoughtful and constructive suggestions. A version of this chapter appears in a special issue of *Mattoid* (*Crossing Boundaries*, *Crossing Cultures*, ed. Jonathan Hart). Reprinted with the permission of Brian Edwards, the editor of the journal, and Jonathan Hart.
2. For an analysis of the relationship between "*titre*" and "titré" (title and titrated), see Derrida 1992, 83–84. Derrida's brilliant study of Baudelaire's poem has completely permeated my own reading. Convinced that the gift is the very figure of impossibility, I also accept the consequences of Derrida's scandalous conclusion for our academic world: I no longer claim that I can carefully distinguish between what I have thought and what I have read, and it is almost pointless to make sure that I am giving my sources as much credit as they deserve. However, I want to thank Colin Davis for letting me borrow *Donner le temps* and Ross Chambers for giving me *Given Time* as a present. I am returning this text as a gift to him.
3. I will look at Van Cauwelaert's novel (1985) in the next chapter.
4. On gifts and on the transgression of the economy of charity in Baudelaire, see Burton 1993, esp. 66.
5. The prose poem is included in the *Spleen de Paris* (published in 1869, two years after Baudelaire's death), whereas *Histoires Maghrébines* came out in 1985. "Counterfeit Money" appeared for the first time in the November issue of *L'artiste* (964) at the time when the journal also republished *La corde* and *Une mort héroïque.* See the "chronology of the publication of the prose poems" in Hiddleston 1987, 114–16.
6. Peggy Kamuf's translation of Baudelaire's poem, which I use throughout this discussion, appears at the end of Derrida 1992; the pages are unnumbered. All translations of "Oh, le pauvre malheureux!" are Colin Davis's.
7. The gift is gratuitous or gratis both for the donor and for the recipient. As the etymological origin of the word suggests, gratuitous is on the side of what does not cost anything. On the one hand, the narrator's fake gift can be seen as what André Gide called "*l'acte gratuit*" since no motivation is ever attached to the potential

harm done to the beggar. On the other hand, this gesture does not involve any kind of expenditure on the part of the giver.

8. The often-quoted phrase appears in Pichois 1973, 2:583. In a letter dated 1866, Baudelaire portrays himself as a Joseph Delorme, "tirant de chaque objet une morale désagréable" (drawing from each object an unpleasant lesson).
9. "Car si l'amour, c'est donner ce qu'on n'a pas, il est bien vrai que le sujet peut attendre qu'on le lui donne, puisque le psychanalyste n'a rien d'autre à lui donner." (1966, 618) ("For if love is giving what one does not have, it is certainly true that the subject can wait to be given it, since the psychoanalyst has nothing else to give him [1977, 255]).
10. For a recent fictionalization of the symbolic and social consequences of *trabendo*, see Merzak Allouache's films, *Bab el-Oued City* (1994) and *Salut Cousin!* (1996).
11. See also "Les yeux des pauvres" (26), where the narrator and his mistress, while having dinner in a restaurant, are observed by a "*famille d'yeux*" (a family of eyes) that the narrator predictably interprets. The introduction to *Histoires Maghrébines*, on the other hand, emphasizes listening and not looking. Equipped with a tape recorder rather than with a camera, the sociologist collects tales and proverbs, anecdotes and memoirs, inviting us to gather around what she calls "*l'arbre à palabre*" (palaver tree) that her interviewees have accepted to "planter au milieu du quartier, de la ville toute entière" (10) (plant in the middle of the neighborhood, of the whole city).
12. The refusal to open one's eyes, the refusal to see, is completely different from the impulse that leads the narrator of another of Baudelaire's prose poems, "Galant tireur" (197–98), to close his eyes before aiming at the target. In that case, the hero closes his eyes the better to see. (He visualizes his mistress instead of the real target, and this symbolic substitution allows him to decapitate the doll he had been missing until then.) Si Bachir does not close his eyes to see better but to make sure he does not see what might be too obvious.
13. This passage is quoted in Mauss 1995, 198, in a footnote devoted to Boas (*Fifth Report on the North-Western Tribes of Canada*: B.A. Adv. Sc, 54–55). Derrida comments on the fact that Mauss does not theorize the relationship between the date, the timing of the transaction, and the gift ("ne théorise pas [le rapport] entre la date et le don" [1991, 62–63]).
14. See Segal 1992 and the link Segal establishes between Derrida, Jean-François Lyotard, and Emmanuel Levinas, especially what Levinas calls "the asymmetry of the ethical relationship, the asymmetry involved in my demanding more of myself than I demand of others" (83).

5. Disarming Stereotypes (pp. 101–127)

1. On *Mais qu'est-ce qu'elles veulent*, see Colville 1993. The author says that the film is "typical of the feminist documentaries produced in most Western countries during the 1970s" (85) and analyses the different female characters interviewed in the film ("a peasant woman, a textile factory worker, an upper middle-class housewife, a young pornographic film actress, an anorexic girl, an older Swiss woman

minister and a widowed concierge from Britanny") (85). The juxtaposition of different feminine professions and female roles is an interestingly early version of one of Serreau's recurrent narratological devices: the splitting of typically unified roles into several comparable characters.

2. See, for example, Montreynaud 1989, 674. According to the author: "C'est la première fois qu'un film de femmes remporte un tel succès" (It is the first time a woman's film has been so successful).
3. This is the opposite of what happens in *L'oeil au beurre noir*, where whiteness is neutralized by the fact that the only nonminority character is supposed to stand for a gender identity rather than represent a recognizable class or race. Similarly, *La crise* goes beyond the opposition between white and black explored in *Romuald et Juliette* or in other films based on the principle of the trio.
4. In "Culture's In-Between," Homi Bhabha refers to Etienne Balibar's conclusion that "the language of discrimination works in reverse: 'the racial/cultural identity of true nationals remains invisible but is inferred from the quasi hallucinatory visibility of the "false nationals"—Jews, "wops," immigrants, indios, natives, blacks'" (Bhabha 1996, 54: the author is citing Balibar's "Paradoxes of Universality" in David Theo Goldberg, eds., *Anatomy of Racism* [Minneapolis and Oxford: University of Minnesota Press, 1990], 284).
5. There has of course always been a discrepancy between political and social ideals and social practices, but stereotypes persist quite independently of the real. In the postwar period, a stereotypical communist dream assumed that class struggle would solve the problems of race relationships. This does not mean that voices were not loudly criticizing the naïveté of assumptions made about natural alliances between working-class white people and colonized black populations, for example. The best example of reaction against the stereotype may be Aimé Césaire's *Lettre à Maurice Thorez* (Letter to Maurice Thorez), in which he explains why he wants to resign from the Communist Party (1956).
6. The old stereotype of "banlieues rouges" for example, has obviously been buried with the remains of the Communist Party, but it was an extremely relevant concept after World War II and even during the War of Algeria when the illusion of seamlessness between race and class could have easily exploded under the pressure of historical realities (see Maspéro 1990 and Bachmann and Basier 1989).
7. See Lionnet 1995, 4.
8. Martin Wagner is not convinced by the "instant friendship" between Michou and Victor. The instant friendship *is* completely implausible, and the film is up against a fictional expectation that normally excludes any instant friendship between two characters who belong to such different cultural and economic universes. Rather than a friendship, however, what the intersection between classes authorizes is a parasitical relationship. At first sight, dependency is on the side of Michou, who sponges off his wealthy friend. At the end of the film, however, it does become clear that the friendship is more symbiotic than parasitical; Victor needs Michou at least as much as Michou needs him: "Vous avez plus besoin de moi que moi de vous M'sieur Victor, mais vous êtes trop con pour vous en apercevoir" (You need me more than I need you Mister Victor, but you are too stupid to realize that).
9. Built on the model of "*sème*" or "*mythème*" the word "*idéologème*" suggests that it

is possible to recognize and isolate the smallest possible common denonimator of ideology between statements. Another way of putting it is to say that it is possible to suspect the presence of a latent stereotypical content in certain discursive situations. Although it is dangerous to assume that unsaid stereotypes function in the same manner as their supposedly more manifest content, the concept of "idéologème" is useful in the case of *La crise* because part of the strategy here is to strip the stereotype to a bare recognizable minimum of discourse. Marc Angenot, who explored the concept, gives as example "le juif" or "la mission de la France" (1977, 24).

10. RMI stands for "revenu minimal d'insertion" (Minimum Insertion Income). Later in the film, Michou refers to it as the "em-ee" (MI) as if it was a common noun.
11. The "touche pas à mon pote" campaign was launched by S.O.S. Racisme in the early 1980s. For a while, the yellow hand that advocated solidarity across ethnic lines was the most popular symbol of the antiracist movements whose rhetoric is implicitly questioned by Serreau's film. Unlike other critics, however, Serreau has no quarrel with the movement's idealism, which explains why her satires never sound bitter, cynical, or hopeless, a pitfall that some sociological research does not always avoid. On important research on the recuperation of antiracist stereotypes by the extreme right, see Wieviorka 1992, Schnapper 1991, and Taguieff 1987. For an analysis that neither accepts nor dismisses the voice of working-class racist white people, see Bourdieu 1993.
12. It has been suggested that *Bouvard et Pécuchet* constitutes the preface that Flaubert intended to write as an accompaniment to the dictionary. In the introduction to the posthumous novel, René Dumesnil quotes the following letter: "Oui, écrit-il à Mme Roger des Genettes, le 5 octobre [1858], oui je me débarrasserai enfin de tout ce qui m'étouffe. Je vomirai sur mes contemporains le dégoût qu'ils m'inspirent dussé-je m'en casser la poitrine. Ce sera large et violent" (Yes, he writes in a letter to Mrs. Roger des Genettes dated October 5, 1858, yes, I will make a clean break of everything that stifles me. I will vomit on my contemporaries the disgust they have generated in me, even if I must rent my lungs. It will be wide and violent) (Dumesnil 1952, 698).
13. Compare with Flaubert's entries: under "colonies," we find, "S'attrister quand on en parle" (1004) (Look sad if the topic is brought up). The word "noire" does not appear, but under "négresses" (interestingly in the plural), one finds: "Négresses. Plus chaudes que les blanches" (1008) (Negro women: hotter than white women). Under "créole," "Créole. Vit dans un hamac" (1005) (Creole: Lives in a hammock).
14. I borrow the definition of humor as an electrical current from André Breton's *L'Anthologie de l'humour noir* (1966).
15. See the beginning of Michel Serres's *Le Parasite* (1980) and his reading of Jean de la Fontaine's fables (1990).
16. Here, the tactic is very close to what Flaubert imagined as the goal of the legendary *Dictionnaire des idées reçues.* In a 1852 letter to Louise Colet written while he was working on *Madame Bovary*, Flaubert says that he is still obsessed with the famous dictionary. "Il faudrait que dans tout le cours du livre, il n'y eût pas un mot de mon cru, et qu'une fois qu'on l'aurait lu, on n'osât plus parler, de

peur de dire naturellement une des phrases qui s'y trouvent" (In the whole book, there should be nothing that I would have written. And after reading that book, no one would dare say anything anymore for fear of saying out loud one of the sentences from the book) (quoted in Nadeau 1969, 291). The objective of repeating stereotypes is to instill fear in people who would be tempted do the same. The difference is that Flaubert's enemy was stereotypical knowledge of sciences, *bêtise* (stupidity) in general, while Serreau tackles malicious forms of racism and exclusionary thinking based on class and ethnicity.

17. The memorability of stereotypical statements dehumanizes the speaker and makes them look and act like mechanical objects. As Henri Bergson put it in his classic 1900 essay *Le rire*, the superimposition of the mechanical over the living is then sanctioned by the "punishment" of laughter (1940, 16).
18. See "Télé: La non-violence sur commande," *Libération* (Feb. 15, 1996), 4. For example, because *La bataille d'Alger* seeks to document and denounce extreme forms of violence (including the use of torture by the French army during the war in Algeria) an electronic device such as the V-chip would immediately turn off the television set and qualify the film as "violent."
19. *Les quatre vents de l'esprit*, vol. 2 *Esca*, 2.2 (Hugo 1985, 1267), quoted in Alexandre 1993, 48).
20. See Tahar Ben Jelloun's similar critique in *Hospitalité Française*:

> "J'entends parfois des gens dire qu'ils sont pro-arabes. Je n'aime ni cette expression ni cette attitude. Qu'est-ce que cela veut dire? Est-ce à dire qu'ils aiment les Arabes, comme si les Arabes étaient une totalité compacte, entièrement bonne et innocente, qu'ils sont prêts à la défendre n'importe où, n'importe quand et pour n'importe quel motif?" (Ben Jelloun 1984, 70)
>
> [Sometimes, I hear people say that they are pro-Arabs. I like neither the expression nor the attitude. What does it mean? Does it mean they like all Arabs, as if Arabs were one undivided whole, completely good and innocent, and they are ready to defend them anywhere, any time, for any reason whatsoever?]

6. Cheating on Sterotypes (pp. 128–149)

1. A first version of the material on Beyala and Ajar has appeared as "«Il faut comprendre quand on peut . . .»: L'art de désamorcer les stéréotypes chez Emile Ajar et Calixthe Beyala," in *Ecriture décentrée*, ed. Michel Laronde, 161–85 (Paris: L'Harmattan, 1997).

When I wrote this chapter, I did not know that I had stumbled upon what was about to become the tip of an enormously controversial iceberg. When reading *La vie devant soi* and *Le petit prince de Belleville*, I was intrigued by certain similarities, but since then, Beyala has been publicly accused of plagiarism, and the curious echoes between the two novels have turned into the deafening cacophony of a public controversy. Meanwhile, the publicity surrounding her name has produced contradictory results. For some, it has stained the author's reputation, for others, it has offered an introduction to her work; but both effects no doubt have added up to increased sales figures.

In May 1996, a tribunal ruled that resemblances between *Le petit prince de Belleville* and Howard Buten's *Quand j'avais cinq ans, je m'ai tué* were indeed instances of plagiarism, and both author and publisher were ordered to pay damages. Later, Beyala was accused of plagiarizing Ben Okri, and the tone of the debate became quite acrimonious as more journalists and critics became involved and as the author began defending herself in print. In February 1997, the popular literary magazine *Lire* published a series of astonishingly similar passages drawn from Beyala's work and that of Paule Constant, Ben Okri, and Alice Walker, intended as devastating examples of deliberate and systematic plagiarism (Assouline 1997, 9). The first page of the article features Romain Gary's *La vie devant soi* and *Le petit prince de Belleville.* The author mercilessly accumulates examples and presents them as colored inserts, facing each other on the page like witnesses called to the stand to confound a suspect. I remember wondering if Beyala would be sentenced to cleaning shopping carts in front of the supermarket all afternoon and if the guardians of authenticity and literary honor were truly watching out for the less informed reader's interest.

I could, I suppose, mourn the sad reality that I have been scooped by *Lire* and regret my lost fifteen minutes of fame. After all, had I not "discovered" that *La vie devant soi* and *Le petit prince de Belleville* had more in common than any coincidence could explain? But why should readers be forced to turn into conquerors who must hurry to plant a flag for fear of being deprived of their historic little phrase? Moreover, once we notice the echoes between two books, should we automatically conclude that, as readers, we have been "robbed" of something: at the time, it seemed to me that in order to feel "robbed" I first had to construct myself as the owner of some literary property, a role I felt reluctant to endorse especially as it was already filled, strictly, by the inheritors, publishers, or authors whose names appear after the copyright sign. Moreover, is it not possible to imagine Ajar in the role of Pierre Marielle leaving jewels on his table to attract his "marvelous child" and thief (*Un deux trois, soleil*)? And do we not remember Marie Féraud's delinquents and the lessons Georgette's father wanted to teach his daughter: after all, does "theft" exist within the same literary family? Georgette probably would not think so, but then again, her brother disagrees. In the end, I chose to interpret those unmistakable echoes instead of trying to explain their presence: perhaps a point could be made about illegitimate filiations and the ways in which both the novels and the relationship between the two novels thematized and emblematized the issues of bastardization and foreignness. The resemblances can be treated as textual events whose social and political significance can be unpacked within the narrative economy of the two stories.

It may well be the case that such an analysis is completely blind to the element of dishonesty involved (or not) in the writing practice, or is ignoring the rights of the true owners. But I also wonder if the values supposedly defended by Beyala's critics are best served by their rhetoric. First of all, there is an unsavory element of blood sport involved in this determined attempt to dislodge the hidden fox. If one reads for plagiarism, then the pleasure and pride of "discovery" can only be tainted by bitterness. And more dangerously, the decision to frame the debate around the unique key-word of "plagiarism," around an invective, makes it practically impossible to ask other questions than whether the charge is true or false and whether she is guilty or the victim of allegations. And such paradigms only appear to reintroduce ethics and responsibility into an essentially corrupt Parisian literary establishment. One of the much-talked-about ironies of the plagiarism issue was that Beyala had just been awarded the Grand Prix de l'Académie française for *Les honneurs perdus.* It may be true that it is important to make sure that the universe of literature is not unduly governed by dusty institutions that award meaningless prizes. But it is not a good idea to foreclose the wider discussion of the preconditions of ethical practice in a world where reading equals buying equals consuming and where stealing is the worst possible crime against the sacred Market (Leclair 1997).

2. Some theoreticians argue that texts from the seventeenth century are not even remotely interested in originality and individual creation and that, as a result, it is anachronistic to assume that stereotypes—more precisely, the concept of repetitive or fixed linguistic and ideological entities—are derogatory before the middle of the nineteenth century. Jean-Louis Dufays's most useful historical analysis (1994) argues, for example, that as long as tradition and convention are respectable and desirable (as he says it was in the prerevolutionary and even pre-Romantic periods), it is out of the question to condemn authors for their lack of distance from stereotypical thought and expression:

   > Avant le dix-neuvième siècle, le stéréotype n'était désigné que par des mots à connotation noble ("lieu commun," "topos," "thème," "fleur de rhétorique," . . .) qui témoignaient de la haute estime dans laquelle on le tenait alors. (57)

   > [Before the nineteenth century, only words with "noble" connotations were used to refer to stereotypes ("common place," "topos," "theme," "flower of rhetoric," . . .), a testimony to how highly thought of stereotypes were at the time.]

   I certainly cannot presume to come to conclusions about texts written before 1850, as I am addressing a decidedly modern corpus, and my conclusions about the reappropriation of stereotypes are linked to a modern social, historical, and literary context. It is possible, however, to conceive of stereotypical thought even during an era that considers the respect of tradition and conformity one of the highest possible virtues. It would be a valuable project to study the differential aspect of clichés and repetitions at times when tradition is the norm and at times when the respect for subversion, at least in literary circles, deconstructs the opposition between conventional and deviant thought. In less abstract words, it is slightly artificial to oppose the Romantics' hatred of stereotypes and the classics' love for repetition. For example, even with the most limited knowledge of Molière's plays, readers may be tempted to wonder if his attacks against the medical establishment cannot be interpreted as a literary and social critique of stereotypical and repetitive narratives about the patient's body.

3. In *La vie devant soi*, Momo, the young Arab narrator, lives with Madame Rosa, an old Jewish woman, a death-camp survivor who is one of the most formidable characters in twentieth-century French fiction. In Beyala's story, the "little prince" is a child of Malian origin who lives in the multiracial community of Belleville. In

Un aller simple, Aziz, an adolescent whose origin is unknown, though he is thought to be Moroccan because of his fake ID, is sent "back" to "his" village. The policeman who has arrested him explains his mission:

> "Le gouvernement a pris des mesures contre les clandestins. Enfin . . . pour les clandestins. C'est une opération conjointe avec les Droits de l'homme et l'OMI, l'Office des migrations internationales. Et il m'a expliqué en gros que pour lutter contre le racisme en France il fallait renvoyer les immigrés chez eux. J'ai continué à me taire, mais ça me paraissait bizarre de lutter contre une idée en la mettant en pratique." (26)
>
> [The government has taken measures against illegal aliens. Or rather . . . in favor of illegal aliens. It is a joint operation with Human Rights and OMI, the International Immigration Office. And he explained that in order to fight against racism in France, it was necessary to send immigrants back home. I did not say anything but it seemed weird to be fighting an idea by practicing it.]

The narrator's choice to remain silent at that point constitutes a refusal to embark in a direct logical confrontation. Fighting the violence of stereotypes with violence and stereotypes is exposed as the ludicrous choice Aziz wishes to avoid.

4. *Un aller simple* is Van Cauwelaert's fifth novel. Some of his earlier texts also received literary prizes (the Prix Del Duca for *Vingt ans et des poussières* in 1982; the Prix Roger-Nimier for *Poisson d'amour* in 1984). The popularity of *Un aller simple* certainly owes a lot both to the publicity generated by the Prix Goncourt and to the fact that the fate of illegal immigrants has unfortunately made it the top of the current-affairs hit parade.
5. See *C'est le soleil qui m'a brûlée* (1987), *Tu t'appelleras Tanga* (1988), and *Seul le diable le savait* (1990).
6. The words "*créolité*" and "*créolisation*" are a direct reference to French Caribbean authors, especially Jean Bernabé, Patrick Chamoiseau, and Raphaël Confiant's *Eloge de la créolité* (In Praise of Creoleness); Chamoiseau and Confiant's *Lettres créoles: Tracées antillaises et continentales de la littérature: 1635–1975* (Creole Letters: Caribbean and European Literary Trails: 1635–1975); and Edouard Glissant's *Poétique de la Relation* (Poetics of the Relation) or *Discours antillais* (Caribbean Discourse). I am also thinking of all the texts that consciously explore the difficulties of decolonized thinking and writing, such as Assia Djebar's autobiographical novels *L'Amour la fantasia* and *Le blanc de l'Algérie*, some aspects of which will be discussed below. Texts that struggle with the pleasures and pains of biculturalism and bilingualism can be said to be creolized even if their attempts predate the use of the word "créolité." In fact, in spite of growing disagreements within the Martinican literary scene, Aimé Césaire himself was working in the same tradition when he proposed to "infléchir le français, de le transformer pour exprimer disons: ce moi, ce moi-nègre, ce moi-créole, ce moi martiniquais, ce moi-antillais" (twist French, transform it to express, let us say, this I, this black I, this creole I, this Caribbean I) (Leiner 1978, xiv).
7. Césaire's vocabulary will disorient all but the most erudite classicists who also have an intimate knowledge of the island, and some Martinicans, as critics were quick to point out, are excluded by the supposedly elitist language. In *Texaco*, the language is creolized or, as Milan Kundera put it in a review, "chamoisisé" [chamoisified] to

the extent that the reader may suffer from the impression that he or she is never in control of the overall meaning (Chamoiseau 1992; Kundera 1992).

8. Quebecois novels are marginalized in a quite different manner than literatures written in countries where French was the language of colonial power.
9. That is, they are not part of the tradition of popular songs and films that depict the working classes and their supposedly down-to-earth poetry and imagery.
10. The feeling of strangeness does not come, for example, from a concerted effort at representing a reality excluded from the conventions of literary representation. What Césaire and his team wanted to achieve in their journal *Tropiques* would necessarily sound strange to metropolitans and Martinicans alike because no one was used to seeing tropical fauna and flora described in print (*Tropiques* 1978). Ajar, Beyala, and Van Cauwelaert by contrast deal with surroundings that are meant to be familiar to a reader comfortable in his or her assumed majority position. No glossary is needed, for example, and the whole debate of colonial versus decolonized language is absent or, rather, skirted. Readers tempted by exotic references must to be content with a few references to "noix de cola" (kola nut) in Beyala's book; other than that, Africa is a structuring absence. As for Van Cauwelaert's Morocco, it is a narrative construction, a sort of ironic Disney World according to Charles Pasqua.
11. The obvious literary forefather is Raymond Queneau, whose character Zazie more or less self-consciously cultivates attention to grammar and stereotypes that both entraps and liberates her from clichés (Queneau 1959).
12. Belleville is also the terrain of Daniel Pennac, whose prose is indebted to Ajar and whose playful manipulations of literary genres contribute to a social critique and a celebration of cohabitation and diversity. See his *Au bonheur des ogres*, *La fée carabine*, *La petite marchande de prose*, and *Monsieur Malaussène* (Pennac 1985, 1987, 1989, 1995).
13. Unlike Beyala's other African novels, *Le petit prince de Belleville* and *Maman a un amant* are set in Paris and are solidly anchored in an urban environment. We know that Loukoum was born in Mali, but his universe coincides with Belleville. If he is a diasporic subject, the definition of diasporic movements is here ironically limited by economic pressures that make traveling difficult. Leaving the neighborhood is out of the question, "returning" anywhere is a nonissue. In *Maman a un amant*, when the whole family decides to go away for a short vacation, their departure is hailed as a most extraordinary event, generating gossip and envy. And yet the destination is far from exotic: the family is going to Lozère, seen as a symbol of dullness and rural boredom: "Nous avons, dit Loukoum, immigré dans la France profonde" (26) (Probably untranslatable or equivalent to what would happen if a Mexican immigrant said, "we left California to immigrate to Saint Olaf, Ohio").
14. I use code switching as a metaphor. I am not referring to sudden and recognizable changes in register or to the insertion of words from the native language, for here there is no native language. Only an unquantifiable level of familiarity and norm changes drastically from one sentence to the next.
15. See Geesey 1995.
16. On the relationship between the collective and the individual part of ethnic identity, see Laronde 1993, 17ff.

17. This could be confirmed by the terror that seizes Madame Rosa in *La vie devant soi* when she thinks that she will be forced to go to the hospital. In her mind the hospital and concentration camps are one and the same.

Conclusion (pp. 150–171)

1. A version of this chapter appeared in *Transculture* (1996): 61–80. The article was first written in French and translated by Jonathan Rosenthal, whom I want to thank for his generous help and for giving me permission to reprint. My thanks also to Sylvie Lindeperg for her reading of the first draft and to Lawrence Kriztman for organizing the MLA session on "Lieux de mémoire."
2. For an analysis of the relationship between education and stereotype, or rather of the stereotypical quality of most metadiscourses about education, see Charbonnel 1993:

   J'ai proposé d'appeler "boulèphorique" (du nom du personnage mis en scène par Erasme dans son Ciceronianus, M. Boulèphore) cette dimension toujours "conseillère" de la pensée de l'éducation, par-delà les genres rhétoriques habituellement recensés. (145)

   [I have proposed to coin the word "boulèphorique"—after the name of Erasme's character in the *Ciceronianus*, M. Boulèphore—to refer to the "advisory" dimension of all discourse on education, beyond already identified rhetorical genres.]

3. Bertrand Poirot-Delpech has fulminated against the apparently logical yet completely arbitrary nature of ceremonies of commemoration. The danger of such "*réminiscences guidées*" (guided memory tours), of "*visites de musée au sifflet*" (whistlestop museum tours), of "*commémoration socialisée et quadrillée*" (socialized and controlled commemoration),

   c'est qu'en somme il deviendrait incongru, illicite, d'évoquer un drame national en dehors d'un compte rond d'années après son déroulement, autrement que dans le cadre d'un devoir accompli comme un seul homme [*sic*], pour la forme, du bout de la mémoire. (Poirot-Delpech, 2)

   [is that, in the end, it would become incongruous, illegitimate to mention a national catastrophe unless a round number of years have gone by. Commemoration would become a perfunctory duty performed by an anonymous crowd, paying lip service to memory.]

4. Every simple theoretical reversal is dangerous, and the pattern is especially visible when the North and the South try to converse, using words such as "feminism," "nationalism," or "civil societies." What is criticized in nations of the West or North cannot be assumed to be the priorities of other geopolitical areas. Gayatri Spivak, analyzing the role played by the disenfranchised woman in what she calls the "old and new" diasporas, writes: "[she] cannot, then, engage in the critical agency of civil society—citizenship in the most robust sense—to fight the depredations of 'global economic citizenship.' This is not to silence her, but rather to desist from guilt-tripping her" (1996, 252).
5. We often commemorate events that we have not been able to prevent. We celebrate

the end of wars as victories against ideologies, but in a sense, it is always already too late. Shouldn't we have a day off to celebrate all those unofficial meetings between ordinary people that resulted in the nondeclaration of a war, in the uselessness of future official peace talks between ambassadors? In the same way that goverments honor the memory of the unknown soldier, would it be possible to celebrate the unknown performance of unknown ordinary citizens who made other commemorative events unecessary?

6. The whole of Djebar's work puts in perspective the ex-colonized Algerian subject's relationship to Berber, Arabic, and French, formulates the problematic and ambiguous connections to the language of the mother, or of the father, or of colonization, and writes with, around, or against those languages that authorize and forbid desire, rebellion, sexuality, or femininity. See, for example, Djebar's 1996, where she describes how her novel *Vaste est la prison* (1995a) plays with three different languages (84). See also Donadey 1991.
7. For another tactic, see Brigitte Roüan's autobiographical film, *Outremer* (1990). Three distinct yet interwoven narratives tell the stories of how three sisters have completely different experiences of the war of independence. The complicated structure of the movie does not choose between the three versions. Instead, through a complicated series of flashbacks and retellings, *Outremer* emphasizes the enormous number of possible narratives and the both incomplete and excessive quality of each sister's point of view.
8. Page references are to the 1992 edition. The novel was reprinted in Paris in 1995.
9. Writing about the literary value of a "lieu de mémoire," Pierre Nora opposes form and content, strategy and what is at stake:

> "La mémoire en effet est un cadre plus qu'un contenu, un enjeu toujours disponible, un ensemble de stratégies, un être-là qui vaut moins par ce qu'il est que par ce que l'on en fait. C'est dire qu'on touche ici à la dimension littéraire des lieux de mémoire dont l'intérêt repose en définitive sur l'art de la mise en scène et l'engagement personnel de l'historien." (Nora, viii)

> [For memory is a frame rather than a content. Something is always at stake, memory is a set of strategies, a being-there that is important not because of what it is but because of what one does with it. Which is to say that this is directly linked to the literary value of *lieux de mémoire*, whose interest finally depends on the quality of the production and on the historian's personal commitment.]

It seems to me that Pélissier's report pleads in favor of a being-not-there of memory. His "literary" report does not function as a form of excess (the quality of the production makes the act of commemoration even more efficient because of his personal talent and commitment) but as a successful erasure of the distinction between frame and content. Without Pélissier's eloquence, the content is not merely altered, it disappears altogether, it is forgotten.

10. Finally, in 1996, a young man confessed to the profanation and publicly regretted having been influenced by the National Front's theses. Once again, Jean-Marie Le Pen is offended by such an obvious misrepresentation of his party.
11. In his article, Alain Peloux reminds us of the following facts:

Trois jours plus tard, une manifestation réunissait 10.000 personnes à Carpentras. Le 14 mai, c'était 200.000 manifestants qui défilaient dans Paris, le président Mitterrand en tête, pour condamner "l'antisémitisme, le racisme et l'intolérance," les propres mots de Pierre Joxe sur le perron de la synagogue carpentrassienne, quelques heures seulement après la découverte des deux soeurs.

[Three days later, 10,000 demonstrators gathered in Carpentras. And on May 14, 200,000 people marched through Paris, led by President Mitterrand, condemning "anti-Semitism, racism and intolerance." Those were the very words pronounced by Pierre Joxe on the steps of the Carpentras synagogue a few hours after the two sisters had made their discovery.]

As for Bernard, he remembers that French cultural life had been deeply affected by the 1990 desecration. On Monday, May 13, 1990,

les six chaines de télévision française—TF1, Antenne 2, FR3, Canal plus, la 5 and M6—ont diffusé lundi soir, en fin de soirée, *Nuit et brouillard*, le documentaire d'Alain Resnais sur les camps et le martyre des déportés durant la dernière guerre. Cette programmation qui a bouleversé les grilles habituelles des chaines, avait été demandé par le CRIF (Conseil représentatif des institutions juives dans le patrimoine culturel). Quai des Belges, Marcel Maréchal lit le poème d'Aragon, "la Rose et le réséda," et *Si c'est un homme* de Primo Lévi.

[Monday, late at night, the six French television channels—TF1, Antenne 2, FR3, Canal plus, la 5, and M6—showed *Night and Fog*, Alain Resnais's documentary on camps and on the deported's plight during World War II. This radical rescheduling of all regular programs had been requested by the CRIF (Representative Council of Jewish Institutions within French Cultural Patrimony). At the Quai des Belges, Marcel Maréchal read "La Rose et le réséda" (Aragon's poem), and Primo Levi's *Si c'est un homme.*]

Several years later, several arrests were finally made. Writing in *L'événement du jeudi* (August 15–21, 1996), Françoise Berger takes the risk of laughing at the uncanny coincidence between a new commemorative controversy and the aftermath of the desecration. Referring to the debate generated by the French government's decision to invite the Pope to celebrate the memory of Clovis, the first Christian king, she writes: "L'un des skinheads de Carpentras a fourni des détails très précis sur l'expédition. Il s'agissait de célébrer l'anniversaire d'Hitler. On a pourtant Clovis, merde!" (14) (One of the skinheads from Carpentras gave very specific details about the operation. The idea was to celebrate Hitler's birthday. What's wrong with Clovis for God's sake?)

12. Although he does not wish to exaggerate the repercussions of the Carpentras affair, Gilles Bresson (1991) suggests that it had direct and lasting consequences on the French political scene:

"La vague antiraciste qui a déferlé après cette affaire a coupé, pour un temps, les ailes du FN qui, après avoir largement profité de celle du foulard islamique du lycée de Creil et de la loi d'aministie sur le financement occulte des partis politiques, a chuté brusquement de 18% d'intentions de votes aux législatives à 13% en mai puis à 11% en juin."

The antiracist tidal wave that followed the event clipped the FN's wings, at least for a while: after taking advantage of the Islamic-scarf controversy at the *lycée de* Creil as well as of the amnesty law regarding the invisible funding of political parties, the National Front saw the number of its supporters plummet (from 18 percent of intended votes for the legislative elections to 13 percent in May and 11 percent in June)].

13. For a detailed contextualization of the book's genesis, see Clarisse Zimra's introduction to "The White of Algeria" in *Another Look, Another Woman* (ed. Lynn Huffer). Zimra presents the English version of the text read by Assia Djebar at the 1993 "Parliament of Writers" hosted by the city and the university of Strasbourg (Zimra 1995).
14. Their history of the "La Courneuve" housing estate shows how myths overlap and contradict each other. Modern estates were a modern answer to shantytowns, representing material and social progress when they were built. They stood for popular solidarity and futuristic dreams. Only later would the image change, replaced by nightmarish visions of gutted mailboxes, dilapidated corridors, delinquency, and violence (Bachmann and Basier 1989).
15. For a different treatment of the "Harki" see also Malik Chibane's character Moussa in *Douce France*.

Bibliography

Ageron, Charles-Robert. 1984. "L'exposition coloniale de 1931: Mythe Républicain ou mythe impérial?" In *Les lieux de mémoire*, ed. Pierre Nora, 561–91. Paris: Gallimard.

Ajar, Emile. 1975. *La vie devant soi*. Paris: Mercure de France.

Alexandre, Didier. 1993. "«Chants du cygne»: Le cliché et sa prévisibilité en poésie." In *Lieux communs, topoi, stéréotypes, clichés*, ed. Christian Plantin, 46–59. Paris: Kimé.

Alloula, Malek. 1986. *The Colonial Harem*. Trans. Myrna Godzich and Wlad Godzich. Minneapolis: University of Minnesota Press.

Amossy, Ruth. 1984. "Stereotypes and Representation in Fiction." Trans. Therese Heidingsfeld. *Poetics Today* 5: 689–700.

———. 1991. *Les idées reçues: Sémiologie du stéréotype*. Paris: Nathan.

Amossy, Ruth, and Elisheva Rosen. 1982. *Les discours du cliché*. Paris: SEDES-CDU.

Anderson, Benedict. 1991. *Imagined Communities: Reflections on the Origin and Spread of Nationalism*. 2d ed. London: Verso.

Angenot, Marc. 1977. "Présupposé, topos, idéologème." *Etudes françaises* 13 (April): 11–34.

Anyinefa, Koffi. 1996. "Hello and Goodbye to Négritude: Senghor, Dadié, Dongala, and America." *Research in African Literatures* 27 (Summer): 51–69.

Apostolidès, Jean-Marie. 1984. *Les métamorphoses de Tintin*. Paris: Seghers.

Appiah, Kwame Anthony. 1992. *In My Father's House: Africa and the Philosophy of Culture*. New York: Oxford University Press.

———. 1993. "No Bad Nigger: Blacks as the Ethical Principle in the Movies." In *Media Spectacles*, ed. Marjorie Garber, Jann Matlock, and Rebecca L. Walkowitz, 77–90. London: Routledge.

Assouline, Pierre. 1977. "L'affaire Beyala rebondit," *Lire* 252 (February): 9.

Audé, Françoise. 1993. "La Crise. Vendre Rambouillet." Review of Coline Serreau's *La crise*. *Positif* (January): 36–37.

Bachmann, Christian, and Luc Basier. 1989. *Mise en images d'une banlieue ordinaire*. Paris: Syros.

Bachollet, René, et al. 1992. *Négripub: L'image des noirs dans la publicité*. Paris: Somogy.

Bal, Mieke. 1991. "The Politics of Citation." *Diacritics* 21: 25–45.

Balzac, Honoré de. 1960. *La Peau de chagrin*. Paris: Garnier Frères.

———. *The Wild Ass's Skin*. 1915. Trans. Ellen Marriage. London: Everyman.

Barbéris, Pierre. 1994. "Introduction." In *Le stéréotype: crise et transformations*, ed. Alain Goulet, 9-13. Coen: Presses universitaires de Caen.

Barthes, Roland. 1957. *Mythologies*. Paris: Seuil.

———. 1973. *Le plaisir du texte*. Paris: Seuil.

———. 1978. *Leçon*. Paris: Seuil.

Baudelaire, Charles. 1962a. "La Fausse monnaie." In *Petits poèmes en prose* (1869), 135–37. Paris: Garnier Frères. 135–137.

———. 1962b. "Le Joujou du pauvre." In *Petits poèmes en prose* (1862), 92–94. Paris: Garnier Frères.

———. 1962c. "Le Galant tireur." In *Petits poèmes en prose*, 135–37, 197–98. Paris: Garnier Frères.

Begag, Azouz. 1989. *Béni ou le paradis privé*. Paris: Seuil.

Begag, Azouz, and Abdellatif Chaouite. 1990. *Ecarts d'identité*. Paris: Seuil.

Belghoul, Farida. 1986. *Georgette*. Paris: Barrault.

Ben Jelloun, Tahar. 1977. *La plus haute des solitudes*. Paris: Seuil.

———. 1984. *Hospitalité Française*. Paris: Seuil.

Bernabé, Jean, Patrick Chamoiseau, and Raphaël Confiant. 1989. *Eloge de la créolité*. Paris: Gallimard.

———. 1990. *Eloge de la créolite/In Praise of Creoleness*. Trans. M. B. Taleb-Khyar. Paris: Gallimard/Baltimore: Johns Hopkins University Press.

Berger, Peter, and Thomas Luckmann. 1967. *The Social Construction of Reality*. London: Allen Press and Penguin.

Bergson, Henri. 1940. *Le rire: Essai sur la signification du comique* (1900). Paris: PUF.

Bernard, Philippe. "Les silences de Carpentras: Un an après la profanation de son cimetière juif, la sous-préfecture du Vaucluse balance entre oubli et l'exigence de la vérité." *Le Monde,* 11 May 1991.

Berrah, Mouny, Victor Bachy, Mohand Ben Salama, and Ferid Boughedir, eds. 1981. *Cinémas du Maghreb. CinémAction* 14.

Berrah, Mouny, Jacques Levy, and Claude Michel, Cluny, eds. 1987. *Les Cinémas arabes*. Preface by Tahar Ben Jelloun and Ferid Boughedir. *CinémAction* 43.

Bersani, Leo. 1995. *Homos*. Cambridge, Mass.: Harvard University Press.

Betts, Gregory. 1995."Wanted Women, Woman's Wants: The Colonial Harem and Post-colonial Discourse," *Canadian Review of Comparative Literature/Revue Canadienne de Littérature comparée* (September): 257–549.

Beyala, Calixthe. 1987. *C'est le soleil qui m'a brûlée*. Paris: Stock.

———. 1988. *Tu t'appelleras Tanga*. Paris: Stock.

———. 1990. *Seul le Diable le savait*. Paris: Le Pré aux Clercs.

———. 1992. *Le petit prince de Belleville*. Paris: Albin Michel.

———. 1993. *Maman a un amant*. Paris: Albin Michel.

———. 1995. *Loukoum, The Little Prince of Belleville.* Trans. Marjolijn de Jager. Oxford: Heinemann.

———. 1996. *Les Honneurs perdus*. Paris: Albin Michel.

Bhabha, Homi. 1994. "The Other Question: Stereotype, Discrimination and the Discourse of Colonialism." In *The Location of Culture,* 66–84. London: Routledge. (Originally published as "The Other Question: The Stereotype and Colonial Discourse." In *The Sexual Subject: A Screen Reader in Sexuality*. London: Routledge, 1992.)

———. 1996. "Culture's In-Between." In *Cultural Identity,* ed. Stuart Hall and Paul du Gay, 53–60. London: Sage.

Bosséno, Christian, ed. 1982. "Cinéma de l'émigration. Emigrés et déracinés à l'écran," *CinémAction* 24.

Bouquet, Stéphane. 1994. "Portrait: Malik Chibane." *Cahiers du cinéma* 476 (Feb.): 11.

Bourdieu, Pierre. 1993. *La misère du monde*. Paris: Seuil.

Bourdieu, Pierre, and Hans Haacke. 1995. *Free Exchange*. Trans. Randall Johnson. Stamford, Calif.: Stanford University Press. (Originally published as *Libre échange*. Paris: Seuil, 1994.)

Bresson, Gilles. 1991. "Le Pen espère encore toucher des dividendes." *Libération*, May 10, 32.

Breton, André. 1966. *L'Anthologie de l'humour noir*. Paris: Pauvert.

Brinker-Gabler, Gisela, ed. 1995. *Encountering the Other(s): Studies in Literature, History, and Culture*. New York: State University of New York Press.

Burton, Richard. 1993. "Bonding and Breaking in Baudelaire's *Petits Poèmes en Prose*." *The Modern Language Review* 88: 58–73.

Butler, Judith. 1996. "An Affirmative View." *Representations* 55 (Summer): 74–83.

Castillo Durante, Daniel. 1994. *Du stéréotype à la littérature*. Montreal: XYZ.

Certeau, Michel de. 1980. *L'invention du quotidien*. Paris: UGE.

———. 1984. *The Practice of Everyday Life*. Trans. S. Randall. Berkeley and Los Angeles: University of California Press.

Césaire, Aimé. 1956. *Lettre à Maurice Thorez*. Paris: Présence Africaine.

———. 1989. *Le discours sur le colonialisme*. Paris: Présence Africaine.

Chambers, Ross. 1971. "«L'art sublime du comédien»: Ou le regardant et le regardé." *Saggi e ricerche di litteratura francese* 11: 189–260.

———. 1991. *Room for Maneuver: Reading (the) Oppositional (in) Narrative*. Chicago: University of Chicago Press.

Chamoiseau, Patrick. 1992. *Texaco*. Paris: Gallimard. (English trans. 1997. New York: Random House.)

Chamoiseau, Patrick, and Raphaël Confiant. 1991. *Lettres créoles: Tracées antillaises et continentales de la littérature: Haïti, Guadeloupe, Martinique, Guyane. 1635–1975*. Paris: Hatier.

Charbonnel, Nanine. 1993. "Lieux communs et métaphores: Pour une théorie de leurs rapports." In *Lieux communs, topoï, stéréotypes, clichés,* ed. Christian Plantin, 144–51. Paris: Kimé.

Charef, Mehdi. 1983. *Le thé au harem d'Archi Ahmed*. Paris: Mercure du France.

———. 1989a. *Le Harki de Meriem*. Paris: Mercure de France.

———. 1989b. *Tea in the Harem*. Trans. Ed Emery. London: Serpent's Tail.

Chibane, Malik. 1993. *Hexagone* (film).

Christian, Barbara. 1996. "Camouflaging Race *and* Gender." *Representations* 55: 120–28.

Cliff, Michelle. 1985. *The Land of the Look Behind*. Ithaca, N.Y.: Firebrands Books.

Colville, Giorgiana. 1993. "On Coline Serreau's *Mais Qu'est-ce qu'elles veulent*? and the Problematics of the Feminist Documentary." *Nottingham French Studies* special issue on French cinema, ed. Russell King, 32 (Spring): 84–90.

Corn, Georges. 1991. *L'Europe et l'orient: De la balkanisation à la libanisation, histoire d'une modernité inaccomplie*. Paris: La Découverte.

Cottenet-Hage, Madeleine, and Jean-Philippe Glennon-Imbert. 1996. *Parallèles: Anthologie de la nouvelle féminine française*. Quebec: L'instant-même.

Delporte, Christian. 1993. *Les crayons de la propagande: Dessinateurs et dessin politiques sous l'occupation*. Paris: CNRS Editions.

Derrida, Jacques. 1991. *Donner le temps*. Vol. 1: *La Fausse monnaie*. Paris: Galilée.

———. 1992. *Given Time*. Vol. 1: *Counterfeit Money*. Trans. Peggy Kamuf. Chicago: University of Chicago Press.

Dhoukar, Hedi. 1990. "25 cinéastes plus ou moins beurs." *CinémAction* 56 (July): 186–91.

Diawara, Manthia. 1992. *African Cinema: Politics and Culture*. Bloomington: Indiana University Press.

Djebar, Assia. 1989. *Fantasia: An Algerian Cavalcade*. Trans. Dorothy Blair. London: Quartet Books.

———. 1992. *L'amour la fantasia*. Casablanca: Eddiff.

———. 1995a. *Vaste est la prison*. Paris: Albin Michel.

———. 1995b. *Le blanc de l'Algérie*. Paris: Albin Michel.

———. 1995c. *L'amour la fantasia*. Paris: Albin Michel. (Originally published by Jean-Claude Lattès, 1985.)

———. 1996. Interview with Lise Gauvin. "Glissements des langues et poétiques romanesques." *Littérature* 101 (Feb.): 73–87.

Donadey, Anne. 1991. "Assia Djebar's Poetics of Subversion." *Esprit créateur* 23 (Summer): 107–17.

Donald, James, and Anli Rattansi, eds. 1996. *"Race," Culture and Difference*. London: Sage.

Dubet, François, and Didier Lapeyronnie. 1992. *Les quartiers d'exil*. Paris: Seuil.

Dufays, Jean-Louis. 1994. *Stéréotype et lecture*. Liège: Editions Pierre Mardaga.

Dumesnil, René. 1952. Introduction to *Bouvard et Pécuchet*. In Gustave Flaubert, *Oeuvres*, vol. 2, ed. René Dumesnil and Albert Thibaudet, 693–710. Paris: Gallimard.

Dyer, Richard. 1993. *The Matter of Images: Essays of Representation*. New York: Routledge.

Encyclopaedia universalis CD-ROM. 1996. "Imprimerie" (search word: "stéréotype"). Paris: Editions Encyclopaedia Universalis.

Fadhel, Abbas. 1990. "Une esthétique beur?" *Cinémas métis: De Hollywood aux films beurs*. *CinémaAction* 56 (July): 140–51.

Fanon, Frantz. 1965. *A Dying Colonialism*. Trans. Haakon Chevalier. New York: Grove Press. (Originally published as *L'an cinq de la révolution Algérienne*. Paris: François Maspéro, 1959.)

———. 1967. *Black Skin, White Masks*. Trans. Charles Lam Markmann. London: Pluto Press. (Originally published as *Peau noire, masques blancs*. Paris: Seuil, 1952.)

Felsenstein, Frank. 1995. *Anti-Semitic Stereotypes: A Paradigm of Otherness in English Popular Culture, 1660–1830*. Baltimore: The Johns Hopkins University Press.

Féraud, Marie, ed. 1985. "Oh, le pauvre malheureux!" In *Histoires maghrébines, rue de France*, 21–26. Paris: Karthala.

Finkielkraut, Alain. 1994. *The Imaginary Jew*. Trans. Kevin O'Neill and David Suchoff. Lincoln, Nebr.: University of Nebraska Press. (Originally published as *Le Juif imaginaire*. Paris: Seuil, 1980.)

Fisher, Hal. 1978. *Gay Semiotics*. Berkeley: NFS Press.

Fiske, John. 1987. "British Cultural Studies and Television." In *Channels of Discourse, Reassembled*, ed. Robert C. Allen, 284–326. London: Routledge.

Flaubert, Gustave. 1952. *Oeuvres*, vol. 2. Ed. René Dumesnil and Albert Thibaudet. Paris: Gallimard.

Foucault, Michel. 1966. *Les mots et les choses: Une archéologie des sciences humaines*. Paris: Gallimard.

———. 1970. *The Order of Things: An Archaeology of the Human Sciences*. London: Tavistock Publications.

———. 1975. *Surveiller et punir: Naissance de la prison*. Paris: Gallimard.

———. 1977. *Discipline and Punish: The Birth of the Prison*. Trans. Alan Sheridan. New York: Pantheon.

Gabriel, Teshome. 1982. *Third Cinema in the Third World, The Aesthetics of Liberation*. Ann Arbor, Mich.: University of Michigan Press.

Garrigues, Jean. 1991. *Banania. Histoire d'une passion française*. Paris: Éditions due May.

Geesey, Patricia. 1975. "North African Women Immigrants in France: Integration and Change." *SubStance: France's Identity Crisis* 76–77: 137–53.

Gilman, Sander. 1985. *Difference and Pathology: Stereotypes of Sexuality, Race, and Madness*. Ithaca, N.Y.: Cornell University Press.

———. 1988. *Disease and Representation: Images of Illness from Madness to AIDS*. Ithaca, N.Y.: Cornell University Press.

———. 1994. "Dangerous Liaisons: Black Jews, Jewish Blacks, and the Vagaries of Racial Definition." *Transition* 64: 41–52.

———. 1995. "The Jewish Nose: Are Jews White? Or, The History of the Nose Job." In *Encountering the Other(s): Studies in Literature, History, and Culture*, ed. Gisela Brinker-Gabler, 149–82. New York: State University of New York Press.

———. 1996a. "Black Bodies, White Bodies: Toward an Iconography of Female Sexuality in Late Nineteenth-century Art, Medicine and Literature." In *"Race," Culture and Difference*, ed. James Donald and Anli Rattansi, 171–97. London: Sage. (Originally published in *"Race," Writing, and Difference*, ed. Henry Louis Gates, 223–61. Chicago: University of Chicago Press, 1986.)

———. 1996b. *Seeing the Insane*. Lincoln, Nebr.: University of Nebraska Press.

———. 1996c. *Smart Jews: The Construction of the Image of Jewish Superior Intelligence*. Abraham Lincoln Lecture Series. Lincoln, Nebr.: University of Nebraska Press.

Gilroy, Paul. 1993. *The Black Atlantic: Modernity and Double Consciousness*. London: Verso.

Girard, René. 1982. *Le bouc émissaire*. Paris: Grasset.

Glissant, Edouard. 1981. *Discours antillais*. Paris: Seuil.

———. 1989. *Caribbean Discourse: Selected Essays*. Trans. with an introduction by J. Michael Dash. Charlottesville: University Press of Virginia.

———. 1990. *La poétique de la relation*. Paris: Gallimard.

Gobineau, Arthur, Comte de. 1967. *The Inequality of Human Races*. Trans. Adrian Collins. New York: Howard Fertig.

Goldberg, David Theo, ed. 1990. *Anatomy of Racism*. Minneapolis: University of Minnesota Press.

Goulet, Alain, ed. 1994. *Le stéréotype: Crise et transformations*. Caen: Presses universitaires de Caen.

Gramsci, Antonio. 1971. *Selection from the Prison Notebook*. New York: International Publishers.

Ha, Marie-Paule. 1995. Review of Said's *Culture and Imperialism. Research in African Literatures* 26 (Spring): 154–57.

Hargreaves, Alec G. 1991a. *Voices from the North African Immigrant Community in France: Immigration and Identity in Beur Fiction.* Providence, R.I.: Berg Publications.

———. 1991b. "La famille Ramdam: Un sit-com «pur beur»?" *Hommes et migrations* 1147 (Oct.): 60–66.

Hart, Jonathan. 1994. "A New Theory of Literature." *Review of Comparative Literature/Revue Canadienne de Littérature Comparée* 21 (Dec.): 705–16.

Hayward, Susan. 1993. *French National Cinema.* London: Routledge.

Hergé. 1946, 1974. *Les aventures de Tintin au Congo.* Tournai: Casterman.

Herschberg-Pierrot, Anne. 1988. *Le dictionnaire des idées reçues de Flaubert.* Lille: Presses universitaires de Lille.

Hiddleston, J. A. 1987. *Baudelaire et le* Spleen de Paris. Oxford: Clarendon and Oxford University Press.

Huffer, Lynn, ed. 1995. *Another Look, Another Woman. Yale French Studies* 87.

Hughes, Philippe de. 1992. *Almanach du cinéma: Des origines à 1945.* Annual supplement to the *Encyclopaedia universalis.* Paris: Editions Encyclopaedia Universalis.

Hugo, Victor. 1985. *Poésies*, vol. 2. Paris: Laffont.

Irigaray, Luce. 1977. *Ce sexe qui n'en est pas un.* Paris: Minuit.

Jarreau, Patrick. 1992. "Enquête: l'Algérie de la deuxième mémoire: 'Rue du 19 mars 1962'" *Le Monde*, March, 18, 17.

Jousse, Thierry. 1995a. "Le banlieue-film existe-t-il?" *Cahiers du cinéma* 492 (June): 32–36.

———. 1995b. "Prose Combat." *Cahiers du cinéma* 492 (June): 37–39.

Kendrick, Michelle. 1994. "The Never Again Narratives: Political Promise and the Videos of Operation Desert Storm." *Cultural Critique* 28 (Fall): 129–47.

Kortenaar, Ken. 1995. "Beyond Authenticity and Creolization: Reading Achebe Writing Culture." *PMLA* 110: 30–42.

Kritzman, Lawrence, ed. 1995a. *Auschwitz and After: Race, Culture, and the 'Jewish Question' in France.* London: Routledge.

———. 1995b. *SubStance: France's Identity Crisis* 76–77.

Kundera, Milan. 1992. "Beau comme une rencontre multiple." *L'infini* 34.

Lacan, Jacques. 1966. *Ecrits.* Paris: Seuil.

———. 1977. *Ecrits, a Selection.* Trans. Alan Sheridan. New York: Norton.

Laronde, Michel. 1993. *Autour du roman beur.* Paris: L'Harmattan.

———. 1997. *Ecriture décentrée: La langue de l'autre dans le roman contemporain.* Paris: L'Harmattan.

Leab, Daniel. 1975. *From Sambo to Superspade.* Boston: Houghton Mifflin.

———. 1993. *Autour du roman beur.* Paris: L'Harmattan.

LeBrun, Annie. 1996. *Statue cou coupé.* Paris: Jean-Marie Place.

Leclair, Bertrand. 1997. "Abraracourcix versus Beyala." *La Quinzaine Littéraire* 710 (February): 31.

Leiner, Jacqueline. 1978. "Entretien avec Aimé Césaire." In *Tropiques,* vol. 1, nos. 1–5 (Apr. 1941–Apr. 1942), i–xxxviii. Paris: Jean-Michel Place.

Lemke, Sieglinde. 1993. "White on White." *Transition* 60: 145–54.

Leveau, Remy, and Catherine Withol de Wenden. 1988. "Le 'Beurs' nouveaux citoyens," *Les Cahiers de l'Orient* 11: 103–13.

Levinas, Emmanuel. 1969. *Totality and Infinity: An Essay on Exteriority.* Trans. Philippe Nemo. Pittsburgh: Duquesne University Press.

Lionnet, Françoise. 1995a. *Postcolonial Representations: Women, Literature, Identity.* Ithaca, NY.: Cornell University Press.

———. 1995b. "Immigration, Poster Art, and Transgressive Citizenship: France 1968–1988." In *Sub/Stance* 76–77, ed. by Larry Kritzman, 93–108.

———. *Autobiographical Voices*. Ithaca, N.Y.: Cornell University Press.

Lippmann, Walter. 1956. *Public Opinion* (1922). New York: Macmillan.

Lorsignil, Cressard, Masurel, Péry, and Rioux, with de Maricourt and Mengin 1991. "Chronologie." In *Encyclopaedia universalia* 1991, 19–94. Paris: Encyclopaedia Universalis.

Maurin Abomo, Marie-Rose. 1993. "Tintin au Congo ou la Nègrerie mise en clichés." In *Images d'Afrique et du Congo/Zaïre dans les lettres Belges de langue française et alentour,* ed. P. Halen and János Riesz, 151–62. Bruxelles: Textyles.

McClintock, Anne. 1995. *Imperial Leather: Race, Gender and Sexuality in the Colonial Contest*. New York: Routledge.

Malkmus, Lizbeth, and Roy Armes. 1991. *Arab and African Film Making*. London: Zed Books.

Manuels-Roret. 1979 [1857]. Nouveau manuel complet typographie. 2d ed. Ed. M. E. Bouchez. Paris: Leonce Lancet.

Marriott, David. 1996. "Bordering on: The Black Penis." *Textual Practices* 10: 9–28.

Martin, Gérard. 1996. "Imprimerie." In *Encyclopaedia universalis*, 773–86. Paris: Editions Encyclopaedia Universalis.

Maspéro, François. 1990. *Roissy Express: A Journey Through the Paris Suburbs*. Trans. Paul Jones. London and New York: Verso, 1994. (Originally published as *Les Passagers du Roissy Express*. Paris: Seuil).

Mauss, Marcel. 1990. *The Gift: The Form and Reason for Exchange in Archaic Societies.* Trans. W. D. Halls. London: Routledge.

———. 1995. "Essai sur le don: Forme et raison de l'échange dans les sociétés archaïques." In *Sociologie et anthropologie* (1950). Paris: PUF.

Mehlan, Jeffrey. 1995. "On the Holocaust Comedies of 'Emile Ajar.'" In *Auschwitz and After: Race, Culture, and the 'Jewish Question' in France,* ed. Lawrence D. Kritzman, 219–34. London: Routledge.

Mélançon, Robert, ed. 1992. *Le lieu commun*, special issue of *Etudes Françaises* 13 (April).

Mizla, Olivier. 1988. *Les Français devant l'immigration.* Paris: Éditions Complexe.

Montreynaud, Florence. 1989. "Trois hommes et un couffin de Coline Serreau." In *Le XXème Siècle de Femmes*, 674–75. Paris: Nathan.

Nadeau, Maurice. 1969. *Gustave Flaubert, écrivain*. Paris: Denoël.

Nora, Pierre. 1984. "Entre mémoire et histoire: La problématique des lieux." In *Les lieux de mémoire*. Vol. 1: *La république,* ed. Pierre Nora, xvii–xlii. Paris: Gallimard.

———. 1992. "Comment écrire l'histoire de France." In *Les lieux de mémoire*. Vol. 3: *Les Frances: 1. Conflits et partages,* ed. Pierre Nora, 11–32. Paris: Gallimard.

———. 1996. *Realms of Memory.* 1: Conflicts and Divisions. Trans. Arthur Goldhammer. Under the direction of Lawrence Kritzman. New York: Columbia University Press.

Pagnol, Marcel. 1931. *Marius*. Paris: Fasquelle.

———. 1932. *Fanny*. Paris: Fasquelle.

———. 1937. *César*. Paris: Fasquelle.

Paulhan, Jean. 1941. *Les fleurs de Tarbes ou la terreur dans les lettres*. Paris: Gallimard.

———. 1966–1970. "Incident de langage dans la famille Langelon" (1938). In *Oeuvres Complètes*, vol. 2, 187. Paris: Tchou, cercle du livre précieux.

Pêcheux, Michel. 1975. *Les vérités de la palice*. Paris: Maspéro.

Peloux, Alain. 1993. "Trois ans après: Profanation de Carpentras: Reconstitution au cimetière." *Le Provençal*, May 7.

Pennac, Daniel. 1985. *Au bonheur des ogres*. Paris: Gallimard.

———. 1987. *La fée carabine*. Paris: Gallimard.

———. 1989. *La petite marchande de prose*. Paris: Gallimard.

———. 1995. *Monsieur Malaussène*. Paris: Gallimard.

Pichois, Claude, ed. 1973. *Correspondance*. 2 vols. Paris: Gallimard.

Pieterse, Jan Nederveen. 1992.*White on Black: Images of Africa and Blacks in Western Popular Culture*. New Haven: Yale University Press. (Originally published as *Wit over zwart: Beelden van Afrika en zwarten in de Westerse populaire cultur*. Amsterdam: Koninklijk Institut voor de Tropen, 1990.)

Pines, Jim, and Paul Willemen, ed. 1989. *Questions of Third Cinema*. London: British Film Institute.

Plantin, Christian. 1993. *Lieux communs, topoï, stéréotypes, clichés*. Paris: Kimé.

Poirot-Delpech, Bertrand. 1994. "Mémoire Guidée." *Le monde*, Jan. 19, 2.

Porter, Dennis. 1983. "Orientalisme and Its Problems." In *The Politics of Theory,* ed. Francis Barker, Peter Hulme, Margaret Uversen, Diana Loxley, 173–93. Colchester: University of Essex.

Queneau, Raymond. 1959. *Zazie dans le métro*. Paris: Gallimard.

Reynart, François. 1993. "Y a-t-il une culture beur? Smaïn, Mehdi Charef, Amina. . . . Ils occupent la scène artistique. Veulent-ils pour autant revendiquer leur identité? Débat" (Dossier: "Les Beurs tels qu'ils se voient") *Le Nouvel Observateur* 1517 (Dec. 2 and 8): 10–57.

Rice-Sayre, Laura. 1989. "Veiled Threats: Malek Alloula's *Colonial Harem*." *Boundary 2*: 351–63.

Rieusset-Lemarié, Isabelle. 1994. "Stéréotypie ou reproduction du langage sans sujet." In *Le stéréotype: Crise et transformations,* ed. Alain Goubet, 15–34. Caen: Presses Universitaires de Caen.

Roberts, Diane. 1994. *The Myth of Aunt Jemina: Representations of Race and Region*. London: Routledge.

Rosello, Mireille. 1996. *Infiltrating Culture*. Manchester: Manchester University Press.

Roy, Olivier. 1991. "Ethnicité, bandes et communautarisme." *Esprit* 169 (Feb.): 37–47.

Roy, Parama. 1995. "Oriental Exhibits: Englishmen and Natives in Burton's *Personal Narrative of a Pilgrimage to Al-Madinah and Meccah*." *Boundary* 2 22.1: 185–210.

Said, Edward. 1980. *L'orientalisme: l'Orient créé par l'Occident* (1978). Trans. Catherine Malamoud. Paris: Seuil.

———. 1993. *Culture and Imperialism.* New York: Knopf.
Schiff, Ellen. 1982. *From Stereotype to Metaphor: The Jew in Contemporary Drama.* Albany, N.Y.: State University of New York Press.
Schnapper, Dominique. 1991. *La France de l'intégration.* Paris: Gallimard.
Schneidermann, Daniel. 1994. *Arrêts sur images.* Paris: Fayard.
Scott, David. 1993. "Air France's Hippocampe and BOAC's Speedbird: The Semiotic Status of Logos." *French Cultural Studies* 4: 107–27.
Sebbar, Leïla. 1982. *Shérazade: 17 ans, brune, frisée, les yeux verts.* Paris: Stock.
———. 1984. *Le chinois vert d'Afrique.* Paris: Stock.
———. 1985. *Les carnets de Shérazade.* Paris: Stock.
Segal, Alex. 1992. "The Annulled Gift and the Repression of Ethics." *Westerly: A Quarterly Review* 37 (Summer): 87–92.
Senghor, Léopold Sédar. 1964. *Poèmes.* Paris: Seuil.
Serres Michel. 1980. *Le Parasite.* Paris: Grasset.
———. 1990. *Le tiers instruit.* Paris: Bourin.
Sherzer, Dina, ed. 1996. *Cinema, Colonialism, Postcolonialism.* Austin, Tex.: University of Texas Press.
Silverman, Kaja. 1989. "White Skin, Brown Masks: The Double Mimesis, or with Lawrence in Arabia." *Differences* 1 (Fall): 3–54.
Smaïn. 1990a. "T'en veux?" Videotape, Reel J2. Trotignon: Warner Music Vision.
———. 1990b. "T'en veux?" Audiotape. Paris: Lance Productions.
———. 1995. *Ecris-moi.* Ed. Olivier Dazat. Paris: Nil Editions.
Spillers, Hortense. 1987. "Mama's Baby, Papa's Maybe: An American Grammar Book." *Diacritics* 17.2 (Summer): 65–81.
Spivak, Gayatri. 1993. *Outside in the Teaching Machine.* London: Routledge.
———. 1996. "Diasporas Old and New: Women in the Transnational World." *Textual Practice* 10: 245–69.
Steel, David. 1996. "Ad-denda. A Decade of Illustrated Books on French Advertising." *French Cultural Studies* 7: 215–22.
Steward, Susan, 1991. *Crimes of Writing: Problems in the Containment of Representation.* Oxford: Oxford University Press.
Taguieff, Pierre-André. 1987. *La force du préjugé: Essai sur le racisme et ses doubles.* Paris: La Découverte.
Terdiman, Richard. 1993. *Present Past: Modernity and the Memory Crisis.* Ithaca, N.Y.: Cornell University Press.
Thomas, Laurence Mordekhai. 1994. *Vessels of Evil: American Slavery and the Holocaust.* Philadelphia: Temple University Press.
Thuillier, Jacques. 1982. "Les deux orients de la Peinture." In *L'orient des Provençaux,* 39–45. Marseille: Imprimerie municipale de Marseille.
Touratier, Jean-Marie. 1979. *Le stéréotype.* Paris: Galilée.
Tropiques (1940–1945). 1978. Paris: Jean-Michel Place.
Tulard, Jean. 1982. *Dictionnaire du Cinema, Les Réalisateurs.* Paris. La Hout.
Uderzo and Gosciny. 1968. *Le bouclier Arverne.* Paris: Dargaud.
Van Cauwelaert, Didier. 1982. *Vingt ans et des poussières.* Paris: Seuil.
———. 1984. *Poisson d'amour.* Paris: Seuil.
———. 1985. *Un aller simple.* Paris: Albin Michel.

Vincendeau, Ginette. 1994. "Coline Serreau: A High Wire Act." *Sight and Sound* (Mar.), 26–28.

Volet, Jean-Marie. 1993. "Calixthe Beyala, or the Literary Success of a Cameroonian Woman Living in Paris." *World Literature Today* 67: 309–14.

Wagner, Martin. 1994. "La Crise." *Sight and Sound* (Mar.): 37–38.

Weber, Eugen. 1991. *My France*. Cambridge, Mass.: Harvard University Press, Belknap Press.

Welch, David. 1993. *The Third Reich: Politics and Propaganda*. New York: Routledge.

Wieviorka, Michel. 1992. *La France raciste*. Paris: Seuil, Points actuels.

Woodhull, Winnifred. 1993. *Transfigurations of the Maghreb*. Minneapolis: University of Minnesota Press.

Young-Bruehl, Elisabeth. 1993. "Discriminations: Kinds and Types of Prejudices." *Transition* 60: 53–59.

———. 1996. *The Anatomy of Prejudice*. Cambridge, Mass.: Harvard University Press.

Zimra, Clarisse. 1995. "Disorienting the Subject in Djebar's *L'Amour, la fantasia*." In *Another Look, Another Woman,* ed. Lynn Huffer. *Yale French Studies* 87: 149–70.

Žižek, Slavoj. 1993."Enjoy Your Nation as Yourself." *Tarrying with the Negative: Kant, Hegel, and the Critique of Ideology,* 200–237. Durham, N.C.: Duke University Press.

Zobel, Joseph. 1974. *La Rue Cases-Nègres*. Paris: Présence Africaine.

Index

University Press of New England publishes books under its own imprint and is the publisher for Brandeis University Press, Dartmouth College, Middlebury College Press, University of New Hampshire, Tufts University, and Wesleyan University Press.

Library of Congress Cataloguing in Publication Data

Rosello, Mireille.

Declining the stereotype : ethnicity and representation in French cultures / Mireille Rosello.

p. cm — (Contemporary French culture and society)

Includes bibliographical references and index.

ISBN 0–87451-834–2 (alk. paper). — ISBN 0–87451-835–0 (pbk : alk. paper).

1. French literature—20th century—History and criticism. 2. Stereotype (Psychology) in literature. 3. North Africans in literature. 4. Africans in literature. I. Title. II. Series.

PQ307.S73R67 1997

840.9'00914—dc21 97–31507